# DAVID SHEPHERD

THE AUTHORISED BIOGRAPHY

# DAVID SHEPHERD

## ARTIST AND CONSERVATIONIST

### J. C. JEREMY HOBSON

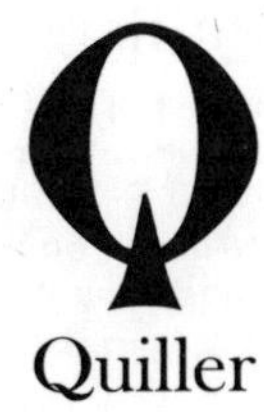

Quiller

First published 2022

Quiller
An imprint of Amberley Publishing Ltd



ISBN 978 1 8468 9332 2 (hardback)
ISBN 978 1 8468 9341 4 (ebook)



British Library Cataloguing in Publication Data.
A catalogue record for this book is available from the British Library.

1 2 3 4 5 6 7 8 9 10

Typesetting by SJmagic DESIGN SERVICES, India.
Printed in the UK.

Quiller
An imprint of Amberley Publishing Ltd
The Hill, Merrywalks, Stroud, GL5 4EP
Tel: 01453 847 800
E-mail: info@quillerbooks.com
Website: www.quillerpublishing.com

For Avril, David's wife – who sadly passed away just as these
pages were at the very last stages of going into print.

'The man may be the head of the home but the wife is the heart'
Kenyan (Kikuyu people) proverb

# CONTENTS

# AUTHOR'S NOTE

In writing this biography I've attempted to portray the artist not only as a young man (apologies to James Joyce for paraphrasing the title of his first novel!) but, as all good biographies should, throughout all aspects of his life: both professional and personal.

Although I'd written over thirty published books beforehand, this was to be my first-ever biography of length. I had previously drawn brief word sketches of many people for magazine articles but never before had to consider anything so detailed. It was then, a daunting task, and one made even more daunting by the fact that it was up to me to create what is likely to be a final account of one man's eighty-six-year lifespan – and a life that certainly included more than most!

A focus on accuracy is obviously most important in any form of non-fiction writing: it's even more crucial when someone's life is already so well documented in books, magazines, radio, television recordings and in the minds of many who have personal reminiscences of meeting their 'hero' and is a 'personality' long admired; both for their artistic talent and contribution to wildlife throughout many parts of the world. Added to which, when one considers I've also written this biography in the capacity of being one of the subject's sons-in-law and that, with any obviously unintentional error I might incur the possible wrath of relatives, then it's probably quite possible to understand the trepidation with which I undertook the task!

Some discrepancies are inevitable – even David's own notes and recollections of particular events vary! Also, as I researched various sources, I began to realise that some of David's paintings which appear as illustrations in various books and magazine articles have been attributed different names. With that in mind, wherever I mention a particular painting within the text, I have given it the title with which I think it was originally catalogued and hope that by doing so, it doesn't cause any confusion.

Writing this biography has been an illuminating insight into the life of a man I thought I knew quite well. It wasn't long into the project that, through my research and talking with many who knew David through different stages of his life, I began to realise that I was acquiring an overall knowledge of a most amazing person. Therefore, should I ever decide to apply and subsequently choose 'David Shepherd: wildlife artist, conservationist and family man' as my specialist subject on a future BBC Television *Mastermind* programme, I'd like to think I might acquit myself with a reasonable number of points!

# ACKNOWLEDGEMENTS

First and foremost, my love and grateful thanks to Avril and all of the Shepherd family who have helped enormously with the compilation of this biography; in particular, the Shepherd 'girls': Melinda, Mandy, Melanie and Wendy – big hugs to you all! Also their various offspring: Thomas, Elliot, Robin, Rosie and Annabel, Emily and Georgina (known to all as 'Peanut'), Luke and Justin. David and Avril's great-grandchildren (Katie, twins Oliver and Matilda, Henry and Freyja) are too young to have known David but they will, as time goes by, most surely acknowledge the part their great-grandfather played in both the world of art and wildlife conservation. Thank you also to Judy Crago, David's sister, for her reminiscences – like her brother, she is a great character and an enormous amount of fun!

Jonathan Shepherd, David's nephew and archivist of the paternal side of the family, has been diligent in his research of family history on my behalf and much of what appears in the section dealing with David's early life would not have been possible without his assistance. Long-time family friends Pamela Jackson and Jayne Le Cras have shared with me their experiences and obvious love of David, his family and his work. Mark Carwardine, conservationist, broadcaster and author, was kind enough to provide me with several wonderful anecdotes (and permission to include his poem *Ode To David Shepherd*, which he read at David's seventieth birthday celebrations – to the accompaniment of laughter and rapturous applause) even though he was, at the time we were in communication, by his own description, 'bobbing about in a boat in the Sea of Cortez' – the wonders of email and modern technology!

Grateful thanks too to Sue Rose – David's PA for the last eight years of his life (and someone who, from circumstances, most certainly got to know David far better than she ever envisaged when she initially applied for the job). Thanks to Jean Winch – business adviser since 2002, and Karen Botha, past CEO of the David Shepherd Wildlife Foundation (DSWF). Also, Kay Roudaut who has a long involvement with DSWF and is the one nowadays responsible for artist liaison and trading – but who, in the past, accompanied David to talk show venues on many occasions. Her input regarding the latter was invaluable.

Particular and most effusive thanks to Julian Birley, one of David's long-term friends and fellow steam locomotive enthusiasts: like David, he is gloriously enthusiastic to the point of obsession – there's no wonder the two of them got on so well! Thanks also to Wilfred Mole for his input regarding steam locomotive *Avril*, and to railway book author and one-time steam engine driver, Geoff Burch. The undoubted knowledge of all three has been invaluable in assisting me on that important part of David's life. Stephen Moor and 'The Grumblies' are a team of model railway lovers who regularly helped David with troubleshooting and maintenance of his model railway at Brooklands Farm. As I would be the first to admit that I know nothing about such things, I am therefore, very appreciative of their assistance with technical matters regarding the railway – also for their wonderful anecdotes and reminiscences of their Mondays spent with David at Brooklands whilst working on his lay-out.

Others to whom thanks are most definitely due include John Bulmer, who really got behind this particular project and discovered the whereabouts of several of David's earliest (and sometimes unknown/forgotten) paintings on both this book's behalf and for the future benefit of the Shepherd family. Thank you to Lisa Pool, Elaine Green and Elaine Lavender of the East Somerset Railway. Thanks too, to Rachel Fannen of the Chesterfield Museum; to Rupert Fogden and Candida Lord of Mallams Auctioneers, Oxford; and to Jonathan Pertwee.

Photographically, my most sincere gratitude to Philip Reeson (www.reeson.com) for his kindness in permitting use of the portrait jacket cover photo of David … and also to Elliot Hobson and everyone who took the various photographs (including the photos of David's paintings) which appear in this book. The names of some have, over time, sadly been lost and they cannot therefore be individually thanked but their input is very much appreciated.

Thank you to Kevin Robertson of Noodle Books regarding the use of David's introduction in *Artist Among the Ashes*. Talking of such things, I have included several quotes taken from both the original and the revised editions of David's autobiography, *The Man Who Loves Giants*; *David Shepherd: The Man and His Paintings*; *David Shepherd: My Painting Life* and *A Brush With Steam*, all four of which were published by David & Charles. Obviously the words and copyright are David Shepherd's (and, since his death, the Shepherd family) and so I was able to use any information gleaned from there at will. I was, nevertheless, extremely grateful to David & Charles for giving their 'thumbs-up' via Ame Verso, their current publishing director.

As well as having been fortunate in having access to the Shepherd family archive and private material, I have also drawn much general information and inspiration from various articles and letters in magazines, books and internet forums. I have, quite cheekily, included extracts from the introduction David wrote in his great friend Rolf Rohwer's 2012 book *Campfire Tales*, knowing full well that, as great friends of the family, Rolf's widow Carole, son Rolf and daughter Kirsten will have no objection whatsoever! Irrespective of that, in accordance with my understanding of the UK's copyright laws, I have not necessarily sought permission to quote very minor extracts from other sources – but have, in all cases, mentioned the origin within the text and would like to assure anyone concerned that I have not taken any quote and used it out of context … or to the detriment of what was intended by the author. In instances where more than a few words have been used, every reasonable effort has been made to contact possible copyright owners.

As a point of interest, the song *Wish Me Luck as You Wave Me Goodbye*, as mentioned in the 'Man of Africa' chapter, was written by Phil Park and Harry Parr-Davies and was first published by Chappell Music Ltd.

# FOREWORD

Long before we became friends with David we were both huge fans of his art, especially his wildlife paintings, which totally captured the spirit of the animals in all their glory. Particularly his magnificent elephants, which back in the 1970s adorned millions of walls in houses throughout the land, treating us to a glimpse of exotic Africa long before safari holidays became affordable to the masses.

The first time meeting David was when he came to the British Wildlife Centre (BWF) in order to study water voles for a future project of his. We immediately bonded over our shared passion for nature and wildlife, and on leaving with a promise of water voles for his pond at Brooklands Farm, it heralded the start of a wonderful friendship – a friendship which really blossomed when we got to know David's wife Avril and there was often just the four of us just enjoying each other's company ... so many lovely memories!

On one occasion, after lunch at Brooklands, David very proudly showed us a secret little door in the wall panelling, which he opened to reveal a tiny room – not a doll's house but a mouse house, home to three perfectly dressed inhabitants with all their furniture perfectly to scale. We were so enchanted by this appealing scene that, rushing back home ... [Judi] painted a miniature mouse portrait that we sent to David to hang on the wall in the tiny room ... much to his great amusement!

On another memorable occasion we all spent a glorious few days relaxing and having fun on Tresco in the Isles of Scilly, where we enjoyed many an hour watching the red squirrels in the Abbey Gardens. The introduction of the squirrels to the Gardens had been one of the BWF's first conservation projects, which in turn had been originally inspired by the work David's Foundation was doing to save endangered species around the world – species that are on the edge of extinction that desperately need all the help they can get.

What a wonderful legacy David has left us ... all those exquisite paintings and a highly respected world-famous Foundation. His enthusiasm and dedication were unparalleled and he continues to be an absolute inspiration to us all ...

**Dame Judi Dench CH, DBE, FRSA and**
**David Mills MBE**

Judi Dench and her 'chap' (Judi dislikes the word 'partner'!) David Mills, were good friends with David and Avril, and Judi has been an avid supporter of the DSWF for over a decade.

David Mills is the creator of the British Wildlife Centre based at Lingfield, Surrey (www.britishwildlifecentre.co.uk), which is home to over forty British species of wildlife ranging from harvest mice to deer. The centre houses Britain's first-ever 'walk-through' red squirrel enclosure – and the couple first met when David invited Judi to officially open it in 2010.

# INTRODUCTION

In 1975, David & Charles published *The Man Who Loves Giants* – an autobiography by David Shepherd. Even though he was only forty-four years of age, he had, by that time, already achieved more than most could have contemplated in three lifetimes. In the second of his two appearances on BBC Radio's *Desert Island Discs* in 1999, interviewer Sue Lawley described David as being 'one of life's lucky people' – an untrue statement as he of all people was definitely very much of the opinion that one should create one's own luck and that life was very much what you made it.

Passionate in everything he did, be it art, wildlife conservation or when involved in one of his many eclectic interests, as his eldest daughter Melinda remembers, he quite often went to extremes '... particularly about musicals, which he absolutely adored ... especially *Me and My Girl*, various productions of which he saw forty-nine times ... including once taking Mum, myself and my sisters to New York to see it on Broadway!'

*Guys and Dolls* was another favourite musical which David and the family saw together on many occasions. As Avril recollected: 'David was strange – he'd much prefer to see the same show lots of times rather see a new one ... he was the same with films too; goodness knows how many times we went to see *Gone with the Wind* ... Once, he booked a whole row of the stalls for family and friends to see one particular viewing.'

Whether cinema or London shows, David was always enthusiastic regarding what he loved. According to Melinda: 'During some performances, Dad would get very animated and excited ... so much so that, as we got older and more potentially embarrassed, as daughters we would almost fight to make sure that the only seat next to him was filled by Mum as she was the only one of us likely to be able to restrain his extrovert enthusiasm.'

Brought up on Gilbert and Sullivan, music of many kinds was a source of joy to David. It was indeed an eclectic mix ranging from show tunes to Abba, from Abba to Mahler and much more in between. However, at least as might be assumed from his choices of music made for his two appearances on radio's *Desert Island Discs* (see Chapter 11) it would appear that his love of Sibelius' *Symphony No. 1 in E Minor* and Mahler's *Symphony No. 8 in E-flat Major* (his overall record of choice on both occasions) remained with him throughout a long period of his life – as did the Glenn Miller composed *Tuxedo Junction*.

## 'A curious man'

Famously, David's career as an artist was launched in 1962 when Boots (primarily a chemist shop) mass-produced a copy of a canvas he had painted called *Wise Old Elephant*, with, as David once described it, a framework of 'filthy little pieces of wood around the edges'. Despite its enormous success (over 250,000 copies were sold in a very short space of time) he made virtually no money from it due to the fact he'd been paid a one-off fee by the producers of the print. At the time, the painting came in for much criticism from the established, somewhat highbrow art world. 'I was called Britain's top pop artist but I had some dreadful publicity,' David was to tell a newspaper reporter many years later.

Interviewed on many occasions by reporters and journalists, their attention was important in that any publicity would help David in his phenomenal fundraising efforts for wildlife conservation and in increasing public awareness for the need for steam locomotive preservation. It was, though, sometimes difficult to establish from the tone of their subsequent articles exactly what they thought of him. In her 2002 article for *The Argus*, journalist Angela Wintle, wrote:

> Shepherd is a curious man. He has so much energy he can barely control himself, and his emotions are never far from the surface. In two hours, his behaviour veers from wild fury to helpless laughter.
>
> He is excitable, enthusiastic and talks non-stop, frequently breaking into raucous laughter which mutates into a whinny ... He wallows in nostalgia and loves 'music which stirs the emotions'. He can't paint when he hears Sibelius: it moves him to tears ... In his head, he lives in a Bridesheadian age of steam trains, hackney carriages and cricket on the village green ... He never tires of repeating his fund of stories and tells me he has an 'ego the size of a planet'.
>
> You can't help liking him though. He has a natural warmth and an infectious enthusiasm.

## Infectious enthusiasm

His warmth and infectious enthusiasm were qualities that endeared him to many, including Her Majesty Queen Elizabeth the Queen Mother, and it was 'enthusiasm' that he mentioned when, asked by her in conversation during a sitting for a commissioned portrait in 1969, 'How do you manage to paint the *Ark Royal* one day and me the next?', he replied, 'There's no difference, Ma'am ... The common denominator is enthusiasm.' The theory regarding the lack of any difference was something obviously long-held by David as it was mentioned in a catalogue for a 1954 exhibition of his paintings where the introduction included the following observation: 'David Shepherd rightly holds with the principle of approaching any subject with the same outlook – as a thing of pictorial beauty – no matter whether it be an avenue of beech trees, a piece of furniture, a portrait, or a jet airliner.'

Enthusiasm aside, he could certainly see beauty in whatever he painted, especially when it came to wildlife and nature. As David himself once wrote: 'Whether it is an English beechwood, a scene of elephants in Africa, or locomotives at Nine Elms, nature creates the most fantastic colours in the evening ... in nature, as well as being beautiful, trees are so important ... tragic though the loss of buildings might be, bricks and mortar can be rebuilt; you can't do the same with wildlife – and it's not so easy with trees either.'

It was David's concern for the natural world and what negative effects the human population was having on it (some intentional, some through ignorance and/or lack of thought) which caused the artist to use his success for its benefit by selling paintings to raise money initially for the World Wildlife Fund (now 'rebranded' as the World Wide Fund for Nature) and then for his own charitable foundation.

It is important to realise that, back in the late 1960s, 1970s and 1980s, David was a 'celebrity' every bit as famous as the easily recognisable names of today and, as a consequence, was greatly in demand for appearances on radio and television (see Chapter 11). Such public platforms gave all-important opportunities to enthusiastically champion his cause. So, despite what may be thought by a younger generation, the BBC Television presenter Chris Packham is most certainly not the first to use his status to promote awareness of the devastating changes to the environment via his support for the Extinction Rebellion group, or his concern for the world's wildlife and habitat. Along with the likes of Peter Scott, David Attenborough and Professor David Bellamy, David Shepherd was championing similar causes well over half a century ago.

### Childhood hero and friend

David was an inspiration to many and a childhood hero to some – including railway buff Julian Birley and media presenter, wildlife photographer and conservation activist Mark Carwardine. Both were to become great friends of David's. Mark's first opportunity to meet his hero was when he was working at the WWF where David was a trustee: 'He had so much energy and enthusiasm and charisma that when he left the room, it felt like a tornado had just passed through.' He was tireless; even at the age of seventy-seven. He told an interviewer for *Surrey Life* magazine that: 'Although I spend most of my daylight hours painting in my studio – I still complete about fifty commissions a year – I venture out to gather reference material and, if I'm lucky, to paint in situ.'

Julian Birley, in addition to becoming a personal friend, is also the former chairman of the North Norfolk Railway where David's steam locomotive *Black Prince* (see Chapter 9) is now kept:

Over the years that I knew David he inspired such fun. The madder the idea the more he wanted to do it. David and I used to drive from Brooklands [David and Avril's home in East Sussex] to the North Norfolk Railway … on a regular basis for a number of years. We used to laugh our way up and laugh our way back. I never tired from listening to his wonderful stories from painting the portrait of Her Majesty Queen Elizabeth, the Queen Mother, who apologised for being late for a meeting with him as she had been 'up the road having coffee with her daughter', to being pushed along the rails in an adapted 1937 Ford Popular car through the African bush by a 100-ton Victorian steam locomotive (see Chapter 9).

During much of David's life, his eclectic interests collided, although in the following example they were, fortunately, metaphorical rather than physical. In August 2009, on the occasion of the fiftieth birthday of his beloved steam engine *Black Prince*, which, before being moved to the North Norfolk Railway, was kept at the Gloucester and Warwickshire Railway, a fly-past of Second World War planes was organised. Aeroplanes from the Battle of Britain Memorial Flight of which David was a great supporter and fundraiser (see Chapter 10) flew low in salute over the celebrations which, although fun and included a huge birthday cake, were primarily intended as a fundraiser for the DSWF.

Friends of David were frequently surprised by unexpected and quite often generous invitations. Stephen Moor, spokesman for 'The Grumblies' (see Chapter 4) who used to descend on Brooklands most Mondays to help maintain and improve David's quite extensive model railway layout, remembers that 'After just a few visits to Brooklands David invited us to the Gloucester and Warwickshire Railway to spend a day with him, his beloved loco and the RAF Battle of Britain Memorial Flight crew. It was a private day and the RAF guys had a go at driving and firing the engine ... at one point I found myself on the footplate getting ready to leave the station with a famous squadron leader pilot in the engine-driver's seat ... it was a quite surreal moment!'

## Big boy's toys

His love of steam locomotives aside, another measure of David's success and enthusiasm for the mechanically large was the acquisition of an old London Routemaster bus (see Chapter 2) which was liveried in DSWF colours and spent time down at the East Somerset Railway before being eventually sold. Although undoubtedly sensible from the point of view of publicity for the Foundation, it is doubtful that even David would have denied that he'd bought it mainly for the joy of possession. As daughter Mandy comments, 'Such things were "trophies"; a measure of his success.'

Another of David's acquisitions was a flatbed Bedford three-ton lorry, on the back of which the daughters loved travelling. Three of the four would frequently load up on the open back – seated on garden chairs – with their parents up front in the cab and pop down for weekend visits to see Melinda, their eldest sister, whilst she was at St Michael's boarding school in Petworth, West Sussex (see also Chapter 6). Great fun, but certainly illegal nowadays and imagine Melinda's embarrassment as they all rolled up at her somewhat prestigious place of education and parked up alongside the other parents' swish vehicles!

A huge lover of Land Rovers – and a great supporter of the British motor industry – David owned several during his lifetime. Before the days of compulsory seat belts, Avril would take their children and those of neighbours to school in a safari wagon type, and one, bought on a whim purely because it happened to be registered for the year in which he and Avril married (1957) was kept in the barn of Maesgwyn, their cottage in Wales. Apart from its use to David out in the wilds of the Brecon Beacons, it was also a vehicle in which several of the grandchildren learnt to drive during their stays up there. For her fiftieth birthday, David bought Avril a Willys jeep – totally forgetting the fact that she couldn't drive it due to there being no power steering and a need to double declutch every time a gear change was required. It was, though, accompanied by something rather more feminine in the shape of an emerald necklace!

Then, of course, there was the famous incident when, at David's seventy-fifth birthday celebrations held at The Dorchester organised as a fundraising event, one of the lots up for auction was a motorised scale model of a Land Rover 'Wincotts Toylander 2 with trailer in DSWF livery' intended for youngsters. Keen to demonstrate its versatility, David squeezed his six-feet-two-inch length into the driver's seat – and promptly drove it off the stage. It caused great amusement to the audience and to David himself who narrated the tale in that year's 'round robin' newsletter included with cards sent to friends and family each Christmas.

* * *

## The Cowley assembly line and lost paintings

Unbeknown to many, several of David's earlier paintings featured artwork of car factories and industry. In February 2020, a canvas of his entitled *The Morris Oxford No. 3 Assembly Line, Cowley*, dated 1955, came up for sale at Mallams Auctioneers, Oxford. It was sold, together with a page from that year's Nuffield organisation's company magazine *Teamwork*, in which David's painting of the assembly line was mentioned:

> ... impervious to the hubbub and curious states ... a young London artist has been setting on canvas his impression of the Morris Oxford coming off the line ... We were a trifle disappointed to find that he belies the usual conception of an artist – no beard or floppy hat, no bow-tie or even sandals! The only unusual thing that we could discover was that apparently he lives on tea and boiled sweets. Certainly none can remember him stopping for a regular meal ...

Although the painting was referred to by David in his original autobiography of 1975 and is thus known, no one in the family had, prior to the auction, ever seen this particular painting. Nor were they aware of the fact that Chesterfield Museum is nowadays the owner of his painting *Kariba First Turbine* 'showing a turbine at Markham Works with two men working on it and orange scaffolding above it'. It was apparently labelled thus for an 'Illustrating Industry' exhibition held in 1958. Given David's prolific output, there must be many others that remain unknown.

***

## David as a fashion icon

Events at The Dorchester and elsewhere might have required David to don a dinner jacket but, never one to be a part of the crowd, his preferred choice from the wardrobe was most often his favourite of a dark green rather than the more traditional black. Despite being usually seen in his trademark safari jacket or gilet, he could scrub up quite well when lounge suits or dinner jackets were required. An *Evening Standard* article of 18 April 1960, mentions that, 'One would not guess Mr. Shepherd to be an artist when first meeting him. A stockbroker would be more likely. "I have no time for artists who go around looking scruffy and unwashed," he said. "If you are going to paint you must be successful and look successful."'

Successful he may have been but, in general terms clothes-wise, unlike Avril, David could never ever have been classed as a fashion icon – although on at least one occasion, he and all the family did appear in an article which featured their attire rather than, as was more common, focus on the artist's painting or wildlife conservation. In the *Sunday Express Magazine* of 20 May 1990, David, Avril and their daughters were all seen wearing 'designer' clothes for a photo shoot at Winkworth Farm. Prior to that, some publicity and press photos of David show him wearing the fashion trends of the time (in the '70s, for example, slightly flared trousers with a colourful kerchief or scarf around his neck) but that was most definitely Avril's doing as David himself didn't really care what he wore. Life was too full to worry about such fads! In her 2002 interview with David (see above) journalist Angela Wintle described David as adopting '... the Stewart Granger safari look even in deepest Sussex. He is tanned and dressed in regulation game warden garb: jeans, khaki shirt unbuttoned to the chest (he often sports a medallion) photographer's jacket, Timberland boots and copper bracelet ... all that is missing are the dry plains of the Serengeti and a herd of wild elephants'.

* * *

### Fit for a queen

Sartorial elegance to one side, David would, when painting, generally favour a particular pair of trousers – for no other reason than practicality. Talking to Stacey Heaney of the *Ulster Star* in 2011, David said: 'I bought a pair of painting trousers at a market. I could have gone to Harrods and paid a fortune, but I bought them at a market thirty years ago, and as I paint I wipe my brush on my right leg. I remember my painting the portrait of the Queen Mother at Clarence House [where David had been told to dress casually and wear what he would normally wear for painting] and she looked at me and said, "That's an interesting colour combination you've got." I still use those trousers and they are so stiff from paint that they all but stand up on their own.'

* * *

*A disciplined work ethic*

Elephants obviously featured in a great deal of David's paintings. They, alongside his extremely atmospheric portrayals of the days of steam locomotives, are the 'giants' for which he is perhaps best recognised. Although in order to obtain the atmosphere and accuracy for which his artwork is known it was necessary to spend time out and about, making sketches and taking photographs, most of the final paintings were done in his studio (see Chapter 3). As one should, he treated the studio as his workplace and went to it daily as assiduously as any London commuter. He was dedicated to his art and extremely disciplined.

Typically, when at home, his studio hours would be 8 a.m. to 10.30 a.m. before a half-hour break for coffee. Back to the studio until lunchtime and then another painting stint from 2 p.m. to 5 p.m. or thereabouts. His work ethic meant that little or nothing would, or should, disturb his daily routine – and in that, he was lucky in having Avril ready and willing to keep family life and daily happenings on an even keel. That's not to say that he was a distant parent; all four daughters remember him as being a brilliant father when they were young.

Although outwardly confident and an amazing self-publicist, he was somewhat insecure and needed constant praise. He was also egotistical. Pamela Jackson, a BBC production assistant who became a family friend (see Chapter 6) and who was also an avid collector of David Shepherd prints, remembers his first visit to her home near Bristol many years ago where 'David ... went from room to room seeing how many of his prints we had – saying "that's one of mine, that's one of mine." It was like a whirlwind going through the house!'

## Chocoholic and a technophobe

He was certainly a man of many parts. Egotistical, outspoken (particularly on the subject of wildlife) complicated, enthusiastic, a lover of fun – and of chocolate! Few lunchtime meals could conclude without a visit to the pantry to pick up a bar of Dairy Milk or similar and, on occasions such as Christmas or birthdays when the family was gathered and, after the meal, all moved into the drawing room for coffee, it wasn't unknown for David to pick up a tin of Roses or Quality Street and throw them randomly at anyone and everyone who was sitting about him.

In an evening, in his later years, if nothing – in his opinion – was worth watching on live-time television then David would delve into the most obscure Sky channels in order to find and avidly peruse programmes dealing with either aircraft or ship disasters. Quite exactly what the fascination was, he never really explained but there are several of his most immediate family who, forced by politeness to watch such things with him, will forever remain scarred! It may just possibly have been the profile of planes that interested him – after all, as a painter of commercial aircraft in his younger years, there would always have been an interest in accuracy. It could not, however, have been because of his interest in their technical mechanics.

Despite a fondness for Land Rovers (in a 2012 interview for *Ink Pellet* magazine, when asked his favourite book title, David remarked, 'I don't have time to read but if I did then the *Land Rover Handbook* would be my choice!') and having a basic understanding of what made a steam locomotive power its way along the tracks, David was not, by any stretch of the imagination, fond of the complications of technology. He left others to deal with business that required the use of a computer, and his lack of tolerance when some inanimate piece of equipment failed to do as he wanted is legendary. Once, when transcribing a Dictaphone recording of David's spoken word into written copy for a book, his secretary of the time was so engrossed in getting the words down on paper that she failed to register what she was actually writing. Thus, it was only when the hard copy manuscript was first read as a draft that it was noticed that much of the information David had recorded was interspersed with several swear words and expletives at points where the machine had obviously refused to behave in the manner which he would have wished.

## Politically incorrect

Kitty Hoare was the first of David's personal assistants and secretaries (see Chapter 3). Sue Rose was the last. Sue describes him fondly as being 'emotional and gushy, good fun but hard work ... he always wanted to be right ... but we did some amazing things together'. On car journeys to various appointments, fundraisers, talks, railway visits and exhibitions – as he did with Julian Birley (see above) – he loved to make Sue laugh. She was someone new to whom he could tell his stories. At other times they sat in companionable silence, apart from when it came to road directions, where David always thought he knew best – and his knowledge better than the Satnav. But then, David had never in his life ever done anything he was told so he wasn't likely to change in his later years!

Unorthodox (and sometimes, in all genuine innocence, very definitely politically incorrect) during the selection process for what eventually became Sue's position as PA, as David looked through the list of applicants (apparently there were over 300) he happened to notice a photo of Sue attached to her CV. 'Can I have this one? She's blonde ...' This is perhaps not as sexist as might first be thought. Bearing in mind his love for his blonde wife and blonde daughters (several times Avril was mistaken for Melinda, Mandy, Melanie and Wendy's sister rather than their mother – a fact which always delighted David) it is more likely that David saw her as the perfect person to fit into Brooklands and its lifestyle. Likewise, when the family's business manager Jean Winch applied for her post in 2002 and came for interview, one of the first questions David asked of her was, 'Do you like dogs?' Fortunately for Jean, she did – and got the job.

## Attempting the impossible!

David's life would, were it ever to be made into a film, be considered somewhat unbelievable and (forgive the pun) one would think a degree of artistic licence would need to be involved. As an artist and conservationist – a fact for which, unknowingly, many generations of wildlife must surely be grateful – his life touched many metaphorically and physically, both within his own family and through his many and varied (quite often influential) friends. The 'Three Generations' exhibitions (see Chapter 4), which proved extremely successful as both Mandy and Emily began showcasing their work alongside that of their father and grandfather, was not unsurprising. Some exhibitions with other artists which David jointly shared at various stages of his life might, however, have raised an eyebrow or two. Whilst there might have been a synchronicity when David's art was shown alongside the likes of internationally renowned English landscape artist Ashley Jackson; one running in conjunction with comedian and amateur cartoonist Spike Milligan was a little more unexpected.

On Twitter, at the announcement of David's death on social media in September 2017, one reply commented, 'His life was too large to fit into one simple, allowable 280-word tweet but, if you wrote a book about a man that did half of what David did, you would be told it wasn't possible.' The following chapters attempt the impossible!

I

# PATRIARCHS, MATRIARCHS, SIBLINGS AND EARLY LIFE

It is well worth beginning this particular section by including a little information regarding David's grandparents and parents, all of whom were fascinating characters and, like David and his siblings, achieved a great deal in their own particular spheres. David's paternal grandfather, Richard, who was born in 1863, was, according to a newspaper obituary after his death in 1924:

A tall, commanding figure ... who at Oxford distinguished himself as few men ever did, getting a First in Classical Moderations, a First in the Final Honours School of Jurisprudence, a First in the B.C.L. and an All Souls Fellowship – a combination of honours of which, though he never boasted of it, he was naturally proud ... He had a profound knowledge of the law ... For some years he had been leader of the Bar in Yorkshire ... He was a very hard worker ... and was never so happy as when immersed in briefs and law books ... in his younger days he was a fast bowler in the Leeds cricket club, and in more recent years occasionally enjoyed shooting in Scotland.

Equally remarkable was Richard's wife Mabel, second daughter of James Oxley and sister of great-uncle Henry (see various references elsewhere in this chapter regarding the latter). In a newspaper article of 1928, it was reported that 'Mrs R. A. Shepherd (Mabel) one of the three daughters to receive £100,000 under the will of Mr J. W. Oxley, the Leeds banker who left nearly £3,000,000, is an invalid widow. Some years ago she was blown down in a gale. Her spine was injured and she has been kept to her bed ever since ...'

Grandparents on David's mother's side were Montague and Mary Williamson. Montague was the son of a northern clergyman and followed his father into the church, being ordained at Exeter Cathedral in 1887. He moved to Cornwall in 1904, and, amongst other appointments, was rector of King Charles the Martyr Church, Falmouth, from 1918 to 1924. Subsequently, he became Archdeacon of Bodmin, 1924–39. In 1937 he was praised for fifty years of ministry; the Bishop of Truro describing Canon Williamson as having had 'an inward gift of being practical ... who never shirked an unpleasant duty'.

Montague's wife was known to David, Peter and Judy as 'Grumpy Granny'. It's highly unlikely that they dared have called this to her face as she was, by all accounts, a very austere-looking typical Victorian lady who, like Queen Victoria herself, was only ever known to have worn black – but, like Victoria, perhaps only since the death of her husband who pre-deceased her by many years. Described as a 'tyrant' by her grandchildren, she lived on the outskirts of Bristol and was looked after for fifty weeks of the year by her daughter (also named Mary) who lived next door and, according to her niece, had 'a miserable life'. As far as the two remaining weeks of the year were concerned, Mary senior's care was the responsibility of her other daughter Joyce (Peter, David and Judy's mother).

* * *

## 'Great-uncle Henry'

Peter, David and Judy's great-uncle is of great importance in the Shepherd story as it was through him that family wealth was obtained. Henry Oxley was seemingly a reclusive character, who had no children. He was great friends with the well-known sculptress Phyllis Bone, who had a house nearby his at Newton Stewart and who also had the honour of being the first woman to be elected a full member of the Royal Scottish Academy in 1944.

Born in 1869, Henry lived in grand style for much of the year at Spenfield House, Leeds, but he also owned Penninghame House and its surrounding estate near Newton Stewart in Scotland. In 1928, on the death of his Leeds-based banker father James, Henry was fortunate enough to inherit the bulk of a vast fortune – amounting to some £2.8 million (equivalent to approximately £120 million at today's values). He was not so fortunate in the fact that 'Estate Duty' (Inheritance Tax) of 40 per cent had to be paid (over £1 million). On Henry's death in 1948, his estate was required to pay Estate Duty at a rate of 75 per cent. On that occasion, over £1.1 million in tax was handed over to the taxman (equivalent to approximately £35 million today).

Interestingly, after being used variously as a private home, a First World War hospital, an open prison for eighty-five inmates and latterly, a holistic centre, Penninghame House, together with 100 acres, came back on the market as a private dwelling in June 2019 with an asking price of £2.6 million.

***

## David's parents

David's father Raymond was born in Leeds in 1899 and spent his childhood at the family home, Cumberland Priory. Before the Second World War, he had owned a small advertising agency in London and, during the war, he was a second lieutenant in the 9th Field Training Regiment, Royal Artillery, working as an education officer, giving talks to the troops on current affairs. After inheriting money from his great-uncle Henry in 1948, he bought and ran Frimley Hall Hotel, near Camberley. Family history has it that, along with its purchase, Raymond also inherited a number of long-term residents, mainly old people, who paid £7 per week and complained endlessly! It was the very last thing he wanted, as David was to amusingly remember in later life:

> Father wanted a young place that would draw people from far and wide to dine and dance. Being very tactful and sensible, he took things very gently at first. For example, the first major change was to transfer the rice pudding from Tuesday to Wednesday, and the blackberry and apple pie from Wednesday to Thursday. This created a major eruption amongst the guests, who had had the same food every day since they arrived before the war. In fact, sitting on the same cushions, in the same position, in the same armchair throughout the war they probably did not even know it was being fought ... After our first dinner dance, most of them left and the hotel gradually took on a marvellous reputation which was soon to become known far and wide.

Away from his complaining residents and hotelier duties, Raymond was a great car enthusiast (especially enjoying the excitements of Talbots and Bentleys) and was also keen on steam railways (both full-size and model) a hobby which was inherited in full by both his sons.

** * **

## The maggot now standing on platform one

In connection with his father's model railway (of which more in Chapter 4) David's recollections of his early life included both Raymond's railway and an apparent early interest in wildlife:

> Even in those very early days ... I must have been crazy about animals. I remember asking my father if I could use one of the cupboards which were part of his railway for my very own 'natural history museum'. He was not too happy about it but he agreed, and one of my earliest memories is of picking up a dead song thrush ... This became the prize exhibit amongst all the feathers and sea shells I had collected from our holidays ... I was far too

young, however, to realise that things gradually happen to dead bodies. My dad was rather cross with me when, returning one evening from his London office, he found 'Watford Station' to be unusually busy. The platform was crowded with maggots wriggling all over the place like drunken commuters. One had even managed to squeeze into the miniature 'Gents' but had got stuck because it was too fat to get out again.

*** 

It is perhaps just as well that Raymond's wife Joyce's care duties towards her mother Mary only amounted to two weeks of the year (see above) as she was an extremely busy lady throughout her life. Born in 1897 and christened Margaret Joyce Williamson (but always known as Joyce) she was brought up in Devon and absolutely adored the country life, dogs, horses and ponies and cattle.

The Williamsons were regarded by David and his brother Peter as being the intellectuals of the family. Their uncle, Charles Williamson (Joyce's brother), most certainly was. As a schoolmaster teaching Classics, he was also an author who wrote books in Latin (actually in Latin, not on the subject of). One of his tomes, *The English Tradition in the World*, was considered 'a political philosophy for today'. Partly autobiographical, it traced the effects of the English countryside on the growth of the 'English Tradition' but, not content with just dealing with how it might have affected life in Britain, Charles went on to discuss the value of that same tradition in all parts of the world.

Joyce rode all her adult life. She owned and bred Welsh Mountain ponies, kept pigs and milking cows (Jerseys) at Frimley Hall, Aberdeen Angus at Oakhill House – and had the honour of owning the champion at Perth Bull Sale (then the biggest and most prestigious such sale sin the country). She was also president of the Farnham and District Fatstock Association before eventually giving up farming altogether and moving to Wastlands, a house at Ewhurst, near Cranleigh.

## Vying for attention

With very little time for children and not being a 'typical' mother (whatever one of those may be!) who knew how to hug her offspring, in an effort to see their mother more frequently, it apparently became David and Peter's mission to try and get rid of any nannies as quickly as possible by devising some really horrible and quite naughty pranks. Their younger sister Judy does not remember this of her brothers but nevertheless, perceived Shepherd legend has it that their personal 'best' was two days!

Joyce apparently made no secret of the fact that, of the three, as children, she preferred the company of Peter and Judy (possibly because they shared her love of horses more than did David) – until that, is, David became famous in adult life when he, according to Judy, very definitely and very quickly, became the favoured one. Part of an article in the *Surrey Advertiser*, published around 1967, does however, tell a slightly different story: 'Mrs. Shepherd commented that it was great fun being the mother of two famous children. Wherever she went she was introduced either as the mother of Judy Crago, the horsewoman (see below) or of David Shepherd, the painter. "It was a reflected glory," she said, "but it was very nice."'

## David's siblings

David's brother Peter was the eldest of Raymond and Joyce's three children. As can be seen in the accounts of their wartime life (see below) he and David had a very close relationship and got up to much mischief together. In adulthood, Peter went on to have an interesting and eclectic mix of careers, some rather more successful than others. After school at Stowe, he went to Cambridge University (Trinity College) and whilst there, was master of the Trinity Foot Beagles. Although in his youth Peter was a keen amateur point-to-point rider and loved riding, it may possibly have been the music master at Stowe who gave Peter his enthusiasm for hounds for, as well as teaching music, that particular tutor was also joint-master of the Grafton Foxhounds.

After graduating, Peter worked in advertising in London: lucrative employment which involved television advertising in the early days of commercial television in the 1950s. In the 1960s he set up a successful finance company specialising in lending to small businesses – a quite revolutionary concept at the time as, in both the 1960s and early 1970s, banks tended to be wary of lending to small concerns and so private financing such as Peter's company was able to provide was the only way forward for some. Throughout his life he became increasingly interested in local government, firstly becoming a West Sussex county councillor, culminating in a four-year term as chairman. Peter's politics were those of a robust Tory, who believed in free markets and enterprise, self-reliance, liberty and freedom from bureaucracy. He was thought to have been the council's most outspoken and controversial chairman, never afraid to ruffle feathers.

Peter's love of horses, riding and racing was ongoing, and he and his wife Elizabeth bred Welsh Mountain ponies. The two, in fact, met at the riding school his mother owned at Frimley Hall (where Elizabeth had come from Wales to work as a groom) and Elizabeth nursed Peter after an extremely serious riding accident in which he fractured his skull. They have two sons, Robert and Jonathan, the latter of whom has done much to ensure that the family history is not lost.

## Judy

David's sister Judy was, in the late 1950s and 1960s, one of Britain's most successful top international riders. In July 1960, she won the British Showjumping Association's National Championships held at Stanley Park, Blackpool, but her delight was marred by the fact that her father Raymond died (at the age of sixty-one) of bladder cancer the next day completely unaware of his daughter's success. In 1961 she married Brian Crago, the Australian horseman who competed as part of the four-man eventing team in both the 1956 and 1960 Olympics on horses Radar and Sabre. In 1962, Judy won the prestigious Queen Elizabeth II Cup at the Royal International Horse Show.

Arguably, her most famous horse was Spring Fever, on which she represented Britain at numerous international shows in the period 1960–67 – and she and Spring Fever were members of the Nations Cup team. Judy also had great success with a second well-known horse, Bouncer, who was loaned to the British team for the Montreal Olympics. Spring Fever's offspring Autumn Folly was subsequently shortlisted for the Olympics with Judy and Brian's son Paul (brother of Felicity) as riders. Paul is, like his mother, a successful international showjumper and knowledgeable equestrian.

For Judy it was not, however, a straightforward ride from school to showjumping success. It involved a great deal of hard work, beginning with her mother's ponies and lessons during her time at boarding school near Arundel, West Sussex. At sixteen, Judy had the option of staying in higher education or going to France to learn the language – she chose the latter. In order to finance her summer showjumping as an amateur rider, once back in England she earned money in London during the winter working in shops and, one year, in the offices of the Bertram Mills Circus. Now in her eighties, Judy remains an active, sprightly woman with twinkly eyes and a great sense of humour. Like David, she has a love of dogs, and has throughout most of her adult life kept a succession of quite characterful Jack Russell terriers, all of which have been descendants of her original bitch from over half a century ago.

## Family pleasures

Brothers and sister all seem to have got on well and shared a similar sense of humour. They have certainly all displayed a great zest for life and, in their later careers, whatever they've put their minds to seems to have been done with enthusiasm, skill and not inconsiderable success.

Childhood holidays were spent at Birchington on the Kent coast. There, if the weather was fine, their father would help them build sandcastles on the beach, although it must be admitted that he was far happier taking them to the nearby level crossing to watch the trains go by. To David and his brother Peter, that was infinitely more exciting than building sandcastles and may well have been (along with Raymond's love of model railways) the beginnings of their lifelong obsession with steam locomotives.

Being the youngest, Judy has no recollections of any time spent at Birchington, but does remember that they occasionally went on holiday to Llandudno in North Wales. She also has memories of periods spent with her parents and brothers at great-uncle Henry's house and estate in Scotland, where the boys rode round on bicycles and where, according to David, 'We used to go out all day into the hills with the gamekeepers and estate workers.' Although Henry Oxley was seemingly 'never very tolerant' of grubby little children (the siblings only saw him for a few brief moments before dinner) they were apparently 'fabulous times' and ones which left an indelible impression on David: 'That of wide open spaces and fresh air.'

At home in pre-war Totteridge, Judy has such clear memories of their childhood activities and passions and the entertaining times they spent with their parents, particularly their father:

We had our first piano lessons with Miss Vernon [all three attained a reasonable level due to her tuition] and used to play duets together and we'd all play wonderful ball games (which Daddy loved inventing) and with his model railways which he loved so much. Whilst the three of us certainly inherited Mummy and Daddy's love of music, I'm not sure where David's artistic talent came from – and which has since popped up in various members of the family.

After the war ended in 1945, we moved to Larkmead, near Theydon Bois … It was a gorgeous house with a glorious music-room … where we … formed our family dance band, the 'Swinging Shepherds'. Daddy was a brilliant pianist … He played by ear and only had to listen to a piece once in order to perform it. David played the drums with considerable zest, Peter the saxophone,

Mummy sang and I joined in with the ukulele and harmonica. Daddy composed the *Normandy Waltz* which won first prize in a competition with the BBC. We had regular visits to see the D'Oyly Carte operas, the Proms and all the old musicals which undoubtedly began our love of the musical theatre.

When we moved to Frimley Hall Hotel in 1948, David and I used to partner each other in the ballroom dancing every Saturday evening ... I'm sure we would have won *Strictly Come Dancing* had it have been around then!

## Wartime life

In Totteridge, David, Peter and Judy were to see much of the war at first hand. It was, according to David, one of the most emotive periods of his life 'to get off the school bus and watch Spitfires and Messerschmitts fighting overhead was paradise for little boys ... My brother and I didn't think about people killing each other even though our father was in the army ...'

The actual harsh realities of war did not, however, go unnoticed by their sister Judy who recalls:

All through the war we used to watch the dogfights during the Battle of Britain and of course we slept in our air-raid shelter behind the house all through the Blitz, whether or not the sirens had sounded. Every morning David and Peter would go out and pick up all the shrapnel and bits and pieces from the air-raids ... I remember being fitted with those horrible gas masks. Then came the doodlebugs: the terrifying V-1 rockets with the flashing blue lights out of the tail and, when the engines stopped, the lights went out and they crashed. Every evening Peter and David would fill in a wall map on which they chronicled and updated the effects of the war.

The two brothers, enterprising even at that early age, would then display their fine collection of souvenirs – pieces of crashed Messerschmitt, incendiary bomb tails, shrapnel and leaflets – and by doing so, raised £60 for 'Spitfire Week' (one of several government national savings schemes intended to encourage the population to buy saving stamps to help the war effort). As David remembered in later life:

> One of the greatest excitements for small boys in those days was to pay a modest sum for the privilege of sitting for a few moments in the cockpits of captured German aircraft. There was always a queue waiting their turn under the not very attentive eye of a rather sleepy Home Guard soldier … I remember trying our very best to 'acquire' one of the instrument dials which happened to be loose. We only managed to make it more so and I do not doubt that it went to the next small boy in the queue … Always keen to add to our collection of war souvenirs, more damage was often done to that aircraft by the time the last person had climbed down the ladder than the Royal Air Force did in shooting it down!

The two brothers must have been a complete nightmare to the authorities. After one particularly heavy night of bombing during the Blitz, a whole load of incendiary bombs were dropped in the fields next to the Shepherd home. At daybreak, David and Peter beat the police to the scene, and before they eventually arrived to clear the area, spent a dangerous but blissfully happy hour or two picking up several bomb tails and even succeeded in pulling one unexploded bomb out of the hole it had made.

Immediately prior to the outbreak of war, the Shepherd family had employed a German maid. David became convinced that she was a spy: 'She would go off to London with her camera and take endless photos of buildings. She left us just before war broke out and returned to Germany – a great help, I'm sure – to Hitler's Luftwaffe.' It was most likely the fanciful thinking of a boy with a vivid imagination but who knows?

About this time, an interesting newspaper court report appeared concerning the Shepherd household. The cutting was, unfortunately, removed from the paper in such a way that neither the name of the newspaper nor the actual date on which it appeared can be ascertained. Further to the mystery is the fact that Judy (the only remaining member of the family able to comment on the matter) has absolutely no memory of any such person(s) being employed by her parents and remembers only Elsie Gale, who was housekeeper during their time at Totteridge. It is, however, too amusing an account not to include:

> Herbert Moser, aged 37, a cook … was charged with stealing three gold watches, a leather suitcase and a quantity of sugar, butter, and marmalade … the property of Lieut. Raymond Oxley Shepherd, of Normandy, Northcliffe Drive, Totteridge, where he was then employed … Mrs. Margaret Joyce Shepherd said that Moser and another male servant were left in the house between August and December last year … When they were left in the house, Moser and the other servant 'abused the trust placed in them by inviting young ladies into the house and running up bills'.

Untrustworthy house staff notwithstanding, with many fond memories of his childhood at Totteridge during the Second World War, David once happened to mention in a radio interview that he'd like to take another look at his childhood home, as a result of which the then current owners got in touch and invited him to visit – which he did. Their kindness began a trend, as when they then sold the house after a happy decade or so of living there, the new purchasers also invited David and Avril (and Judy – and subsequently, Judy and her daughter Felicity) to lunch on several occasions.

### *Prep school and* Nursery World

David and his brother both attended Kingsfield Preparatory School at Oxhay, Hertfordshire. David was a weekly boarder and, according to his sister, was regularly homesick and used to cry most Sunday evenings when it was time to return after the weekend break. Whilst very definitely an outgoing extrovert in later life, David's mother remembered him as being a 'rather nervous little boy' so Peter's presence at both Kingsfield and also later at Stowe must have given him at least a little reassurance.

Kingsfield was originally founded in about 1933, but was re-founded by a certain Wilfred Sobey in 1940. Sobey ran it until

1970 when he retired and so it is likely that the two Shepherd boys would have been taught by him and/or his predecessor, the Revd R. E. Newton. Another likely teacher would have been Godfrey Pullen who taught gym, cricket, boxing, football, athletics and swimming. He also taught geography and English and had been an officer in the First World War. Pullen was a brilliant raconteur, and legend has it that during one riveting account he gave in class of a daring wartime exploit he had starred in, one boy, transfixed by the excitement, was prompted to ask, 'Gosh! And did you get killed, Sir?'

Going to the cinema was frowned upon by the Kingsfield authorities – it was considered 'packaged entertainment' which was, to them, an uncreative use of young brains. But if the cinema was frowned upon, comics were viewed by them with real distrust and all except *The Eagle* (which had a Christian editor) and the *Children's Newspaper* were banned from the premises. Presumably then, an issue of *Nursery World* could only have been perused at home but, no matter where it was, the young David must have seen a copy and decided to enter a painting competition contained within its pages. There wasn't, however, much artistic talent involved as all that was required was to fill in with coloured crayons the printed outline of a tiger. No matter, David entered – and won the first prize of a book token.

## Time at Stowe

Despite their father having been educated at Charterhouse, Surrey, both David and Peter were sent to Stowe in Buckinghamshire (perhaps, as David later surmised, in the naïve belief that, during the war, 'Hitler's Luftwaffe would never fly north of Watford').

Stowe, as a house (originally the seat of the Lord Viscount Cobham) remains one of the grandest buildings of its architectural type but is nowadays best known for its school, which still retains much of its original garden and Lancelot (Capability) Brown inspired landscape. Opening as a school for the first time in May 1923, J. F. (John Fergusson) Roxburgh was its first headmaster. He remained in that position until 1949 and was thought of fondly by many of his pupils, including David, who remained in contact with him for many years after leaving Stowe – and even invited 'J.F.' as he was widely known, to supper at Winkworth Farm on several occasions.

* * *

*1949 Leaver's Report*

David left Stowe School the same year as his headmaster J. F. Roxburgh who, in David's Leaver's Report, wrote the following comments: 'He is a vigorous and determined worker who tackles every job with enthusiasm. He should be able to achieve good success in later life and I wish him all good fortune.'

L. H. Reid, David's tutor, was no less effusive in wishing him well for a life after Stowe: 'He has taken [school life] in hand with admirable energy and enthusiasm, and is to be congratulated heartily on the results he has achieved. No member of the side is more deserving of success. I am very sorry he is leaving and wish him the best of good fortune and the realization of his immediate ambition.'

* * *

In a newspaper report covering John Roxburgh's retirement in 1949, journalist H. de Winton Wigley mentioned that the outgoing head had 'caused Stowe to be conspicuous for its freedoms. "J.F." has outlawed artificial restrictions ... There is hardly any out of bounds ...' That philosophy clearly suited free-thinking David and there is no wonder that he spoke so fondly of his time there.

Interestingly, most school entries and exam notifications refer to 'Richard', David's first name. Christened Richard David Shepherd, it is perhaps understandable that the school records tended to use his first given name; more surprising is the fact that he seems to have been addressed as Richard by some of his fellow pupils too. A letter from a certain Geoffrey Duckworth written in September 1949 congratulating its recipient on attaining his Higher Certificates, begins 'My dear Richard,' and goes on to say, 'Very many hearty congratulations ... I agree entirely with

Mac [who he?] that you were an excellent monitor, and [I] much appreciated all you did last term to make my unarduous [sic] job even less so!' Purely out of interest, some of David's very early paintings were signed 'R. D. Shepherd' rather than, as is most commonly seen, 'David Shepherd'.

All that to one side, what of David's academic achievements? In his autobiography *The Man Who Loves Giants*, he rather glosses over such things saying that he left Stowe with 'not much more than Higher School Certificates in geography and English – and a dream of becoming a game warden in Africa'. In fact, various school certificates show that throughout his time at Stowe he regularly achieved credits and passes in subjects such as English language, English literature, history, geography, Latin, French (written and oral) elementary mathematics and biology.

Away from the desk and the examination room David excelled at cross-country running and was regularly selected to represent his house (Chatham) and the school – and was one of only a handful to have been awarded their House Colours for cross-country. Sporting as far as cross-country running went, he was less keen on rugby: 'I could not understand the fun of being buried in mud under heaps of writhing bodies and having one's collar bone broken.' It was trying to avoid becoming involved in rugby that persuaded David to take up the far gentler option of art: 'Here was a world almost like a club, where the most artistic amongst us donned yellow waistcoats and went faintly Bohemian on Thursday afternoons.'

With a combined respect and admiration for Stowe's first headmaster, together with the obvious love of the school itself and its environs, it is no surprise that David was to maintain a lifetime's association with the school (Wendy, Avril and David's youngest daughter, was also a pupil). He remained a loyal and devoted 'Old Stoic', visiting often throughout his life and holding exhibitions there. David also painted portraits of a number of Stowe headmasters upon their retirements, including Donald Crichton-Miller, Robert Drayson, Christopher Turner and Jeremy Nichols, and was president of The Old Stoic Society for the period

1993–94. The admiration and long association were mutual, and Stowe continues to include the David Shepherd Wildlife Foundation amongst the various charities it supports.

Headmaster Anthony Wallersteiner remembers David's eightieth birthday celebrations at the school – a dinner and exhibition – and that, in his opinion, 'David was one of the brightest stars from the generation of pupils who flourished under the founding headmaster … and he exemplified all the virtues we want to see in Stoics today. An amazing man – truly inspirational.'

## Avoiding National Service

When David left school aged eighteen, he entered into a world which, as Roland Quinault, writing in a 2001 edition of *History Today* pointed out, was very unlike Britain as we know it now:

> The most obvious difference was in the physical fabric of the country … the legacy of the Second World War was still everywhere to be seen. In the major cities, and particularly in London, there were vacant bomb-sites, unrepaired houses, temporary prefabs and gardens turned into allotments. The countryside was peppered with wartime military bases, many now abandoned, others reactivated in response to the Cold War … British society was still strongly influenced by war. Most grandfathers had served in the First World War, most fathers in the Second, and most young men were … called up for two years of National Service.

David, however, avoided National Service due to genuinely suffering from hay fever, but perhaps not quite to the same extent as he made the medical officers believe! The story he told in later life was that when asked to report for the necessary medical, just before he did he took himself off to where an inordinate amount of pollen would exacerbate his condition. It was an ingenious trick which apparently saw him excused the regulatory two-year stint undergone by many of his contemporaries – and would leave him free to pursue his dream of becoming a game warden in Africa.

2

# THE LONDON SCENE

'The London Scene' would come to mean a very different thing in the late 1960s when Carnaby Street, Twiggy, fashion and society photographers David Bailey and Patrick Litchfield were at their zenith. In the 1950s, however, at the time when David was just beginning as an artist, its buildings and streets formed much of his subject matter. The railings on the Victoria Embankment were also where he first exhibited and sold his work on Sunday mornings, but most importantly, London was where being trained by Robin Goodwin very definitely put David on the road towards an extremely successful artistic life – and gave him the finances to influence a great deal of wildlife conservation and railway restoration.

*On the street*
After his abortive attempt to become a game warden in Kenya (see Chapter 7) and his success in selling bird paintings there in order to fund his passage back to Britain, David wondered whether there might possibly be an artistic career ahead and, with that in mind, applied to the Slade School of Fine Art in London. Again, as with his idea to become a game warden, his application was met with short shrift; one of his paintings of seagulls on

plasterboard which he submitted along with his application, was described by the interview panel as being 'a painting of birds with dubious ancestry, flying in anatomically impossible positions, over a lavatorial green sea'.

Others might have become downhearted and disillusioned by two such rejections in a relatively short space of time, but not David – although he was, at the time, famously considering becoming a bus driver, it being the only thing he could think of to do to earn a regular income. Then, equally famously, quite by chance, he happened to meet the well-established marine and portrait artist Robin Goodwin at a drinks party in either Winchester or London (records and recollections vary!) as a result of which David's career path changed direction as surely and steadily as an AEC Routemaster bus might negotiate the busy London streets.

*Paralysed with fear*

During conversation at the party, the two agreed to meet at Robin's studio in Tite Street, Chelsea – rented by Robin from the artist Augustus John – where it was decided that Goodwin would teach David the subtleties of art. However, right from the outset Robin pulled no punches when it came to making his pupil realise the harsh realities of becoming an artist. According to David:

> The first day … was traumatic. He said 'I am going to tell you a few basic things now and if you're not prepared to accept them, you can get out of my studio for good. First of all, just because you think you are an artist and the world owes you a living, don't imagine you are any different from anyone else, you are not. An artist, or a pianist, is no different from a farmer or electrician. You are going to be working seven days a week in your studio, using every hour of daylight that God gives you. You have to be there at nine o'clock in the morning in November when it is so dark you can't see the canvas and paint to pay the bills.' Piling on the agony, he continued, 'I'm never going to say anything good about anything

you do for the next three years because I am going to assume that you know the good things. I am only going to tell you the bad things.' I felt like bursting into tears. All my illusions about being an artist had been shattered in one blow.

It appeared that David could forget any illusions about being a solitary artist stuck away in a lonely garret too. Rather than easing his pupil gently into an artistic life by working in a studio, Robin very quickly took his protégé out onto the streets of London. 'I've got a commission to paint Westminster Bridge; come on, you're coming with me,' he told David. Then, as David was later to write in his autobiography *The Man Who Loves Giants*:

> We both hopped on a bus. Robin had his easel, covered in paint from years of hard work; I had my brand new one. We alighted and, within a matter of minutes, Robin was painting away quite happily right by the bus stop, completely oblivious to the crowds around him. I was paralysed with fear; here I was in the middle of London. I tried to pretend that it was a better composition down the steps, behind the wall in front of County Hall. In fact down there I couldn't see anything anyway, and, of course, Robin saw through this straight away. 'Come on up here and paint beside me.'
>
> For the first three days, I don't think I touched the brush onto the canvas. Every time a bus went by, every few seconds, about thirty people craned their necks to see what we were doing. But this was good discipline and would enable me to paint in almost impossible conditions in future years.

* * *

## Natural talent

'Some people believe that to become a professional artist you need natural talent. I'm the first to admit that I had none. Anyone who sees my first attempt at an oil painting, *Seagulls*, will agree.

I am living proof that a person with enough determination can, in fact, be taught to paint.'
David Shepherd, August 2004

* * *

Irrespective of curious onlookers peering from the top deck of buses, Robin's habit of training David out in the streets of London always created a crowd around the two artists. Even on a Sunday there were quite often several dozen people wanting to take a look at their work as it progressed and this could, on occasion, cause the most basic of problems: with their view obscured, Robin and David couldn't see the subject they had chosen to paint. They were also subjected to unwanted advice of the 'I wouldn't do it that way if I were you' type. As David reminisced in *My Painting Life* (1995) 'We always had a way of dealing with those who really wouldn't get out of our way – a quick step back, flourishing a paint-covered brush, worked wonders.'

Less easy to deal with were the requests to 'move along' from the London policemen. Although the artists and their easels were not necessarily causing an obstruction, the fact that they frequently had so many people watching meant that, on occasion, the crowds were – a situation which was obviously annoying just when they were progressing well with their respective paintings. According to one particularly officious young constable, it seemed a licence to paint was required as a result of an archaic law from the past which required application for a permit if one's easel had three legs, but not if it only had two! Determined to make the artists aware of this earth-shattering piece of knowledge, he had not, however, reckoned with Robin and David's previously successful tried and tested method of reacting to a request to move on:

'Have you got a permit to do that?' he asked, slightly officiously. We both knew how to cope with the situation ... [He] had, like so many others, obviously had the idea that all artists were pretty crazy up top and we played on this supposition. Robin and I dropped our lower jaws and adopted a completely vacant expression without issuing any audible sound at all. It worked like magic. The policeman, obviously thinking we were completely mad, walked on – and we continued painting.

In similar vein, there is a famous black and white photograph taken in 1969 of a smartly booted and suited David standing in the middle of the road behind an extremely large painting of an elephant. Titled *The Dust Bath*, it was painted to help raise funds for the Bell Ranger helicopter (see Chapter 8) and was being moved to a gallery before being taken to America for auction. In the photograph, both painting and artist are seen obstructing the London traffic, and on one side a taxi is attempting to get by while on the other, a very young-looking police sergeant looks on somewhat bemused and very unsure as to how best to deal with the situation!

Being challenged in such a way on several occasions eventually caused David to compare himself with the street artists of Paris: 'I believe if one painted in the middle of the Champs-Élysées they would divert the traffic around you, as an artist in France is part of the daily scene, and is accepted as such. But in London you are invariably regarded as a menace ...' Nevertheless, David recalled being out on the London streets as being 'wonderfully happy, hilarious days'. Just one example of things that amused him was the time when, at the beginning of a day's work, his palette fell face downwards, and on picking it up he discovered that there were fourteen little coloured pyramids on the pavement. Inevitably, during the course of the time he stood there painting, the public traipsed through the small piles of paint and their footmarks went off in all directions – a little bit of street art long before the likes of modern-day artist, Banksy.

Amusing though such instances were, the impracticalities of painting in a street environment rather than in a studio quickly became obvious to David, who had many a painting spoilt by minor dust storms created by the London traffic, or even when insects and flies had landed slap-bang in the middle of fresh paint and then proceeded to crawl their way across other parts of the canvas, creating an entirely different dimension to that which was intended. When this happened, many hours would then be spent back at the studio flicking off unwanted debris with a palette knife and touching up the base paints.

* * *

During the days spent training with Robin, the two would quite often go down the Thames, and over a period of time painted many pictures between Chelsea and Woolwich. One of their favourite viewpoints was from Bowater's Wharf across to St Paul's and Blackfriars. In those days the river was full of shipping activity and steam-powered tugs pulling barges were everywhere – and, unlike today where it is dominated by huge modern buildings, the skyline was virtually unobscured and was dominated by the dome of St Paul's – which is just how architect Sir Christopher Wren intended it to be. Exactly how the scene looked at the time was captured by David in his painting *Smokey Thames*.

On one particularly windy day, the two were painting on Cherry Garden Pier, which juts out into the Thames near Tower Bridge. Caught by a sudden gust of wind, Robin's canvas took off into the Thames and was last seen bobbing along towards Greenwich accompanied by some of his best brushes.

* * *

## Life on the Embankment

For many years, one of the best showcases for aspiring artists was to display their work at the open air 'free-for-all' art exhibition held on the Victoria Embankment every May. For the artist it provided an ideal way for their efforts to be seen by a wide audience without the need to pay a gallery a sometimes extortionate percentage (and that always assuming one could find a gallery prepared to exhibit one's work on their walls). Arguably more importantly, it gave the public the chance to view an eclectic mix of painting styles.

During the 1950s, relatively few people owned much in the way of art and if they did, they were generally cheap prints, biblical quotations or Victorian samplers and certainly not originals – a privilege hitherto of only the wealthy. Times were, though, beginning to change and David, amongst several others, recognised the Embankment as being the place to best showcase their work. Indeed, people often used to go there straight from the opening of the Royal Academy Summer Exhibition (which took place at roughly the same time) and frequently comment on what a refreshing change it was to see some 'real' painting at last. Quite exactly what was meant by that can only be guessed.

Being in the open air, Embankment exhibitions did, however, cause the artists a sleepless night. The system was for them to arrive the evening before and, just as soon as Big Ben struck midnight, to put up a painting and by doing so, thus officially claim their pitch. They could then either go away and risk their precious picture being stolen, or stay there for the duration. No one ever knew where their pitch was likely to be until staking their claim but, as David found, 'The great thing was, apart from the fact that there was no selection committee or hanging fee, we would always be next to someone new. You could come and go as you pleased and, sell for whatever prices you thought reasonable and the public loved it. Enormous crowds would come in through the lunch hour every day, particularly in warm sunny weather. Besides, being on the Embankment, you never knew who was going to come out of The Savoy hotel in the way of potential purchasers!'

Wealthy people one might assume, but even those with a bulging wallet were not necessarily keen to pay what an original painting might have been worth. As David remembered:

The very first painting I sold, on the Embankment, was a small English landscape priced at £25. The buyer haggled me down, pound by pound, until I gave in and settled for £12. I then had to carry the picture to his car, which turned out to be a Rolls-Royce – complete with chauffeur. I swore I'd never be beaten down like that again. Even struggling artists should recognise their own worth.

Sitting there, hoping to sell a painting, made some onlookers imagine the archetypal poor struggling artist who had fallen on hard times – and that was certainly the case when one of David's fellow pupils from Stowe happened to pass by: 'One day I was sitting opposite my pitch in the sunshine, wearing my old school tie. An "old boy", walking through the exhibition in his lunch hour from his city office, complete with bowler and pinstripe suit, looked aghast to see me apparently on my "beam ends". I have never seen such a pompous expression on anyone's face; he obviously thought that I was letting down the school.'

Despite some looking down their noses, others greatly appreciated the work which David exhibited on the Embankment, and in 1955 he was featured in a short Pathé news film, *Embankment Artists*, which included a shot of him hanging his painting of a TWA Constellation flying over New York which the narrator described as a 'masterpiece of detail' and a 'fascinating study'. David's time on the Embankment was also noteworthy for the fact that, among the many people he met were the mainstays of Solomon & Whitehead (Guild Prints) Ltd who later published almost all of his print editions.

## No nudes are good nudes

One of the problems David experienced whilst training with Robin was the lack of opportunity to do life drawings and, because of this, Robin advised David to go to Guildford Art School – advice that proved less than inspiring, and David left before completing the full term. Although Robin couldn't afford to pay for professional models, he did, however, manage to get a couple of girls to come and pose for nothing, in their spare time. Their kindness gave David the chance to paint one of the few nude pictures in his portfolio. It was also about this time that David was beginning to get introductions to various businessmen who might be potential buyers of pictures. One such lived in Esher, right in the heart of the stockbroker belt:

I loaded all the pictures into the back of my car and drove to his house. I showed him landscapes and pictures of London, and then his eyes fell on my little nude. He grabbed it with both hands and ran triumphantly into his dining room, where he hung it up on the oak panelling. It could almost have been painted especially for the setting, but his wife would not let him have it; 'My dear, how can we possibly eat our dinner with that in the room?' It is sad to think that even in this enlightened age there are still many stupid people who have that ridiculous attitude towards the naked form.

## *Art and the critics*

Although the Slade School of Fine Art may have been scathing of David's efforts, in 1954, the prestigious Royal Academy seemingly felt differently. For no reason other than belligerence, David submitted a painting – one of the frontage of a little antique shop, entitled *Moon & Hodge: Antiques* – for their Summer Exhibition; never for one moment expecting it to be accepted. It was, but it wasn't given pride of place however, and was, according to David, 'hung above an electric plug socket almost at floor level, in gallery heaven-knows-what-number'.

The fact that such exhibitions at the Royal Academy and elsewhere were, in David's personal opinion, more a place where influential people could be seen at a private champagne and canapés fuelled function rather than being staged for the benefit of artists and their work, was long a bone of contention. To them 'it was just a social event at the beginning of the London season' whereas, to the artist, being exhibited there could make, enhance, or break their reputation. Critics – whose reviews people read and took note of – were often present at such gatherings and many were not held in high regard by the artists, David included.

During a long lifetime of painting and being in the public eye, it's inevitable that one attracts critics – and to some, their criticism might cause sleepless nights. David, however, learnt to take their words with the proverbial pinch of salt and a positive attitude. In response to a question posed by a journalist for the London-based *Metro* newspaper in 2009, David told him in no uncertain terms that 'I've got a pretty jaundiced opinion of critics – especially after the one that described my *March Sunlight* painting as being representative of "sexual awakening" and that the icy pools of water at its base were indicative of "a sexual longing" [see Chapter 3] and, if they've got that idea, you can't get it out of their minds ... The art establishment, which frankly makes me sick, is all full of snobby people – I can't stand it. That's why I know so few people in the art business.'

* * *

## A pseudo culture

One critic, many years ago – Roger Limbrick, who was at that time a teacher at London's Chelsea School of Art – wrote, 'Shepherd's work is dreadful. It's a pseudo culture. The difference between his work and real art is the difference between a Weetabix snack and a proper English bacon and egg breakfast.'

* * *

Professional reviewers notwithstanding, amateur critics abound in whatever sphere one works. When painting *London* (see below), whilst the painting was still wet on the easel, one of David's friends walked into the studio and straight away commented, 'You've got one arch too many in Waterloo Bridge.' With the amount of work and research he had put into it, David was surprised but looked again at the photos of that particular stretch of the Thames and discovered that, on this occasion, his critic was correct and he was left with no option but to paint out the whole of the bridge and start afresh.

David had certainly had time to get used to criticism under the tutelage of Robin Goodwin. There were several instances where the master pushed his pupil to the absolute limit. He was, however, as David remembered, 'Quite marvellous at knowing just how far to go without breaking my spirit. Several times, in a screaming temper, I was on my way to my car parked outside, all ready to pack it in for good and go home. On one of the more emotional of these occasions he leaned out of the window and shouted down at me, "Come on back you silly little blighter, I am still teaching you so you must be worth teaching." That was, as far as I remember, the only kind thing he said in three years; but it made sense. It was no good telling me that everything I did was good, which it wasn't, because I would have learnt nothing.'

## The streets of London

Despite the name, Shepherd Street in Mayfair has no connection with David or his family. It was, though, such an attractive part of London that David was to eventually paint thirteen pictures of there and the immediate surroundings. The one actually titled *Shepherd Street, Mayfair*, painted in 1954, was one of David's first to be reproduced as a fine art print. However, although copies were sold as a print, the original painting, despite being offered for sale at the time for only £25 (which was, though, probably a fair amount in the early 1950s) never did sell and has been kept in the family ever since. Despite that, other paintings of the area sold more readily. Being in the part of London it was, the locale was of great interest to tourists, especially Americans who regularly used to walk through because of its 'old-world charm'. There was then (with the exception of *Shepherd Street*) often a passing casual clientele who would quite happily buy David's paintings straight off the easel even though, in some cases, they still had to be completely finished, varnished and framed.

Although most of David's London scenes were street views, one – and it was a massive one measuring 2.4 m (8 ft) by 1.5 m (5 ft) – showed London from the air. The logistical problems associated with a painting of that size were obvious and, unable to find anyone able to fly him over the scene (see Chapter 10) the painting, simply titled *London*, was completed as a result of referring to a series of aerial photographs as no one single photo could cover the wide angle David wanted to portray. One great advantage of being a painter rather than a photographer is that it allows for 'artistic licence', and so, rather than it be a totally contemporary scene, David chose to paint the period when the Festival of Britain site had been cleared on the South Bank and the Shell Centre was beginning to go up in a forest of girders and scaffolding. The Royal Festival Hall had been completed but the old and historic shot tower, a prominent feature of that part of the Thames at the time, had yet to be demolished. Painting *London* was a lengthy process and at certain points of doing so, the picture and all its necessary structural detail became quite tedious so David relieved the pressure by adding several quirky elements such as extra London buses and even, in Westminster Square, his own car and his sister Judy's horsebox!

Not all his works during this period were general scenes of the capital and its streets. In some of his paintings, David chose to depict just a part of a scene, a vignette, a snapshot of a street corner or shopfront. 'I have always felt that the English do not care as much about their heritage as they should. Since the days when I was painting in London, so many of these lovely old shops have been swept aside by the property developers in the name of progress, to be replaced by anonymous modern concrete. If not succumbing to that treatment, they have been vandalized out of all recognition, with beautiful woodwork and gold-leaf lettering replaced by the horrors of the plastic age.' A typical example is his painting of *The Curio Shop*, the frontage of which attracted the artist 'because [it] was crammed full to bursting with copper and brass pots and pans, all glinting in the sunlight'.

Although as his painting career diversified and wildlife conservation took up much of his time, David painted less and less of London, in 1994 he painted *Westminster '66*, a painting of several Routemaster buses going over Westminster Bridge with the Houses of Parliament in the background. It was in that year, that David asked the Friends of the London Transport Museum if he could have a bus for his charitable foundation for use as a promotional vehicle. They agreed that an exchange could be arranged – a bus in return for a painting. When completed, *Westminster '66* was to hang in the London Transport Museum in

Covent Garden, whilst out on the road a fully restored Routemaster bus was driven all over the United Kingdom promoting the cause of the tiger, the rhino, and other endangered species.

## *An affection for the city*

In 1959, as part of an article for *Shell Aviation News*, David explained how he developed an increasing affection for the city as a source of endless painting material – despite the dirt and smog before the advent of the Clean Air Act and the subsequent sandblasting of some of the capital's best-known and structurally diverse buildings:

In spite of its apparently chaotic mixture of architectural styles, all enveloped in a perpetual haze of dirt and soot, here nevertheless, to my mind, are to be found subjects which would have delighted Rembrandt. For London as Canaletto painted it is gone. London then was surely cleaner and more feminine, as is Paris today. But at the same time she was lacking in the dramatic character that she now has ... but painting London is beset with problems.

I maintain that the warm browns of mellow brickwork and greeny-greys of soot-encrusted stone are far too subtle to get from sketches and photographs. (These last always seem to make London look for all the world like a Mediterranean seaside resort.) But so few artists will put up with the conditions ... that pictures of London with the real atmosphere of the city are rare indeed.

The dirt and dust, of course, is appalling. It settles in the wet paint like wasps to a pot of jam ... One can have no idea how dirty London is until one stands for eight hours at a time on the pavement with a wet painting.

***

## 'Smog', pollution and the artist

For years London was synonymous with 'smog', a word coined at the turn of the twentieth century and which was used to describe the city's infamous mix of fog and smoke. These 'pea-soupers' were actually caused by suspended pollution of smoke and sulphur dioxide from coal fires, both household and industrial. Even in the times during which David and Robin were painting their London scenes during the 1950s and early 1960s, there were still occasional 'pea-soupers' that affected London life and, particularly in the smokier districts of east inner London, it wasn't unusual for there to be as much as a 30 per cent reduction in winter sunshine hours caused by suspended pollution – a problem that was only alleviated by parliamentary legislation and the introduction of the Clean Air Acts of 1956 and 1968.

* * *

Although London was eventually to become less of a source of painting subject matter over ensuing years, of course David would continue visiting London (much-changed since his first experiences of Britain's capital city) throughout his life, be it to see print publishers, visit television and radio studios for interviews, organise exhibitions at galleries such as the Tryon or The Mall, and, as part of fundraising events at the Natural History Museum, The Savoy or The Dorchester (see Chapter 11).

Putting all that to one side, it would be wrong to end this section of David's biography without reiterating the gratitude that he would forever feel for his artistic tutor and the days spent learning from him during his time in London: 'I'm certainly glad I went to that party and met Robin Goodwin. After the three most momentous and character-forming years of my life, he finally said, "David, you are on your own, I can't teach you any more."' On his own David may have been as far as the art world was concerned, but he was to remain close friends with Robin until the latter's death in 1997. In their almost half a century of friendship they and their families socialised and interacted on a regular basis, and even ended up having homes close to one another in Surrey.

3

# HOME IS WHERE THE ART IS

By the beginning of the 1960s, Robin Goodwin and his family were living at Burgate House, a Queen Anne property built in 1734 and situated equidistant between the villages of Dunsfold and Hascombe, Surrey. It was Robin's wife Biddy who first drew David and Avril's attention to the fact that a house just up the road from them had recently come onto the market and it was one in which they might possibly be interested. 'It will be just right for you,' she opined – so, in 1962, along went the couple to take a look. They saw it and agreed; both David and Avril fell in love with Winkworth Farm at first sight and were not at all daunted by the prospect of moving from a relatively modern (and small) Oakhill Cottage to a vast farmhouse which had its origins in the Elizabethan period. They did, however, wonder whether they could afford it. David initially approached his bank manager for a loan but he, with the suspicion typical of anyone having to deal with supposedly penniless and itinerant artists, was a little reluctant to say the least. However, the year coincided with David's first Wildlife One-Man Exhibition at Aylmer Tryon's gallery in London (see Chapter 7) and whilst at that point no one could have predicted its outcome, David invited his bank manager along to the preview. It proved a shrewd and fortunate move as all but four of the paintings had sold by the end of the evening.

Also fortunate in terms of delaying a possible purchase by other interested parties was the fact that there were probate complications that prevented the conclusion of a quick sale. In addition, whilst viewing was taking place during 1962 there were several weeks of exceptionally bad weather, which were undoubtedly off-putting to other potential purchasers. So, with Winkworth happily still on the market, and flushed with the success of his recent exhibition, David made a second approach to his previously reluctant bank manager. This time the bank took a more favourable view and agreed to lend the money necessary. In April 1963, David and Avril plus three very young daughters (the fourth had yet to be born) found themselves the new inhabitants of a property which was to prove to be their beloved family home for almost forty years.

## A slice of 'Olde England'

Winkworth Farm was, as David later recalled, 'a glorious, half-timbered black and white, farmhouse dating from about 1560 … the late owner had expended his love and energy on the garden, and the house needed a tremendous amount of superficial work done'. There were, for instance, no signs of any fireplaces, since they had long all been bricked up. So on completion of the sale and never a person to delay when a particular project had been decided upon, one of the first things David did was to remove all the 'cheap panelling' and take a sledgehammer to the bricks he found in the sitting room in the hope of finding the original inglenook fireplace. His hunch proved correct. Despite only having moved into Winkworth in the spring, David and Avril hosted Christmas 1963 for both sets of parents – during the course of which Avril remembered the two mothers walking arm in arm and overhearing one saying to the other, 'I wonder if these two know just what they've taken on?' They need not have worried. Sir Edwin Lutyens had influence on the house, and Gertrude Jekyll had been instrumental in the design of the garden;

it would, therefore, have been unthinkable if David and Avril had not continued with what those two eminent people had begun. An article by Chris Webb in *The Telegraph* in 2017 explained more:

> Edward Lutyens took a shine to Winkworth Farm that resonates to this day … [to whom] it owes much of its charm … in 1895 [he] remodelled the mid-18th century barn on the right of the property, joining it to the house, and lengthening it to make a hallway. His hand can be seen in the corner windows, which were favoured by him, in tiles set end-on into walls, and in some Bargate stone window surrounds. His closest pupil, J. D. Coleridge, designed a rear extension.
>
> Sir Edwin's friend, Gertrude Jekyll, planted part of Winkworth's garden, and a garden wall and terrace are attributed to her …

The gardens in particular (which had also been influenced by some further work in 1914, by the architect F. W. Troup) benefited from the youth and enthusiasm of the new owners. With Winkworth came 'Mr Thorpe' (always respectfully referred to as 'Mr' by both adults and children alike) a gardener who was very keen and full of ideas. So too were his employers, and together they further enhanced the gardens and pleasure grounds. On Mr Thorpe's retirement, Ken Ellison, Chris Boyson, and subsequently Dave Penney took over the gardening mantle – and with the latter's help, Avril created a quite spectacular 'secret garden' of her own.

Not so secret was the back door to the house – which most visitors used because the main door was not obvious or easily accessible due to the walled frontage. With David's love of English country life, the area around the rear entrance soon began to look like a snapshot of a bucolic scene from Agatha Christie's tales of Miss Marple and her imaginary village of St Mary Mead. The letter box was of the type from which the postman was probably more used to collecting letters than he was delivering them, and, to the right of the door was a shopfront proclaiming the owners to be 'Winkworth and

Daughters 1963'. It was, in fact, a quite literal 'front' for the walk-in family larder, an idea created and brought to fruition via David's ever-active mind. During his time training with Robin Goodwin in London he had painted several similar shopfronts, and after visiting a show house at the Ideal Home Exhibition where a friend had created something similar, he decided to follow suit. Its Victorian-period design was accurate from its bow-fronted window and old-etched glass pub door (with a bell that tinged as the 'customer' entered) to the window full of old advertising and grocery items, and even included an old-fashioned delivery bike complete with its front basket.

In the house, Avril's creativity and natural flair for period design was soon very much in evidence – but even so, David's input, especially when it came to the subject of wall colour, was apparent. The sitting room was originally three rooms and, in 1990, David had the idea of removing the partition walls in order to create a spacious L-shaped room. Interviewed for *Period House* in 1996, Avril said 'I wish we'd done it years ago.' The dining room was painted coral: 'David chose the unusual colour ... I thought it was very brave at the time, but I love it now as it looks so warm.'

A house the size of Winkworth took a great deal of furnishing; items were bought as and when money allowed and pieces most fitting to the style of the age of the building were found in antique shops, auctions and house sales. The dining room table and chairs were the only items of furniture that were bought with the property. 'We were very young then and couldn't afford much,' Avril told *Period House* reporter Christine Parsons, 'but we had to buy this set as even the auctioneer agreed that they really should stay with the house.'

Outdoors could be seen many things of interest found elsewhere by David and subsequently brought home to satisfy his love of the countryside, rural history and British tradition. By the lake stood an old gypsy caravan and, as one came down the drive, the sight of a fairground showman's caravan greeted the visitor. Red and yellow in colour, when David and Avril moved to Brooklands Farm, near East Grinstead, it went with them – as did the archetypal red telephone box rescued from the scrapyard during the time Post Office Telephones changed to British Telecom in the early 1980s. Designed by Sir Giles Gilbert Scott and seen as a British cultural icon in many parts of the world, there's no wonder David chose to 'fly the flag' by having such a telephone box on prominent display in his garden. As daughter Melinda says, 'It was one of the toys he always wanted – and got.' Once moved to Brooklands Farm, however, it became more of a minor feature at the side of the house (and a place in which to store wild bird seed and hide the spare house door key for any members of the family that required access).

### The artist's studio at Winkworth

In an interview for *Surrey Life*, published early in 2011, David recalled that 'When we sold the house, the estate agents described the living room as having space for an elephant – I don't suppose people had a clue about just how many elephants and tigers came to life in my studio at Winkworth Farm!'

Once established at Winkworth – and very much on the ascent as far as his artistic career was concerned – David had a quantity of roof tiles removed and replaced with glass over a room in what was known as the 'new' wing (built in 1784) in order that more natural light could come through onto his easel. He painted thus for twenty-five years but, as the traffic increased on what had hitherto been a relatively quiet country road which ran past the front of the house, he began to notice that, as the same road had by then been discovered by 40-ton articulated trucks whose owners found it saved them a few pennies in diesel fuel between Guildford and Horsham, he was painting 'to the sound of screeching brakes and crunching wing mirrors as they met and struggled past on the lane outside the window'.

The situation had become 'intolerable' and the Shepherds were at the point of putting Winkworth on the market, when David had the idea of somehow moving his studio away from the road and the increasing amount of noise, which broke both his concentration and ability to listen to his eclectic mix of music. As he painted, and depending on his mood, this might well have included anything from Mahler to Glenn Miller, or any one of a selection from his beloved musicals.

Although David was always a man of action and rarely refused to be beaten when faced with a problem, somehow dragging a part of the house away from the hustle and bustle of the road was obviously not an option. However, with thinking somewhat reminiscent of 'If the mountain won't come to Muhammad, Muhammad must go to the mountain', in the late 1980s he heard of the work of Peter Barker, an architect who specialised in moving old barns, and contacted him for a possible solution. 'He told us of a 400-year-old Surrey barn some ten miles (sixteen kilometres) away at Parkhurst Farm, Dunsfold,' recalled David, '... a listed building which, unbelievably, the farmer had got permission to demolish. This beautiful building was taken down, beam by beam; each ancient piece of oak was numbered and then the whole building was re-erected in our garden.' It became the perfect studio – and David was no longer troubled by the sound of diesel engines, squealing brakes and breaking wing mirrors.

## Brooklands Farm

Despite the new studio, the overall peace and quiet at Winkworth was not to last. The road became even busier than before and there were numerous bumps and scrapes between vehicles and the wall that overlooked the front gardens of the house. The road also had a narrow pavement well-used by walkers en route through Hascombe village and up to the Winkworth arboretum at the top of the hill. Sightseers would often brazenly stop and look over the wall into the property (and occasionally even sit on the wall for a picnic before throwing their unwanted rubbish into the garden) and the house itself would be frequently photographed – as a result of which, it famously appeared as a very popular jigsaw puzzle which, although David and the family received nothing in the way of financial recompense, presumably made the jigsaw manufacturer a fair profit. It was definitely time to move on and so, after well over three decades, the search for a suitable home which could eventually be as equally loved as Winkworth was begun.

After looking at several possibilities over the following two years, in 2000 David and Avril eventually purchased and moved into Brooklands Farm at Hammerwood, near East Grinstead. Like Winkworth, it had lots of history and was originally a true working farm. The Museum of Rural Life, based at Reading, has an eight-page catalogue containing details of a 1918 upcoming sale/auction of the 'Live and Dead Farming Stock and Furniture at Brooklands Farm, Hammerwood Estate, East Grinstead, Sussex' so perhaps this is around the date that active farming ceased.

Brooklands really was 'home from home' as it had so many similarities with their beloved Winkworth. It was roughly the same age and style and, like Winkworth, had both formal and pleasure gardens, woodland and natural ponds running alongside paddocks (which were periodically grazed by sheep belonging to a neighbouring farmer) – all in all, some 7.6 hectares (19 acres). In their brochure, estate agents Hamptons described the house as being 'a fine Grade II Listed detached house dating from possibly as early as the fifteenth century with later additions'. Furthermore: 'the elevations are of part stone with stone mullion windows, timbering with plaster infill panels, part tile hanging and leaded light windows under a Horsham slab and clay peg tile roof'.

The brochure then went on to detail Brooklands' 'many outstanding and original features' and described the drawing room as being an 'elegant' and 'beautifully proportioned room with a fine inglenook fireplace … [next to which] is an … impressive sitting room with a minstrels' gallery and a deep inglenook fireplace. An unusual feature is the deep well with its transparent top and spot lighting'. The well was indeed an unusual feature. Prior to David and Avril's arrival, it had lain hidden away and neglected but, with the new owner's love of history, the work of bygone artisans and his renowned quirkiness, it was soon restored to its former glory. When any first-time visitors arrived, David would delightedly roll back the tapestry rug that covered the 'transparent top' so that, via its spotlighting, they could see down its impressive depth to the water far below.

As with many such houses, although there was a dining room with polished oak floor, beams and an open fireplace, it was the farmhouse-style kitchen where the family mostly congregated for mealtimes – unless, of course, the numbers were too great such as at Christmas, significant birthdays or weddings, on which occasions the gallery adjoining David's studio would often be used.

## The artist's studio at Brooklands Farm

Initially, there was no place perfectly suited for a studio at Brooklands and David spent the first few years painting in one of a block of four stables. As at Winkworth, it was to prove necessary to replace some of the roof with glass panels to let in sufficient (and, most importantly for an artist, the correct type of) natural light. Again as at Winkworth, the problem of a lack of designated studio was solved in typical David Shepherd fashion by the purchase and removal, piece-by-piece, of a second period 'Sussex barn' from Horsham (once more sourced and supplied by architect Peter Barker) which was then re-erected some distance from, but in full view of, the house. Not only was there the barn with its studio and large vaulted gallery used to display paintings to potential clients (and also, on occasion, as the venue for family gatherings) outdoors was a small courtyard complex, at the opposite side of which was a further barn. It was on the ground floor of this particular building that David housed prints of his paintings and his rather large doll's house, whilst the room above was dedicated to his model railway set-up (see Chapter 4).

Prior to the 'new' barn construction, there was, however, a building of similar size and structure which was, to put it kindly, in less than good repair. Nevertheless, when approached regarding its possible removal, there were strong objections from the planners at Mid Sussex District Council who, because it was considered a listed building, were somewhat reluctant for it to be demolished. Never one to take 'no' for an answer, David reapplied and was more successful second time around. The earlier objections were considered something of an over-reaction and permission to demolish the original barn and replace it with the one from Horsham was granted.

* * *

## Strictly no swimming!

One of the first things David did on the purchase of Brooklands Farm was to fill in the existing swimming pool. The grandchildren were furious! It was, though, bearing in mind its location under a line of trees, somewhat sensible as otherwise, at certain points of the year and in some climatic (heavy wind and rain) conditions, it is likely that more time would have been spent clearing leaves from the pool than in swimming.

* * *

### *Tunnel vision*

At both Winkworth and Brooklands, David's barn conversion studios were connected to the main house by an underground walkway, at the entrance to which was a salvaged prison door from Falmouth jail, behind which the last man in England to be convicted of cannibalism was once incarcerated. That somewhat startling fact quite possibly requires further explanation! In 1884, a four-man crew sailing from England to Australia were shipwrecked with almost no food. When the seventeen-year-old cabin boy became ill, two of the men, by the names of Stephens and Dudley, decided to kill and eat him. Five days later they were rescued and charged with murder (for some unrecorded reason the third man was not apparently charged). Although their lawyers argued that killing the cabin boy was a necessity for the survival of the three other men, the two accused were nevertheless convicted of murder and sentenced to death – a sentence which was later commuted to six months' imprisonment. The door, like the red telephone box, the showman's caravan and various other quirky items, accompanied the family in their move from Winkworth to Brooklands and, subsequent to the sale of Brooklands Farm in 2019, it is now in the care of Melanie and her family where it remains an interesting object of conversation for those seeing it for the first time.

Having moved his studio away from the main house at Winkworth, David decided that, in the event of rain – and umbrellas being somewhat passé – in order to prevent potential clients getting wet during their short journey from coffee and being entertained by Avril in the house, he would install a tunnel. It was created by knocking a hole below ground through the outside wall of the house in what was once a wine cellar and digging a deep trench, which was then walled and roofed. At Brooklands a similar underground passageway was built, and David loved to take first-time guests from the main part of the house and through what appeared to be a cellar door near the utility room but which, in fact, led immediately to a set of stairs and down to the tunnel. Along a limestone paving-flagged lit corridor (the lighting coming from brass GWR and GNR carriage lamps set in wall-mounted sconces) would echo the footsteps of David and his guests before they then emerged up another set of wooden stairs into David's studio – and from there, into the gallery.

The construction of the tunnel was not straightforward, nor inexpensive. In 2002, David told *The Argus* journalist Angela Wintle that he had 'spent money like water' on their new place but that he wanted to enjoy the fruits of his labours: 'I don't want to die with my money in a tin,' said David. Ironically, the water analogy he used turned out to be an apt one. The Wealden clay upon which Brooklands stood meant that the ingress of water and the water table was an issue – and even when the initial problems were eventually sorted, a very heavy rainstorm could still occasionally cause problems and a little minor flooding. Nevertheless, the tunnel was a constant source of delight to David, and it was a popular game of some family youngsters (and some adults!) to make a point of being recognised by new guests entering the tunnel from the house end for the first time – and then to dash across above ground and greet them again as they came up the steps from the tunnel into the studio!

## Trees all around

The very first opportunity David had to do anything positive about ensuring the future well-being of trees in his own surroundings was brought about by the purchase of Winkworth. Most interestingly, one of the previous owners had been Dr Wilfred Fox who had a particular love of trees and had in fact, created the Winkworth Arboretum (now owned by the National Trust) situated virtually next door to where the Shepherd family were living.

That tree species can be so different in their needs was not lost on David. 'Plane trees, for instance, survive where others can't, even in big cities ... just take a look at those in Berkeley Square in London. Sadly so few people do ... we're all in a mad rush.' Plane trees or not, David planted many specimen varieties at both Winkworth and Brooklands. Impetuous and yet undeniably enthusiastic, in an interview for *The Countryman* magazine in 2015, he admitted to errors in his various planting regimes: 'I've made some horrendous mistakes ... Throughout my long life, I've met lots who know far more than me ... that's why I think organisations such as the Countryside Restoration Trust are important. Volunteers are so vital; officialdom wouldn't bother.'

Whilst (despite any supposed 'mistakes') much arboreal was achieved during the Shepherd family's long custodianship of Winkworth Farm, it was perhaps at Brooklands Farm in East Sussex where David had most influence on his immediate environment. 'I'm impatient,' he said in *The Countryman* article '... and I'm getting older ... I can't wait for 250 years for trees to grow and so as soon as we moved in I bought some root-balled well-established trees.'

***

## Important hedgerows

When anyone visited Brooklands, if they had half an eye for the countryside, they couldn't help but notice trees: both those that make up the surrounding area and also those which had been planted far more recently by David for the enjoyment and benefit of future generations. Obvious too, were the hedgerows that intercepted the gardens and the wild areas – none of which existed before David and Avril bought the place. Concerned by the loss of 'thousands of miles of hedges in the British countryside', David made a conscious effort to try and redress the balance by doing what he could on his few acres of East Sussex – and whilst doing so, was careful to only plant hedges that contained typical British species.

* * *

There are, though, some who have looked upon David's love of trees and his subsequent depiction of them in his paintings from a very different angle. Many years ago, when writing of one of his most popular paintings of the English landscape, a particular reviewer from the *Evening Standard* pontificated that David's painting *March Sunlight* – which shows an elm tree budding in the early spring – was representative of the artist's 'sexual awakening' and that the icy pools of water at its base indicative of 'a sexual longing'. It was a comment that much amused David and was a story he was to tell many times in his books, interviews and wherever and whenever there was an audience to listen.

The *Evening Standard* reviewer's somewhat bizarre comments notwithstanding, when asked what it was about a tree standing proud and erect in the British countryside that excited him, David's answer was far more comprehensible: 'It is its "character", shape, the browse-line created by cattle, and the rooks in its top-most branches; the fact it's stood for generations and will, I hope, continue to do so for many more years to come.' During his painting career, trees and their position in the English landscape provided much subject matter for the artist. Elms in particular were much loved by David. Describing his painting *Winter Elms*, he wrote:

> Of all the great English trees, the stately elm is by far my favourite. Tragically, it is now almost a thing of the past due to the ravages of Dutch elm disease.
>
> Fortuitously, over the years I have been sketching and photographing elm trees all over England. There is no more beautiful sight, I believe, on a cold winter day than the silhouettes of bare elms, their fine tracery of branches spreading like a fan across a cool grey sky. The rooks' nest in the very uppermost branches of the tree, and the seagulls about to land on the damp earth below, complete the scene. To me this is the very magic of the ever-changing English climate in its subtlest of moods.

### Cadgwith Cove and the Brecon Beacons

During much of the time both living at Winkworth and Brooklands, the Shepherd family enjoyed the use of two other homes – supposedly intended as places for relaxing and dog-walking – one in Cornwall (purchased whilst David and Avril were still living at their first house, Oakhill Cottage) the other (bought after the Cornish property had been sold) in the heart of the Brecon Beacons.

A second home to which one can escape as a break from work and eager clients is something to which many aspire and David was no different, except, of course, that he was never likely to be the type who could just switch off and rest, so it was inevitable that both the house in Cornwall, and subsequently the one in the Brecon Beacons, gave inspiration for work as well as family pleasure. This was particularly true of their house at Cadgwith Cove where David often painted outdoors and also met a retired Cornish fisherman, whose portrait he was to eventually paint – and from whom he learnt one of life's little lessons:

> Rambo had the sort of face and personality which was God's gift to a portrait painter. His very complexion breathed the salt spray in which he had lived for seventy-six years …

I didn't know him that well and, in my ... ignorance, went into a great long speech about what hard work it was [to be an artist's model], that it was not just a matter of sitting and being painted, that I would pay him for his efforts because it would be hard work on his part and so on and so forth. When he did manage to get a word in edgeways, he said, 'I think I sat for at least half a dozen artists last year so I do know a bit about it.' I felt so small that I wanted to disappear down the nearest hole; it taught me ... never again to be quite so patronising.

## Cadgwith

From Winkworth, the young Shepherd family would periodically travel down to Cornwall and Todden Croft, their house at Cadgwith. It was well before the area had become very popular with tourists – and certainly before there were any decent motorways or straight roads to take the family from Surrey to Cornwall – and was, therefore, a long journey, during the course of which David kept his daughters entertained with stories of mice and their families (see Chapter 4).

The cottage was perched high on a rock overlooking the cove and harbour. Even today, Cadgwith is still most people's idea of what a typical fishing village should look like, with colourful fishing boats winched up safely and picturesquely on the shingle beach. Many of the cottages – the Shepherds' included – were originally made of the local serpentine rock with walls measuring up to a metre (just over three feet) thick before being faced with 'cob' (a mixture of clay and straw) then painted white. Due to this part of Cornwall being far distant from the slate-producing regions, most roofs are thatched. Attached to part of the property was 'The Chalet', which originally had a tin roof before being thatched during David and Avril's tenure. It was, however, known by most of the locals as the *Highland Fling* due to the fact that much of its structure had been built from the ship of that name which was wrecked off the coast of Cadgwith in 1907.

## *Maesgwyn*

Owning and enjoying the comforts of Maesgwyn, the house in the Brecon Beacons, meant a much shorter travelling time from home, but even so, the lanes which took one up to the house were extremely narrow and twisty and most certainly couldn't be negotiated at speed. At the top and over the cattle grid situated there, it was necessary to turn right down a farm track and into a natural dip in which the house was situated. Once at the isolated cottage it was a peaceful haven surrounded by not much more than the Brecon Beacons, sheep and herds of native Welsh ponies which lived rough all year long. It was perfect for walking the dogs and, when strenuous exercise palled, the bookshop town of Hay-on-Wye was reasonably close by.

A stone-built, slate roofed three-bedroomed (although the small one at the back was to become David's studio) property, there was a large barn attached. A lake close by, although beautiful, had an eerie atmosphere due to being affected by the Chernobyl disaster in April 1986. Despite being some 2,000 miles away, parts of Wales came under the influence of the infamous and much-damaging blast of radioactive particles which were released into the air after the disaster. Although initially in denial regarding the effect a tragedy that occurred so far way could have in Wales, as the trees surrounding the lake withered and died and an apparent absence of wildlife around its edges and in its water manifested itself, David became increasingly worried about Chernobyl's likely legacy – and rightly so, for as rapidly became evident, both flora and fauna suffered as well as the livestock (particularly sheep) of Wales and Cumbria.

## *Time to move on*

Despite the effects of such an international tragedy as Chernobyl, the frequent holidays and weekend breaks at Maesgwyn were, as with Todden Croft in Cadgwith Bay, much enjoyed by many family members and, in addition, gave both David and Avril those all-important breaks away from an otherwise extremely hectic daily life, and there were tears shed when the Welsh cottage was eventually sold in 2013.

Winkworth and Brooklands had also given immense pleasure to the Shepherd family and friends over the years but they could never, by any stretch of the imagination, have been considered economically practical, particularly when it came to heating. But, even with advancing age David would in no way contemplate living in a 'modern' house far more likely to be suited to both his and Avril's needs, and so they remained at Brooklands to the very end of David's life. In July 2019, Avril moved to a more modern (1930s) and certainly more manageable house situated on the Surrey/West Sussex borders.

When it came to selling both Winkworth Farm and Brooklands, it required an imaginative estate agent to market the property in a positive manner, as what ideally suited the Shepherd family for work and daily living was quite likely to prove a somewhat strange layout to the average buyer. When Winkworth came up for sale again in May 2017, due to its connection with Sir Edwin Lutyens, Margaret Richardson, a trustee of the Lutyens Trust, was asked to comment – and said, 'I know the house. It's a bit of a dog's dinner, but it is absolutely lovely.' Although she was most likely referring to various other amendments made to the property by several various owners, there can be no doubt that whenever the history of the property is next written, it will include the many quirky additions made whilst under Shepherd management!

In the agents' brochures appertaining to the sale of Brooklands, rooms used for a specific purpose by David were given a verbal make-over; thus the space in which he had kept his doll's house, for example, was entered in the selling details as being a playroom. On reflection, however, perhaps the two things were not too dissimilar as no one can possibly deny the artist's love of toys, large or small!

4

# A LIFE IN MINIATURE

Anyone who knew David would most certainly agree that he was a complicated contradiction. Whilst he steered through life at high speed and with the thrusting tenacious characteristics of both the steam engines and elephants he loved so much, he also had endless patience and was able to sit or stand for hours wire-brushing thousands of individual rusty rivets before then replacing them in one of the locomotives he was renovating. This quite unbelievable patience was also very much in evidence in the construction of a life in miniature, especially when it came to the creation of his model railway (scale buildings from bits of cards, trees from string); furnishing a doll's house, and building sequestered homes for tiny model mice. For the 'man who loved giants', these hobbies were the enchanting polar opposite to the steam engines and all things large.

As a child, David made Airfix models and tiny cardboard steam engines and carriages – all with an eye and attention to painstaking detail, an attribute that was to see him able to concentrate on the tiniest but nevertheless all-important brushstroke when painting as an adult. It also became evident when he first began to construct his miniature railway and people it with characters, houses and buildings, trees and hedgerows, most if not all of which he constructed himself and in perfect proportion. His first 'proper' model railway included the old tinplate Hornby trains. As he was to remember, 'No matter how often they were trodden on, kicked or dropped, their clockwork interiors always responded to the enormous push and pull rod sticking from their cabs, providing one didn't lose the key!'

Birthdays and Christmases during David's childhood in the 1930s were never a problem when it came to relatives thinking of a present for the young enthusiast:

> There were always cows, chocolate vending machines, porters' wheelbarrows, signals, milk churns – the possibilities were endless – and I was fortunate in having quite a number of aunts and uncles. Like all little boys, I would flatly refuse to go to sleep on Christmas Eve. I would lie awake as long as I could, gazing in agonised anticipation at the stocking at the foot of the bed. In the morning a big red box with the magic word 'Hornby' written on it would always be sticking out from its top.

### Tri-ang 'TT' and a question of space

His interest in model locomotives (one should, as David would have undoubtedly told you, always refer to the power that pulls in such situations as being either the engine or the locomotive – a 'train' being merely the wagons and carriages that follow) was undoubtedly fuelled by the enthusiasm of his father but, graduating from his childhood Hornby set, David's most serious involvement with model railways began as an adult at Winkworth Farm. His first layout was of 3 mm scale with 12 mm track gauge, commonly known as 'TT' and developed by toy manufacturer Tri-ang during the late 1950s/early 1960s. It was apparently seen as a smaller option to the popular OO/HO systems already in existence, but the popularity of TT eventually lost out to the introduction of the even smaller 'N' gauge which subsequently made it commercially unviable for Tri-ang to continue production. Nevertheless, David stuck to the TT models throughout his life despite the obvious difficulties in obtaining what rapidly became obsolete stock. He built a nucleus of around a dozen locomotives: some straightforward Tri-ang items and some built from kits, but all of which, as with most of the smaller model railway scales, operated on 12 volt DC fed through the rails to a motor fitted usually in the locomotive boiler.

Eventually though, time (and space) sadly ran out at Winkworth when it came to the subject of his model railway. As David was to opine, 'As usual, I took on far too much ... The original layout was housed in a room which was eventually commandeered for use as the Foundation's first-ever office [see Chapter 8] ... so the whole layout had to be taken apart and the models and buildings put into the attic ... neglected in favour of work ... a full-scale railway and other things that were taking up my days ...' It very much looked as if the layout might remain in the attic forever, but David was not a man to say 'never say never' and in 1989 commented that '...one day I hope life may slow down just a little, although I doubt it, and then I will be able to resurrect the model and start all over again'. He never did slow down but, nonetheless, the whole railway set-up was re-erected bigger and better than ever after the family's move to Brooklands Farm in 2000 – and in its own designated room too!

## *A hole through the chimney*

At least neither Winkworth nor Brooklands had to be structurally altered in order to accommodate a particular piece of model railway track – unlike at the childhood home at Totteridge. As has already been established, David's father Raymond (and his brother Peter) were as enthusiastic about railways, both full-size and model, as was David. In fact Raymond's enthusiasm was such that he created a quite unusual tunnel in order to achieve a more realistic layout. Reminiscing, David was later to write:

> If the present owners of the house in which I spent my childhood wonder why the chimney smokes in the best bedroom, I can tell them. It is because trains used to run there before the war. My father had a beautiful O-gauge model railway. Like many model railway

enthusiasts, he took over the best bedroom for his layout. He located Watford just beside the door and Carlisle over at the other side of the room, in the dormer window. He couldn't make the room any bigger so, in order to achieve a more realistic curve between Euston and the North, he bored a hole right through the chimney breast somewhere near Rugby ... this was inclined to cause problems when we lit a fire downstairs but at least the railway looked more realistic!

* * *

## 'Miniature' or 'model'?

As this chapter goes under the heading of 'A Life in Miniature' perhaps now is the time to clarify the situation – at least as far as railways are concerned. A miniature railway is generally regarded as a small-size railway able to carry passengers (e.g. the Romney, Hythe and Dymchurch Railway in Kent). A model railway is essentially a development of the 'train set' concept, being built on a fixed baseboard with both railway and non-railway scenery (rivers, hills, etc.) and intended to look like the real thing but small enough to fit in the spare room, shed or wherever. The extent of detail obviously depends on the individual and their own interests and modelling capabilities.

* * *

### *'The Grumblies' to the rescue!*

To some, kit-building and 'scratch' building provides the perfect opportunity to build up a collection based on a particular railway at a particular time in very fine detail. From that point of view it has to be said that David was not a serious railway modeller – he liked to see trains running through the scenery but wasn't too worried about whether or not a particular locomotive had the correct diameter driving wheels or was matched with the correct period coaching stock.

In 2007, David got into conversation with one of the team in the carriage sheds on the Bluebell Railway. As it happened, it was just at the time when David's railway was being rebuilt after the move from Winkworth and, possibly as a result of all the years it had been kept in storage, it was not working at anything like efficient capacity. By good fortune, the person in the carriage shed just happened to be chairman of the 3 mm Society (a specialist society support group formed in 1965 in order to help TT enthusiasts) and he knew of society members in the area surrounding Brooklands Farm who had considerable modelling skills and experience. More importantly, they would be happy to help another 3 mm modeller. Thus the relationship between David and those who were eventually to become known as 'The Grumblies' was formed.

As Stephen Moor, one of their members explained, 'We answered to the collective name "The Grumblies", not because we were in any way grouchy but as a useful password ... "The Grumblies are coming on Monday" is all David ever needed to know whenever his PA told him of our intentions ... We favoured Mondays as it seemed best for most, especially those that were still working ... there were [generally] six or seven of us in the team over our ten years from 2007 ... usually four or five per visit.'

It was always an enjoyable day out for the team ('The Shepherd household always provided a good lunch!' remembers Stephen) and if he should happen to be at home on a Monday or whatever other day they arranged to visit, David frequently joined them in the railway room situated to one side of the barn he'd had transported and converted into his studio and gallery (see Chapter 3). Whilst David's contribution towards the running of the model railway was very much concerned with the scenery ('What he could do with an old bath towel had to be seen to be believed!'), The Grumblies did all they could to maintain the railway in working condition. The original wiring was, however, to remain forever a source of complicated confusion to them. According to Stephen Moor:

[It was] always a mystery to us. It was mounted – as is usual – on the underside of the layout's baseboard but (in its rebuilding) the baseboards had been placed on purpose-built tables so it was impossible to gain access to the wiring which was now sandwiched between the two. We had to resort to cutting chunks out of the tables from beneath so that we could then get to the underside wiring … with one of us laying uncomfortably on the floor flat on our backs, David would invariably come into the room and see a pair of feet sticking out from underneath the layout and undiplomatically accuse whoever of taking a nap!

As a gesture of appreciation for all the pleasure David's layout had given the team (and in grateful recognition of all the lunches provided by Avril and David in the kitchen at Brooklands) The Grumblies made a unique and thoughtful presentation: 'After several years of enjoying ourselves working on the railway, we decided to leave a more permanent reminder and presented David with a model of *Black Prince* in the right scale to work on his model railway. This was built from a kit by one of our members and it was a real treat to see David's reaction when he saw his much-loved locomotive running on his own model railway.'

After David's death in 2017, his model railway, so beloved by The Grumblies and others, was taken to Somerset where steam buff Gordon Fry of West End Garage, Bruton, kept it safely in storage. In 2021, the East Somerset Railway were in negotiations to have the 'village' part of it as a main, permanent display intended to showcase David's enthusiasm for, and skills at, model work.

## Grandpa's Workshop

Whilst David may have painted miniature, perfect scale originals to adorn the walls of his Georgian doll's house (see below) he wasn't in the habit of painting scenes of his model railway. He did, though, famously paint *Grandpa's Workshop* which featured Bert Perriman, Bert's grandson Andrew, and a model of a steam locomotive, a London, Brighton and South Coast Railway Atlantic. David explained how it all came about:

I had wanted to paint a subject like this for many years, bringing together my love of model-making and my passion for steam ... After much help from friends and quite a lot of detective work, we tracked Bill Perriman down near Lancing in Sussex.

Model makers are a very special breed of people and there will always be those who hope to catch me out. I was advised that there were many essentials that I must put in the painting to make it authentic – the Oxo tin of bits and pieces, jam jars full of nails and other paraphernalia which may seem rubbish, but to the model maker will, one day, perhaps be of some use. ... Typically, Bert had hidden himself away in his tiny workshop at the bottom of the garden. There, amongst the orderly chaos of the tools and bits and pieces that are so much a part of a model-maker's world, he was able to relax ... Young Andrew lived next door to his grandpa ... [and was] crazy about steam trains too. Having run back from school and pausing only to grab a packet of crisps from the larder, he rushed round to lend a hand.

* * *

## Not the most comfortable locomotive

David was not averse to visiting miniature narrow-gauge railways – especially one run by his long-time friend and fellow railway enthusiast Julian Birley. *The Railway Magazine* carried this report:

International wildlife artist and preservation pioneer David Shepherd has visited the Bala Lake Railway [Gwynedd, Wales] to experience the delights of a locomotive at the opposite end of the scale from his BR Standard 9F 2-10-0 ... *Black Prince*.

Accompanied by his wife Avril, David visited the award-winning line. ... [and] took a turn on the footplate of Julian Birley's Quarry Hunslet 0-4oST named *Alice*.

Five of Julian's restored slate wagons were attached to *Alice*, and David soon discovered just how light a touch is required to ease the locomotive into action ... David thrived ... on the slightly crowded footplate, and thoroughly enjoyed himself during the 90-minute return trip along the lakeside.

He said afterwards that *Alice* was 'not the most comfortable locomotive as there is no seat unlike *Black Prince*, and perching on the rear rail of the footplate is not conducive to overall comfort.'

* * *

## *Underscored and underlined*

The standard livery for most British Railways steam locomotives was black, often with a thin red, cream and grey 'lining' (trim). The process of painting this trim required a great deal of skill but it was a part of model railway life that modellers took very seriously. Nowadays, most affix a 'trim' to their model locomotives by the far easier expedient of using ready-made transfers, but back when David took possession of the full-scale *Black Prince*, it was a job done by eye, a steady hand and a careful brushstroke. To have it done on *Black Prince*, David decided to have a bit of fun with a signwriting model maker, but unfortunately for David, the end result wasn't quite what he anticipated:

In one of my more unfortunate moments when *Black Prince* was stabled at Longmoor, I decided to see what she would look like 'lined out' in red. I knew a sign writer, who in his spare time lined out model locomotives for people. I rang him up: 'Would you like to line out a locomotive for me in red?' 'What size is it? Is it OO or O gauge?' 'Well, actually it's neither. I don't have the engine with me, but if you don't mind coming with me to see it, I'll take you over to where she lives.'

We drove to Liphook and turned right, on to the road to Longmoor. He still had absolutely no idea of the task that awaited him. He thought I was taking him to a friend who had a model railway.

We reached Longmoor and got out of the car. By now, he was beginning to wonder. We went round the corner and there was *Black Prince*. To say the least, he was quite surprised. However, he agreed it made a change from model locomotives, and he lined out *Black Prince*, but she looked so terrible that I very soon turned back to her original unlined black.

## There's a mouse in the house

During their long trips from Surrey to Cadgwith Cove and their holiday cottage in Cornwall, David would keep his young daughters entertained with tales of Marmalade and Montague (the latter possibly named after David's maternal grandfather) imaginary mice whose exploits also featured in bedtime tales at Winkworth Farm. As Melanie remembers, 'His imagination with these stories was amazing.' Not content with stimulating the girls' imagination, he also made Melanie, for her collection of felt mice, a 'wonderful "mouse-house" … from a polystyrene gin barrel …'

It was these stories, plus Melanie's collection, that was to cause the family to begin a whole mischief of model mice – and David to construct little mice homes in the most unexpected places around both Winkworth Farm and Brooklands. Melinda remembers that 'The original bread oven in our Tudor house became a kitchen scene with miniature wooden furniture and felt mice.' Fortunately, being of roughly the same period of construction, both houses had bread ovens – thus enabling a similar home to be set up when the family moved to Brooklands in 2000. A source of interest and amusement to adult and child visitors alike, these little characters were illuminated by lights, and as one looked into their private world it was like viewing something from *The Borrowers* books by Mary Norton. Elsewhere, mice were dotted around various rooms and were quite likely to be seen in any nook or crevice, or tucked into any irregularities in the wooden ceiling beams. So too, if one looked carefully, were tiny plasticine elephants made by Melanie which, along with the mice, were also placed in the unlikeliest of places.

## A period property – in miniature

The doll's house, although 'miniature', was certainly not small when compared to what most would think of as being a doll's house. Bought many years ago, the excuse for doing so was that it would make good entertainment for the Shepherd girls and perhaps, in the fullness of time, for any children they might have. The real reason was, though, mainly to indulge David's love of small-scale and miniatures. David and Avril went to buy it together and as they manhandled it out of the shop a passer-by remarked that 'someone was going to be a very lucky child' – at which Avril pointed to David and told the stranger, 'That's the lucky child!'

No matter for whom it was purchased, it was a magnificent Georgian-style building of which any architect, let alone child, would have been very proud. Complete with railings and outdoor balconies, the interior was furnished to scale (1:12) and even included miniature David Shepherd original paintings hanging on the walls. The lighting and every piece of furniture was absolutely correct down to the tiniest detail when it came to style and period.

* * *

## Red Teds and Fortescue

Red Teds was a bear given to David by his mother when he was one year old. Although nowadays showing signs of wear and tear, he is still very much a part of the Shepherd family and, along with Fortescue the Owl, is now in retirement. Fortescue – another from David's early years – being small enough to sit in a suitcase, regularly accompanied his owner throughout his adult life on his frequent trips both home and abroad.

* * *

5

# DOTTY ABOUT DOGS – AND OTHER ANIMALS

In some biographies it might seem strange that a person's love of animals should feature before their family and friends (see Chapter 6) but not in this case. As David's nearest and dearest can testify, his undoubted love for them could, however, sometimes appear secondary to the affection he showed to his dogs. It's the opinion of Mandy that David occasionally favoured them to his daughters because they didn't answer back, especially when she and her sisters were in their rebellious teenage years. At the start of any telephone calls home made during his frequent trips away, David would invariably ask after the likes of Cookie and Willow before enquiring after the health of family members.

*Dogs and all about them*
Avril recalled that when she first knew David, any visitors to David's parent's home would be greeted by five corgis – and that they were not always the most welcoming of animals! Once she and David were married and living at Oakhill Cottage (close to David's parents) the young couple soon obtained Simba and Susie,

two golden retrievers. As David was to write in the first edition of
*The Man Who Loves Giants*:

> Not long after our wedding ... we went down to Yeovil together
> while I fulfilled a commission from Westland Aircraft to paint in
> their factory ... Off I would trundle to work every day. My wife,
> in the meantime, had gone chasing off to buy a golden retriever
> puppy. We both considered this to be the most essential item of
> furniture in our new home ... I was busy painting Whirlwind
> helicopters in the paint-shop when Avril wandered straight into
> the factory through the security gates – apparently with permission
> from the managing director – carrying two little golden bundles in
> her arms. They waddled around the paint-shop, puddling all over
> the place, and we bought both of them.

Back at Oakhill Cottage, the two pups quickly settled in and Avril
regularly took them for long walks with David's father and his
dogs around Frensham Ponds. On one particular occasion, all the
dogs went running ahead and disappeared out of sight. Very soon
a man appeared from the direction in which they had disappeared
screaming and yelling 'Take those bloody dogs away!' He was,
as Avril described the situation in her inimitable and unflappable
manner, 'very angry'. Seemingly the dogs had run into a film set
and totally ruined a particular scene which would, according to
the apoplectic man (who, it transpired was the film's director)
have to be completely re-shot. Quite which film it was that they'd
disturbed is unknown but the area around the Frensham Ponds
has long been used as a location for such things.

At Winkworth and from thereon, David and Avril were never
without dogs – a trait which has obviously passed to all four
daughters who have rarely been without one or more of their own
throughout their adult lives. The golden retrievers were replaced
in time by flatcoat retrievers and an Old English sheepdog called
Wilton because, as sixteen-year-old Melinda explained to a
magazine reporter in 1974, 'he's just like a carpet'. It was, though,
to be the bearded collie breed with which David and Avril really

fell in love. The first was Muffin but all of those which followed were regularly painted by David, either as subjects on their own, or incorporated into a more general and appropriate scene such as *Cottage Companions*.

As members of the Southern Counties Bearded Collie Club (SCBCC) David and Avril regularly attended the annual strawberry teas, taking with them whichever of the dogs was sharing their lives at the time. One such was Bonnie (who was actually Melinda's dog), a name which also proved to be popular with many of the other collie owners of the era as, on one particular occasion when Avril had cause to call to the animal for which she was responsible, a good number of the canines at the event came happily bounding towards her, no doubt in anticipation of a treat.

It's typical of David that such fun was mixed up with fundraising, and as well as donating prizes on such occasions (quite often signed prints of *Our Bearded Friends – Cookie and Willow*; *Muffin's Pups*; *Muffin* and *Playtime*) he did a great deal to help with fundraising efforts, both directly for the SCBCC and also more generally in association with the *Dogs Today* magazine. In 1994, on the death of Muffin, David wrote her obituary for *Dogs Today* and in her letter of response, editor Beverley Cuddy thanked David for sharing his feelings with their readers and said, 'There have been many moist eyes when reading about your wonderful friend.'

### A childhood full of animals

David's sister Judy clearly remembers the animals from their childhood, both whilst growing up in Totteridge during the war and during their teenage years at Larkmead and Frimley Hall Hotel – and even some of the names they were given:

We had goats which we used to milk and make butter because of the rationing and we had two goat kids born on Easter Day which we called Allé and Luia. And Mousie, the Shetland pony we learned to ride on, along with three tortoises, a cat called Hannibal because he used to climb over everything and of course, our beloved dogs – Pekes in those days – which were all named after characters in *The Mikado*.

Then, after the war we moved to our beautiful Larkmead house, near Theydon Bois, where we spent a wonderful three years. Mummy ran a children's riding school so we had a lot of ponies, and she put a photo of David on the front page of her brochure with a cup and rosette after winning a show class on our lovely pony Bracken. Peter [David and Judy's brother] and I were very cross and jealous because he and I were supposed to be the riders in the family and David supposedly hated horses – but actually he was quite good with them!

Then we moved to Frimley Hall Hotel... [and] Mummy continued with her riding school so we still had the ponies, as well as the cows and pigs and of course the dogs [corgis by then] and cats. We had two Jersey cows we called Ermintrude and Esmerelda which we used to milk (or I did!) and a cat called Batterpuss because it purred like Battersea Power Station, and a hamster called Middlesex because we didn't know if it was a boy or a girl. Our corgis included two puppies we bred called Wide and Small – Small was shorthand for 'smallest growler in all the world'!

Corgis – all descendants of the original ones first owned by the Shepherds whilst living at Theydon Bois – were, as Avril was later to discover (see above), regular and constant companions to Raymond and Joyce, and Joyce was never without one almost until the day she died in 1978. With regards to Mousie the pony and the various goats of their childhood, David wrote the following:

Early in the war, the day came when, like so many people, we had to lay our car [a Morris Eight] up for the duration. We turned to four-legged transport and bought a little Shetland pony called Mousie, with a trap, and we used to do all our shopping by this romantic form of conveyance. Shetland ponies are tough little things and Mousie used to happily trot all the way to Finchley,

Mill Hill or Barnet. On arrival, we would tie her up outside the shop ... [and] Mousie lived in our family until the ripe old age of thirty-six.

We also kept a large and varied number of goats during the war. We were able to let them loose in a field just a few yards from our house and they were a valuable source of milk, butter and cheese. I remember endlessly turning handles on primitive butter-making machines while the air-raids were going on. I suppose it was all worth it; it was, in fact, because like so many people we scrounged little extras from the fishmonger and butcher. This was an integral part of the British way of life during the war and, on reflection, was I suppose a bit naughty, but my mother and I would be standing in the inevitable queue in Whetstone for meat or fish and, as so often happened when halfway up the line, the fishmonger or butcher would say, 'No more.' Then it was always remarkable what came out from under the counter as a swap for a pound of goat's butter!

We used to buy our goats [transported by rail] from all over the country and I remember one frightful crisis when the London and North-Eastern Railway Company rang up from King's Cross, having done an immense amount of detective work, to tell us that a goat, lost in transport, had at last been found; it was in the station and it had eaten all its identification and address labels.

* * *

## Mice ate the Morris Eight!

There is an interesting aside to the fact that when the family car had been laid up for the duration of the war and Mousie the Shetland pony had taken over transport duties, the Morris Eight car had become a storage place for animal feed. When the time came at the end of hostilities to get the vehicle back on the road again, it was discovered that the local mouse population had been extremely active and, in addition to helping themselves to any animal feed available, had eaten all the interior of the roof lining and passenger seats.

* * *

Both as a young boy and into early adulthood, David had a particular affection for pigs and thought them very clean and intelligent. One Large White boar, a part of the farmyard scene when the family lived at Frimley Hall Hotel, was a much-loved pet that would squeal its delight on seeing David and was happy to be scratched and tickled for as long as David was willing to do so. According to Judy, David would apparently lie down in the straw with it and it was not unknown for both pig and human to doze off together, both happy in each other's company.

## Trot on!

Along with the childhood livestock companions and various dogs, other animals featured in daily life once David and Avril had moved to Winkworth Farm. Never a fan of cats because of the damage they cause to songbirds and other wildlife, one was found injured at the roadside and was smuggled into one of the outbuildings where it was nursed back to full health by animal-mad Melanie who kept it a secret from her father for quite some time. However, as is the way with most daughters who can invariably wrap their fathers around their proverbial little finger, David was eventually persuaded to let the cat (called Mouse!) into the house where she lived quite contentedly.

That famous persuasion was also brought into action when it came to the prospect of acquiring a pony. Melanie recalls that 'When we were old enough it was inevitable that at least one or two of us daughters would start being interested in horses especially as Dad's mother [Joyce] bred Welsh mountain ponies.' Horse-mad Wendy remembers that for a long time the answer to the request was always 'No!' But then 'we eventually got our way. We had to earn it mind you, and do all our own chores … in being emphatic on that, he taught us all that nothing is free in life.' Furthermore, before finally agreeing, David insisted that *all* the girls had to prove that they could look after a pony in addition to their ever-growing menagerie of guinea pigs, rabbits, dogs and ducks. With this in mind, a large part of the garden was temporarily fenced and two of Joyce's prized mares arrived for two months' trial.

The girl's due diligence paid off, as a result of which Chota, a 14-hand New Forest pony appeared. He proved as good as gold until the girl's had got their confidence – at which point they all unanimously agree that he became 'extremely naughty' and regularly unseated whoever happened to be riding him before then galloping home with reins and stirrups flying. As Mandy was to mention at David's memorial service in 2018, 'When Chota used to bolt home to Winkworth Farm with no one at the helm, Mum would head off to look for us and Dad would take the sweating pony for a fast ride around the block to teach him a lesson.'

One thing led to another. Any horse likes to be with other equines (they are, of course, a herd animal) and so a companion was found in the shape of Oxo, 'an adorable and characterful donkey.' Being a knowledgeable horse-person, it is no surprise that the advice and assistance of David's mother was sought in order to search out a donkey most likely to fit in well with the household. Joyce's assurances that she had found a suitable animal: 'He's quiet and has never brayed in all the time that I've had him,' was sufficient to persuade the Shepherd family that her paragon of a find should come and live alongside Chota. Then the noise began. It eventually transpired that Joyce had only actually had Oxo in her yard for a day and he was to turn out to be anything but quiet! Nonetheless, despite this he stayed and David's daughters could frequently be seen riding both Chota and Oxo in and around the countryside surrounding Winkworth, with both animals helping to forge wonderful memories of many happy times.

In spite of David's childhood riding lessons, the pony and trap jaunts with Mousie the Shetland, occasionally mounting the naughty Chota – and when visiting Wendy in Wyoming where he and Avril would ride out to the mountains 'Western-style' (see Chapter 6) – it seems that he had no particular desire to have a horse of his own. This is perhaps surprising as both the countryside surroundings of Winkworth and

Brooklands were ideal riding country. Possibly his thinking was that he was away from home too often and, despite the fact that both his sister and daughters describe him as being a more than competent equestrian (he won several horse shows and events as a youngster) it just wasn't a practical or feasible option.

Despite hardly riding in his adult years, all the times he'd spent around horses and ponies in his youth had instilled a fondness and understanding of equines that manifested itself in much of his horse-related artwork, especially that depicting shires and farm horses of a bygone era. *Spring Ploughing* features two shires at work and was inspired by A. E. Housman's poem, *A Shropshire Lad*. Shires appear again in *Shires on Holiday*, a painting commissioned by Whitbread Breweries which shows galloping 'off-duty' dray horses, and again in *The Old Forge* where one is having new shoes fitted by the farrier. *The Lunch Break* portrays both man and horse in the 1920s whilst *Somerset Harvest* evocatively depicts both the hard work and romance of the harvest fields during the same era.

Rural and mechanical were often combined. Amongst David's working sketches is one which, in the foreground, shows a horse and hay wain being loaded by a couple with pitchforks while in the background stands a soldier (possibly Home Guard) watching over a crashed German plane. As to the background inspiration for such bucolic provincial sketches and paintings, some were real places whilst others were either a composite of several, or came entirely from David's imagination: 'I love to recall the days of my childhood when life seemed to go by at a much more leisurely pace ... it is though, sometimes very difficult, if not impossible to find the perfect backdrop to use to show off the main subjects to their best advantage. I use photos but I'll never paint from other people's ... I need to take them myself so as to get the right atmosphere.'

## Ducking the issue

As part of his vision for Winkworth Farm, David created a lake. The following year Canada geese arrived to breed – and they and their offspring returned year after year. One youngster was not, however, as fortunate as its siblings and, because of a defect to its wing (probably a condition known as 'Angel Wing' where the last joint is twisted and the wing feathers point outwards) it couldn't fly off in the autumn when the others did. Like the tale of *The Ugly Duckling* by Hans Christian Andersen, Avril remembered that it overwintered on the lake by itself until the others returned the following spring – and did so for four years before it was eventually taken by a fox, much to the dismay of David and the family. A pair of Australian black swans also lived on the lake. Aggressive towards the young Shepherd girls, there was less sadness when they disappeared overnight, taken, so it was thought, by travellers who had set up camp not all that far away.

Somehow, somewhere (these things just seem to happen in the Shepherd household!) a flotilla of Muscovy ducks appeared. Unlike wild geese, the Muscovy is a very definite domestic breed and generally reluctant to fly, so, although no one can actually remember their arrival, the nucleus of the stock must have, at some point, been deliberately included into the Winkworth menagerie by one or other of its human inhabitants – and were seemingly given free rein.

Whilst the image of David seen by most is that of a man possessing passion, unpredictability and a frenetic, energetic lifestyle, there was a quieter, gentler, certainly caring side to him that was often only seen by his wife and daughters. This, from Melanie:

When I was studying for my O levels, the annual Muscovy duck hatching began. As the usual boiler location was already booked, another of the mother ducks laid her eggs in Dad's lorry garage. At hatching, the ducklings catapulted to the ground to follow mum down to the lake. However, one of the eggs didn't quite hatch and the mother wouldn't leave so I took the egg away and the family group headed safely to the lake. With Dad's help we gently broke open the shell and brought out this rather pathetic wet little creature. Once dried she very much came to life and so began our love affair with a cheeky little duckling we named Ziggy. Sleeping on my pillow at night behind my ear, learning to swim with her gammy leg, sleeping in my dungaree pocket in the daytime, getting stronger every day in the bath, and digging ten times a day in the flower beds for her worm meals, she thrived. She loved to be with company all the time and so was mostly in the kitchen but was often found walking down the corridor to the sitting room. At mealtimes Dad would lift her on to the table where she went from plate to plate picking all the best bits ... especially peas ... from everyone.

Notwithstanding all that, ducks, either as guests at the dinner table or on the lake alongside the wild geese, were not the only poultry to reside at Winkworth. As a child – and according to an interview he gave to *Your Chickens* magazine in March 2017 (poignantly, his last ever – and how inconsequential a topic considering his lifetime achievements) – David's involvement with poultry seemingly began at a very early age: 'My family had chickens and turkeys when we were living in Totteridge ... and a few months before Christmas, we used to buy day-old turkey chicks for fattening. During the worst nights of the Blitz I remember that they would all be brought into the house for safe-keeping. Why on earth we thought that, had the house received a direct hit, they would be safer in the kitchen than out in the garden, I can't imagine!'

At Winkworth Farm, his childhood enthusiasm was momentarily rekindled and the family had a flock of Rhode Island Red chickens. Twelve of them were housed in a shed and run under a walnut tree but after a further visit from a fox who this time managed to dig under the wire-netting enclosure, so great was the upset and trauma that it was decided that such carnage and heartbreak did not need to be endured again. That said, when asked in the same interview for *Your Chickens* magazine whether or not he would ever consider keeping chickens in the future, David remarked that he was 'very enthusiastic about the idea of one day doing so', particularly when it came to the prospect of possibly re-homing commercially-kept birds nowadays championed by the likes of the British Hen Welfare Trust (BHWT): 'Commercially-kept chickens [are] one of the most abused things on the planet ... People treat [them] as machines and it's cruel ... particularly their live transport ... so I can't imagine anything more rewarding than rescuing and re-homing ex-intensive birds and watching them enjoy life as nature intended.'

### *Two for the price of one*
Once the Shepherd daughters had outgrown their early teenage years, and also outgrown both their beloved Chota and Oxo, the grassy paddocks at Winkworth were left somewhat bereft of livestock. Some years previous, David had been inspired to undertake a painting, *Highland Cattle*, depicting five quite majestic-looking beasts in a Scottish landscape:

> The Victorian landscape painters of the nineteenth century seem to have had an obsession for painting threatening storm clouds swirling around the brooding scenery of Scotland, crofters herding sheep along the stony mountain paths, and, it seemed inevitably, Highland cattle drinking at the water's edge ... travelling in the Highlands and coming round a corner on a remote mountain road I actually came face to face with these friendly and indeed, highly paintable animals. I could now see why they appealed to my Victorian predecessors, and I hope that, in my painting I, too, have managed to do justice to these marvellous wild and woolly animals ...

Obviously smitten by these 'wild and woolly animals', as one of David's significant birthdays approached, and knowing his admiration of the breed, Avril thought it might be a good idea to gift her husband a Highland cow as a surprise, and with that in mind made enquiries regarding doing so. After all, although the relatively gentle slopes of Surrey were not in any way reminiscent of the 'brooding scenery of Scotland', it wasn't as if they were short of grazing. As it happened, both Avril and David got the surprise as it turned out that the cow had been in calf when Avril was making all the necessary arrangements and when it was actually delivered to Winkworth, it arrived with a calf (a bull) at foot! Family friend actor Frank Thornton (perhaps best known as Captain Peacock in BBC Television's *Are You Being Served?* and as Truelove in *Last of The Summer Wine*) and his wife Beryl happened to be visiting at the time and so the two bovines were ceremonially named Beryl and Frank in their honour. However, as bull-calf Frank grew he took to being rather boisterous and to chasing David around the paddock, as a result of which their tenure was relatively short-lived, with Beryl eventually being offered to a breeder and Frank to a farmer.

## A step away from the norm

In addition to Highland cattle, the Hereford breed also featured several times in David's paintings. *Fred, After his Shampoo* is of a Hereford bull portrayed just after being washed and groomed in readiness for a show, while *Old Ben's Cottage* has a Hereford in the foreground. *The Orphans* depicts a group of bullocks of indeterminate breed, but it is, however, in one of his earliest paintings of cattle that it is first possible to recognise the light and atmosphere for which David was to become so well known. Painted at a time when he was more used to putting images of aeroplanes on canvas, *Reading Cattle Market* was very definitely a step away from the norm. As David was to comment many years later:

I cannot really remember what inspired me to paint this scene. What I do know is that after I'd finished my training I had plenty of time to choose my subjects, and a cattle market made a change

… Furthermore, this highly paintable scene was not unlike a steam locomotive shed. The sun cast beams of light through the cigarette smoke, and the back views of the marvellous characters sitting in the audience gave me plenty of material as they watched the hustle and bustle of the cattle auction; there was certainly plenty of atmosphere!

Over the years, David was a patron and supporter of many animal welfare charities, including the West Surrey Badger Group, and Compassion in World Farming (to whom he donated several paintings to be auctioned at their events – thus helping to raise all-important funds for farm animal welfare). So, although at the outset it might have seemed strange to have included David's passionate love of dogs, family pets and farm livestock prior to describing his family and friends, perhaps now, after reading of this particular and extremely important aspect of David's life, it is quite understandable!

6

# FAMILY, FRIENDS AND ROYAL CONNECTIONS

How different David's adult life might have been had he not had the good fortune to meet Avril as he painted portraits of aeroplanes in the 1950s – and how fortunate that she eventually agreed to marry him (see below). Never has the expression 'behind every great man there is a great woman' ever been so true. Throughout the whole of their life together Avril was very definitely the absolutely crucial part of both work and family life and was much loved by her daughters, grandchildren, family members and countless friends. As David admitted in an interview for *The Argus* newspaper in June 2002, Avril proved the perfect foil for him:

> … because she lets my tantrums ride over her. It's amazing she has stuck with me all these years but I would be lost without her. I can't even boil an egg. If I were on a desert island, I would be dead in a week.
>
> I can't go abroad for more than two days because I start missing her. I said that to Sue Lawley [on David's second appearance as guest on *Desert Island Discs*] and she said: 'Gosh, people don't say that sort of thing any more.' Well, they should … my wife takes all the knocks, that's why she's a blooming saint…

The patience of a saint was, at times, certainly required by Avril. At certain points of his immensely creative life, David was, by his own admission, virtually impossible to live with. In the newspaper interview (see above) he told journalist Angela Wintle, that 'Sir Edward Elgar was the same. There were times when he was so daunting, his wife would leave his lunch on a tray outside his room. I can thoroughly understand that.'

The proverbial path of true love didn't always run smoothly. David and Avril first met at a dance at Camberley and when the obviously smitten David suggested that he walked Avril home, she refused saying (in a white lie) that someone else had already agreed to do so. Nonetheless, determined and persistent (as he was with everything in life) he eventually persuaded the initially reluctant Avril to embark upon a courtship which would, some eighteen months later in 1957, eventually lead to a long and extremely happy marriage, even if by a somewhat unusual set of circumstances.

On a walk from Waterloo station, it took David until reaching Battersea Power Station to pluck up sufficient courage to ask Avril to marry him. She refused. Returning home rejected and somewhat deflated, David told his parents that he'd proposed – but failed to inform them that Avril had declined his offer. Scheduled for lunch with the Shepherd parents the next day, Avril turned up at their house in Frensham to be greeted by hugs, congratulations and 'welcome, daughter-in-law' type comments from David's mother Joyce. It was, as Avril said, 'an awkward situation' but one which she amazingly went along with and fortunately, never had cause to regret despite some initial opposition from her stepfather who thought it possibly a risky business to marry an artist.

In certain senses, Avril and David had similar characteristics, one of which being that neither were ever able to sit down and relax (something that has also very definitely been passed down to their daughters who, like their parents, always have to be busy at some project or another). If there were things to be done then Avril would do them, no matter what the day or occasion. She was famously late for their wedding, not because it was tradition, more that up until half an hour before needing to prepare herself for church, she'd been painting the bannisters of their new home, Oakhill Cottage and, although arriving looking as lovely as ever, nevertheless appeared at the altar with white gloss paint firmly engrained under her fingernails!

For the first few years, before recruiting outside assistance, Avril was David's PA and secretary, and entertained clients with famed hospitality. She also kept her sometimes tempestuous and occasionally manic husband in order. As one family friend wrote at the time:

This is where Avril Shepherd proves to be David's perfect partner, for while David crashes around the house looking like a rogue elephant with toothache seeking out a letter or some other object which he is certain somebody has deliberately hidden – but which invariably turns up in his pocket – Avril goes quietly about the business of running the house, charming her guests and generally ignoring the crashes and thumps, the curses and ravings and slamming of doors.

David is quite magnificently flappable; Avril is supremely unflappable – and somehow this balance works wonderfully …

At Winkworth, Avril fortunately had an ally in Kitty Hoare. Kitty was the first of David's personal assistants and secretaries – and she very quickly got the measure of David and his erratic moods and refused to be fazed by them. When things got too heated she would bring him back in line with a severe look and a few well-chosen words: 'Mr Shepherd, I do not have to stay and listen to this …' was usually sufficient. Despite his undeniably volatile nature (he did, though, calm down greatly during the last quarter of a century or so of his life) his PAs and secretaries were very fond of David and generally remained for several years before moving on for reasons of their own rather than being daunted by his behaviour.

* * *

## 'Queen of the Cruise'

The cruise ship MV *Monte Umbe* was built for the services to South America and her basic route was Bilbao-Coruna-Vigo-Tenerife-Rio de Janeiro-Santos-Montevideo-Buenos Aires. From 1960 however, she was also used for a limited number of cruises from Bilbao or Barcelona each summer, visiting ports as far afield as New York and Leningrad. In 1968 *Monte Umbe* began a new service from Liverpool to Tenerife carrying 360 one-class cruise passengers. In 1969, much to David's horror, Avril booked the whole family on such a cruise and, despite David's initial misgivings, apparently a thoroughly enjoyable holiday ensued. The adventure was made even more memorable by dint of the fact that Avril won the title of 'Queen of the Cruise' and was awarded a beauty queen-type sash and a bottle of champagne. Her young daughters were delighted but her husband even more so – and, quite rightly, was extremely proud of his extremely attractive wife. Some forty years on, the event is still remembered as part of the Shepherd family history.

* * *

*Shepherdesses – David's daughters*

Melinda, the first of the four daughters, was born in 1958 but, unlike many of today's fathers, there was no sign of David at her birth. As Avril remembered, 'He dropped me off at the hospital and then went home to await the telephone call.' When it came, his mother insisted on him having lunch before visiting the new mother and child – a fact that quite understandably, upset Avril who made it known that she was, to say the least, somewhat disappointed and a little angry. He must have taken note, for he never made the same mistake when the other three daughters were born!

Whilst babies may not have been David's forte, he interacted wonderfully with his daughters once they were able to walk. Although he tended not to dress them or get involved with anything of a practical nature ('It was quicker to do it myself,' said Avril), he nevertheless spent countless hours playing games, organising running races and telling stories – so much so that all four girls recall their childhood at Winkworth with great love and affection.

Melinda recalls that it was 'blessed with many varied and rich memories – not that we necessarily appreciated it at the time … Family life was never dull. There was always something going on … On occasions if one of our pets was ill, it wasn't unusual to see it in the kitchen next to the Aga – what visitors must have thought about Mum, legs apart in order to avoid stepping on injured or ill animals whilst cooking a magnificent meal would most certainly be frowned upon nowadays … but then I'm sure some people saw us as a slightly eccentric family anyway!'

Mandy too remembers their upbringing as being 'untraditional' but that 'so much was learnt from an amazing stream of visitors … extraordinary wildlife experts from every corner of the world, and legends who shared Dad's love of wildlife such as Jack Nicklaus who gave us a golf lesson on the lawn with an umbrella, and James Stewart who tried to ride our donkey!' Melanie was also there to witness that particular occasion: 'His feet were virtually walking on the ground he was so tall and long legged …'

Even at a young age, Wendy realised that her father was a person of inspiring drive and passion: 'Dad was an amazing man in so many ways … family was foremost for him and he genuinely loved us dearly. He always wanted us to be happy. It was a special childhood, full of excitement, travel and learning.'

In later life, it was Wendy's love of horses that led her to work and live in America – where she married Curt and had two sons, Luke and Justin. Before that though, her equine career had begun as a groom for the renowned British polo player Claire Tomlinson. Whilst Wendy was in her employ, David met a sculptress at an art convention and, during conversation, learnt that she lived on a ranch in Wyoming and that the family played polo – and that there was possibly a job as a groom for Wendy. As Wendy says, 'I'd read *My Friend Flicka* as a child so off I went … and stayed':

When Mum and Dad visited they loved the mountains and both even rode out on horses Western-style ... We once took them to a Native American ritual site called 'Medicine Wheel' ... a forest ranger proudly told Dad that the site was probably from the 1300s – to which Dad replied that his kitchen was older than that!

We had so much special time whenever they came over to stay ... trips to the mountains and paint-ball fights with the boys ... where Dad would cover himself in ketchup so as to look as if he'd been shot! Shopping became a game and he'd chase them around the store. He told a perfect stranger that the boys were out of control, to which she replied: 'No Sir, it's you who is out of control.' Little did she know!

So even though we'd only see Mum and Dad a couple of times a year, Dad made the most of it and had fun with the boys. If we were in the UK on a visit, he took them to London to see classical concerts and gave them an eclectic love of all music – as he had his daughters when, in his studio at Winkworth, we'd all dance to the show tunes of *Me and My Girl*!

When his daughters were at school, in the manner of all children they could easily be embarrassed by their parents, particularly in what they, or rather David, wore. His favoured item of apparel was a sleeveless safari gilet which he would almost invariably be wearing whenever he turned up at their school parents' evenings or social functions. 'All the other dads were there in their smart business suits – and there was Dad wearing his usual safari jacket,' remembers Melinda. There was, as touched upon elsewhere, also the embarrassment to Melinda when, rather than arriving at her boarding school in a smart car as did the majority of her friends' parents, David, Avril and her three younger sisters occasionally turned up in a Bedford flatbed three-ton truck; her siblings travelling on the open back and waving wildly in a manner reminiscent of a scene from a *St Trinian's* film.

The height of David's immediate artistic success happened to coincide with the years of his children's education.

Clients, commissions and commitments often meant that David was unfortunately too preoccupied to attend school events such as sports days or, if he did, he'd turn up at the last moment in the hope that the girls would think he had been there all the time. On at least one occasion he was caught out. Knowing that he'd been a late arrival (despite his insistence that he'd been there for the duration) Melinda spun him a story of how she'd won a race at the sports day: 'Yes, I know darling … you were absolutely marvellous … I saw it all from beginning to end.' She hadn't won the race – and he had not seen her not win it.

### David's daughters – their adult life and parental influence

The question is often asked whether it is nature or nurture that makes children what they become in adult life. It's an interesting concept, particularly when it comes to David and Avril's daughters. All have their mother's blonde hair and stunning youthful features. They have also inherited her skills as parents to their own children. Frequently asked whether she has any of her father's artistic ability, Melinda will say 'no'. She has, however, a definite skill for interior design – and that ability is most certainly inherited from her mother. David, who, for much of his life attempted to educate on the subject of conservation, might well be said to have been a teacher, a profession which Melinda has followed in mainstream schooling, both at primary and secondary level.

Mandy is, as is well known, famous in her own right as an artist. Her style and choice of painting medium does, however, differ from that of her father. Also, she and David took directly opposite routes in the art world. As is evidenced in Chapter 10, whilst David was first known as an aviation artist and then one who painted wildlife, Mandy's artistic interest was firstly wildlife and then aviation and the military.

Melanie, for over two decades the CEO of the David Shepherd Wildlife Foundation, has obviously inherited David's passion for wildlife and its conservation and is, incidentally, extremely skilled in silver-work – art in another form. 'Passionate' is not too strong a word and it is through Melanie's dedication that so many opportunities to fundraise on behalf of the DSWF, and thus endangered wildlife, have been enabled.

Although Wendy inherited, as she describes it, 'a small talent for painting', she was quite determined to be her 'own person'. She became a little rebellious and did 'her own thing'. Even though David was not best pleased about her not using her brain in a better way than working with horses, as Wendy argues, 'He followed his passion … and I followed mine.' 'Perhaps,' she says, 'I'm a little more like Mum in that I've chosen to be in the background, proud of the Foundation and in what Dad achieved, albeit in a supporting role … Dad had high standards and an incredible work ethic which I've tried to follow … and to teach our boys.'

## Grandchildren and great-grandchildren

Melanie's eldest daughter, Emily, is an artist – hence the Three Generations initiative originally comprising David, Mandy and Emily (see below) and, in 2019, created #SketchforWildlife on social media. In January of that year, she took on the challenge of producing 365 thirty-minute daily sketches or paintings priced at £100 each, with 100 per cent of the money going directly into wildlife conservation. By the following January she had hit, and then surpassed her target, having produced 400 paintings and sketches within her self-imposed time scale. Emily's sister Georgina (known to all as 'Peanut') was the head of programmes and policy at the DSWF and is now its CEO, so together they are most certainly continuing their grandfather's legacy.

Wendy's eldest son, Luke, lives in Wales with his wife Holly, whilst Justin, her youngest, remains in America and in October 2020 married his fiancée, Ivy. Melinda's twins, Thomas and Elliot, are married to Krystal and Lynzie and each has a child, Katie and Henry. Robin, the elder of Mandy's three daughters (the other two being Rosie and Annabel) is also married and has twins, Oliver and Matilda. Sadly, of the young, upcoming generation of great-grandchildren, Katie is the only one David ever met – and with whom he was immediately besotted.

### The 'Three Generations'

Although it might sound more like a singing group than a family of artists and conservationists, the 'Three Generations' was actually a perspective of family life instigated by Melanie in order to bring together the idea of art and conservation (an idea enhanced further in the hugely successful Annual Wildlife Artist of the Year competition as described in Chapter 8). It was a brilliant concept – and relatively easy to stage as the main participants, David, Mandy and Emily, were readily to hand and, conveniently, formed three generations.

A review of the 2010 Wildlife Artist of the Year exhibition by Raymond Andress – at which the 'three generations' put on a joint showing, explained all of the three artists' differing styles quite succinctly:

> David Shepherd the grand old man of wildlife painting is now eighty years of age and still painting. His retrospective at this exhibition shows a selection of his work over a lifetime. He is famous and rightly so, for his portrayal of the heat and thorn scrub of East Africa, populated by various spectacular animals ... His daughter Mandy ... has inherited her father's talent for depicting wildlife ... [but] with a dry brush, impressionistic yet detailed technique. The third-generation artist on show here is David's eldest granddaughter Emily Lamb, painting in a more abstract style she combines indigenous people with wildlife to great effect. She is ... original and talented ...

The review (much longer than the part quoted above) ended with the disclaimer that its author had not, in any way, been compromised by either 'a quick peck on the cheek from Mandy ... or by free wine!'

### Friends

Sometimes family and friends intermingle – and can seemingly be easily confused! Richard Radcliffe recollects that the first time he ever met David was in connection with the DSWF.

He had gone to Winkworth in a business capacity for a meeting at which it was hoped he could advise on how to attract more legacies:

I went into his home and he came into the room and called me 'darling'. He was actually addressing Melanie who had, unbeknown to me, come into the room behind me. So I replied 'Hello dear'. After recovering from mutual giggles his old dog came into the room and broke wind very loudly. It took about five minutes before either of us could talk. With tears of laughter rolling down our faces we talked about legacies and death and life. He then looked at his watch and said: 'Oh my God, I'm late for a funeral,' which reignited giggles.

Nigel Colne is a trustee of the DSWF and a great family friend – and first met David well over twenty years ago:

As a Director of M&S I held a sporting charity evening with a specific cause as the focus. I had always had an interest in African wildlife and knew of David … and of the Foundation he had established …

I spoke to Melanie … and offered to make DSWF the beneficiary of this event and was delighted when David and his wonderful wife Avril agreed to be our guests on the night (which I have to admit involved a modest amount of gambling!).

Ever courteous, a day later I received a lovely letter of thanks from David – full of gratitude but with a handwritten addition – 'I managed to lose six quid!' That was David's impish sense of humour and fun but I realised he combined this with a passion and anger over the way that mankind was treating his only home – our Earth – and our treatment of the wildlife within it.

Pamela Jackson was to become a great friend of the family, but initially she met David and Avril as a result her being a member of the BBC Television crew who filmed *The Man Who Loves Giants* (see Chapter 11). As a junior assistant at the time, Pam was charged with finding the entire production crew accommodation during the period they were filming the sequences with David at his studio and at other places relevant to David's career in Britain, before then going out to Africa to film the remainder of footage required. It proved not to be an easy task and, almost distraught with the difficulties of doing so and with all likely B&Bs and hotels in the locality rejected for one reason or another, she was eventually saved by David and Avril's kindness in offering to put up several of the crew, including herself, at Winkworth Farm:

We ... spent a lovely few weeks filming David in his studio and other locations. We all tried to help around the house – washing up, taking the children to school, etc. One night I went to bed and found the children had made me an 'apple pie bed' and then put plastic spiders in it. They then waited outside my door to hear my reaction! David thought this was extremely funny! I remember us sitting round the table for dinner at night and, as a young girl who had recently joined the BBC, I was constantly amazed by all the famous people David would mention in conversation or who called him on the phone.

* * *

## Jesus for tea

David Winter, the long-haired Forestry Commission worker chosen by David to be his model for *Christ on the Battlefield* (see Chapter 10) virtually lived with the Shepherd family at Winkworth for the weeks it took the artist to complete the painting, and it was therefore inevitable that the Shepherd daughters, all very young at the time, took to referring to him as 'Jesus'. As David commented in his autobiography, 'Any attempt their schoolmistress might have been making to give them religious instruction was hopelessly undone because they used to say when they went back to school the next day, 'We've had Jesus to tea.' Although truthful in the eyes of the young girls, their teachers apparently took a sceptical view and, on one occasion, according to Melinda, 'accused us of blatant lying'.

* * *

Mark Carwardine is known to many through his television presentations and programmes for BBC Radio 4, all of which discuss a wide variety of wildlife, travel and conservation topics. He also knew David extremely well for almost forty years and describes their first meeting – in the company of some other extremely well-known people!

> I was twenty-one years old and it was my first week working at the World Wildlife Fund (as it was called in those days). At the time, I was very shy and quiet. All my childhood heroes – great movers and shakers in the world of conservation – were there for a trustees meeting. But to my horror, after the meeting, the director came up to my desk and asked me to give some of them a lift to the railway station. I nearly passed out. My car at the time was a very old Citroën 2CV with a gaping hole in the floor, covered by a mat, and it had a seriously leaky roof. It also had a nasty habit of cutting out when I least expected it. So I went down to reception and there, waiting for me, were David Attenborough, David Bellamy, Peter Scott and David Shepherd. They squeezed themselves into the car and off we went. Halfway to the station the heap of scrap conked out. Forty years on, I still come out in a cold sweat remembering David Bellamy and David Shepherd pushing us along the road, while David Attenborough and Peter Scott sat inside barking instructions on how to jump-start it in gear. But it was the beginning of many great friendships and, David in particular, became a very important person in my life.

*Famous friends; heads of state and royal connections*
In a lifetime of art and fundraising, there have been many encounters with film stars, world leaders, comedians and

celebrities, many of whom have also aided David in his wildlife conservation efforts – and who have been mentioned throughout these pages. Some though, rather than mere acquaintances, have become long-standing family friends. David's appearance on television's *This Is Your Life* in February 1990 (see Chapter 11) included a few of them, but of all the internationally known actors and film stars that came into David's life, it was perhaps James 'Jimmy' Stewart and his wife Gloria who seem to have been the ones of which David, Avril and the whole Shepherd family remember with the greatest affection.

The Goons: Spike Milligan, Harry Secombe, Peter Sellers and Michael Bentine, for one reason or another, also featured in David and Avril's life, especially Michael Bentine. After Bentine's death in 1996, his widow Clementina remained in constant touch. Actor Frank Thornton and his wife Beryl were long-time friends of the family and visited the Shepherd home regularly – one particular visit happening to coincide with the arrival of two Highland cattle at Winkworth, an account of which appears in Chapter 5. With David's love of nostalgia and fond memories of his childhood during the Second World War, it seems quite appropriate that 'Forces' Sweetheart' Dame Vera Lynn should have been a friend. She often visited Brooklands and David and Avril were regular visitors to her home on the south coast. She described David as being 'a great visionary whose dedication and work in the fields of conservation and wildlife protection are legendary'.

Rolf Rohwer, a professional hunter in Zambia and Tanzania (see Chapter 7) became an extremely close friend of David and his family. As David was to write in the introduction to Rolf's autobiography *Campfire Tales*, 'Above all, for me personally, he was simply my best mate.'

At any large family party, or at one of David's (and latterly Mandy and Emily's) exhibitions in London or elsewhere, one was quite likely to bump into sporting stars, actors, politicians, comedians, musicians, immediately recognisable conservationists and singers, all included and invited as friends rather than for who they were in the minds of the public. None, however, had been painted as a portrait, unlike Kenneth Kaunda, who eventually became a particularly special friend of David's through conservation and his connection with Africa.

Long before their friendship however, Anglo American Corporation had commissioned David to paint a portrait of Dr Kaunda for their boardroom and it was with a certain degree of trepidation that he agreed to do so – and for a variety of reasons, as the artist was later to explain in *My Painting Life* in 1995:

Because he was a busy man, I could only paint him when he was having a brief holiday in the Luangwa Valley National Park. With the heat and the dust, and the ever-changing light, not to mention the hippos making revolting noises in the lagoon just behind me, this was hardly the place to paint a Head of State. Nevertheless, with his great co-operation, we managed. There was no dais on which we could put him so we piled a couple of tractor tyres on top of each other. We then put a Woolworths chair on top and sat him on that, under a tree. Being the good man he is, he was so helpful: I said, 'I don't like your shirt, Sir.' He said, 'Okay, I'll borrow yours,' – and he did.

HRH Prince Michael of Kent was a personal family friend – as was Prince Bernhard of the Netherlands, with whom David did a great deal of conservation work (see also Chapter 8). Over the years, Prince Michael attended several of the DSWF fundraising dinners and his presence always lent a little gravitas to the event. The same could not always be said of David however! Pamela Jackson has long dined out on the following anecdote from the time she was in Africa with David whilst working with the BBC for *The Man Who Loves Giants*:

We went to film in Germiston Railway Sheds where, we were told, I was the first woman to enter. All went well during the day but, eventually, I needed a loo. I told my boss who informed one of the South African Railway officials. The next thing I heard was a whistle being blown and then dozens of men pouring out of one of the sheds. When it was empty I was told to go in and use the 'facilities' which were at the end of this enormous, empty shed. To say I was embarrassed would be a vast understatement but, even worse, as I came out of the shed everyone was stood outside watching and waiting for me! Another whistle blew and all the men were allowed back into the shed to continue working. David and the crew thought this was hysterically funny ...

Although Pam may have told the story to her more intimate friends, and she knew it had amused David at the time, she never thought her tale of embarrassment would reach royal ears – but it did – at a DSWF fundraising dinner:

My partner and myself happened to walk past David as he was talking to Prince Michael. The next thing I knew David grabbed my arm and said to the Prince, 'I must introduce you to this person.' I thought this was lovely of David and felt very honoured. However, I was not so pleased when David said to His Royal Highness that he had something very funny to tell him about me and duly related my Germiston Sheds toilet story! I am not sure what Prince Michael thought but I do know that David couldn't stop laughing ...

## A riot with the Queen Mother

Another person David got to know quite well as a result of painting their portrait was HM Queen Elizabeth, the Queen Mother. The portrait was commissioned by the King's Regiment, as she was their Colonel-in-Chief:

I painted her in 1969 and had six, one-hour sessions. It was a riot. Not many people have had six-hour sessions with the Queen Mum. She actually offered me another because she said: 'I so enjoy talking about Africa with you Mr Shepherd. I never have time to talk about anything for more than two minutes because I'm too busy shaking hands.'

One of the things that moved me most was that she was so trusting. She said some very controversial things about individuals in the Royal Family. We were in this lovely room overlooking The Mall and she said: 'They should never have been allowed to put that ghastly Hilton Hotel on Hyde Park Corner. People on the top floor can see right into my daughter's garden.

At the end of the last session I gave her a tiny original painting of a lion. I would imagine that each member of the Royal Family is given so many presents that it would take a warehouse to accommodate them all. Nevertheless, I would love to think from her reaction that, when she accepted the painting, it did mean something really rather special to her.

It was some ten years later that it was arranged that I would show her my finished portrait of HMS *Ark Royal* (see Chapter 10); from all accounts this was one of her favourite ships ... [at Clarence House] ... I was shown into the sitting-room where [I] placed the painting on an easel. One of the first things I noticed was my little lion painting on the mantelpiece. When the Queen Mother came in and saw me looking ... she said, 'Mr Shepherd, you know I haven't just put that on the mantelpiece today because you were coming. It has been there ever since you gave it to me.' I was touched beyond measure ...

When she died in 2002, I went to her lying-in-state. I had to. I cried my way through the Great Hall.

## *Railway connections*

As a lover of steam engines and being involved with the various railway enterprises, it's no surprise that David had many friends with similar interests. As well as those mentioned elsewhere (see Chapters 4 and 8) others included the delightful and totally eccentric Sir William (Bill) McAlpine who was credited with saving the world-famous locomotive *Flying Scotsman* and who was its owner from 1973–96.

During their friendship, Sir William visited David and Avril at their home and, in turn, they visited Fawley Hill, Sir William's Buckinghamshire estate where, alongside a full-size private railway (which included the original station from Somersham in Cambridgeshire and also pillars from the original Wembley Stadium) he also had a menagerie of goats, deer, wallabies, rheas, emus, peacocks, alpaca, meerkats and capybaras.

Bill and his second wife Judith were the instigators of the annual Fawley Hill Steam and Vintage Rally weekend, an event which David frequently attended and where he was, on occasion, asked to give talks. The gathering raised money for several charities and, as well as the opportunity to ride Bill's steam locomotive, visitors could also share the delight of his century-old fairground and look around a wide spectrum of transport (vintage cars, traction engines, horse-drawn ploughs, buses and boats) brought onto the estate especially for the occasion. In keeping with their host's eccentricity, specially invited guests mingling with the public would include a madcap assortment ranging from pop stars to historians, from racing drivers to Spitfire pilots. It was a heady mix for any onlooker to enjoy – especially when, as was seen on David's very last visit, it was possible to observe Sir William and himself careering around in an overgrown golf buggy giggling like little schoolboys!

*Terence Cuneo*
A friend with both a connection to steam locomotives and to the art world was Terence Cuneo. Unlike David, Terence had been successful in gaining admittance to the Slade School of Art and had begun his working life working as an illustrator for magazines, books and periodicals before spending much of his time during the Second World War painting for the War Artist's Advisory Committee – for whom he provided illustrations of aircraft factories and wartime events. One interesting, incidental and idiosyncratic thing about Cuneo's work, bearing in mind the stories David told to his daughters (see Chapter 4) is that, somewhere in most of Terence's paintings, is included a mouse.

It was after the war that Terence was commissioned to produce a series of paintings showing railways and locomotives, but his portfolio was eventually to include portraits of famous and influential people (Her Majesty the Queen and Field-Marshal Montgomery to name but two). His work covered a huge range of subjects, including African big game. With so much in common it is perhaps no wonder that he and David became good friends and the two actually painted together quite frequently during David's early years as an artist.

* * *

## A friend from space

Inside the Shepherd home, family photographs showed David and his wife Avril with royalty and celebrities encountered throughout the years.

The various visitors' books collated over the decades bear even more evidence of a brush with fame. It is, though, most illuminating to know that out of all those encountered, David considered meeting Neil Armstrong to be one of the greatest highlights of his life – and mainly because of the profound words uttered during a casual conversation. Whilst recounting the astronaut's re-entry towards earth after his successful mission to the moon, Armstrong remarked, 'David, as I came back, I saw how fragile the earth looked.' With that, and already well aware as a result of his lifelong effort in wildlife conservation, David could only agree.

7

# 'A MAN OF AFRICA'

David was once referred to as being 'a man of Africa'. His great friend Kenneth Kaunda called him a 'Zambian and fellow countryman' and, in a 1990 issue of *Queste* (the magazine for 'owners, enthusiasts, supporters and friends of Rolls-Royce and Bentley motor cars') Melvyn Reynolds, authoring an eight-page feature article on David's art and interests, told his readers that David's 'empathy for elephants ... has gained [the artist] an international reputation and earned him the Swahili name "Tembo", meaning elephant man.' It is an impressive group of sobriquets, particularly when one considers that, as fate could have so easily dictated – and had David not been so tenacious – his first trip to Africa might well have been his last and his subsequent painting career consisted of depictions of commercial aircraft and bucolic English scenes rather than of wildlife to be found in the country he came to regard with immense affection.

David's account of how he (unsuccessfully) attempted to become a game warden during his first-ever visit to Kenya in 1950 is well-documented but, nevertheless, a small part of it is worth repeating due to the fact that it was an episode which was hugely instrumental in both forging his future career and creating a love of Africa and its wildlife.

At the age of nineteen I left Stowe with just one dream in life, I had to be a game warden in Kenya. My only qualifications were a Higher School Certificate in Geography and English, and a very great deal of arrogance, including the assumption that I was God's gift to Kenya's national parks …

My dad did nothing to discourage me … He adopted the generous philosophy that if that's what I wanted to be, he would not stand in the way. So preparations were made for me to go for five years. It was to be the greatest adventure in my life, and I went into it blind … I was far too excited to even contemplate what I was committing myself to. In fact, all I had was an invitation from a coffee farmer up in the highlands of Kenya, a friend of one of my uncles, who had agreed to take me on for a few weeks whilst I found my feet.

The day came when I was to go down to Nairobi to see the National Park Administration. I honestly did believe in my arrogance and stupidity that all I would have to do was knock on the door of Mervyn Cowie's office – he was the chief game warden in Kenya at the time – and say, 'Here I am, I'm David Shepherd, and I've come to be a game warden.' He would then say, 'Yes, we know all about you. How marvellous. Here's a job.' He didn't. The interview was very short and not so sweet. I realised then that there was no reason whatsoever why they should give me a job … First of all there was no vacancy, and if there had been they certainly wouldn't have given it to someone who didn't know the difference between a zebra and an antelope.

* * *

## Frimley district news

In a short piece headed 'Animal Studies' published in the 14 March 1952 issue of the *Camberley News and Bagshot Observer*, it was reported that:

'While big-game hunting [sic] in Africa, Mr. David Shepherd, of Frimley Hall hotel, took photographs of several wild animals.

These pictorial studies were shown to Anthony Steel when he visited the Odeon, Camberley, on Saturday. He wrote in the album "What excellent photos. It brings back memories of my own trip to East Africa. Best wishes."'

(Anthony Steel was a British actor – and one of his major roles was as a game warden in the 1951 film *Where No Vultures Fly*, a film inspired by the life of Colonel Mervyn Cowie – yes, the very same man to whom David applied for a job as a game warden in Nairobi!)

* * *

### Elephants, ducks and a passage home

Despite his negative response, Cowie did, however, provide David with his first opportunity to see elephants in the wild. A Nairobi National Park employee happened to be taking a photographer to Amboseli the following day and offered the recently rejected would-be game warden a lift.

'It was raw, unspoiled Africa,' recalled David in *The Man Who Loves Giants*. 'The three of us slept under the stars with only a mosquito net. Lions walked through the camp at night and we found their pad marks the next day beside our beds. Nowadays, Amboseli is a fully-fledged National Park, full of people and the paraphernalia that have to go with them – notice boards, tracks, lodges, toilets and the rest of it. I saw it in the raw and I was lucky.'

Lucky indeed for, on that trip, not only did he encounter elephants for the very first time – an experience never forgotten despite the innumerable subsequent encounters during many other visits to Africa in ensuing years – it caused David to be 'hooked forever by the incurable disease of Africa'.

Nevertheless, getting up close and personal with elephant herds as an accomplished and well-known artist would have to wait a while longer. In the meantime, after Mervyn Cowie's somewhat abrupt rejection there was the small question of a need for employment for the remainder of David's first trip to Africa. The fact that he had (albeit limited) experience of the trade due to his father Raymond owning the hotel at Frimley obviously stood him in good stead as, after applying for a job in the Sindbad Hotel in Malindi, David was paid £1 a week as an odd-job man and driver. However, as far as a career was concerned, pleasant though the interim employment may have been (David became lifelong friends with the hotel's owners, Peter and Polly Mumford), it wasn't a lifetime goal for an ambitious man and a passage home eventually needed to be secured. Ever resourceful, the fledgling artist began painting bird pictures to sell to whoever might be persuaded to buy them locally:

> It was hilarious to be sitting on the beach of the Indian Ocean working away at mallards flying in over the Lincolnshire fens against a badly painted moonlight, but this was all I could do, being totally untrained. And I painted them on plasterboard because that was the only material I could get in Malindi. I painted seven of them and I shoved them all up in the hotel; I sold the lot for £10 each.

In a typically self-deprecating way, David later commented, 'I can only assume that the people of Malindi must have been totally culture-starved in those days.'

How different a scenario when, a couple of decades later, David's work exhibited in Africa was greeted with great enthusiasm, and buyers eager to purchase one of his paintings were prepared to queue for literally hours in order to do so. Famously, at the Everard Read Gallery in Johannesburg in 1969, David's one-man show was a complete sell-out. The exhibition's success even caused *The Star* newspaper there to publish a cartoon by 'Fedler' depicting rather bored-looking elephants in an open enclosure surrounded by dozens of artists and their easels, whilst running madly behind them all a uniformed zookeeper was shouting: 'Sorry, no time to explain – I've got to get my sketch pad!' On the ground was a discarded front page of *The*

*Star* with the headline: 'ELEPHANT PAINTINGS – MAMMOTH SELLOUT!' Painting elephants in the style of David Shepherd was obviously considered the way to go as far as public popularity was concerned – and an assumed way of acquiring instant wealth from their sales!

In the early 1950s however, the plasterboard bird paintings were a means to an end and their sale paid for his passage home – tourist class – on the Union Castle steamer, the *Dunnotar Castle*.

* * *

## A media star

The popularity of David's paintings at the height of his success should never be underestimated. In the late 1960s and 1970s his work earned him immense recognition, and by 1974 he had been at the top of the popular print market three times. His depictions of African elephants and other animals could be found in homes all over the world, and whenever a show was organised, potential buyers would beat a path to the door of whichever venue the show had been organised, no matter in what country.

For one particular event in London, seven Americans flew across the Atlantic and returned on the same day and, because there were so many people wanting the pictures available, David and the exhibition organisers had no option but to ask would-be buyers to put their names in a hat. The Americans thought this a very fair way of doing things (two of them were eventually successful purchasers) but, according to David, 'A chap who had come to the show from a taxi ride away objected very strongly at not being able to buy a picture immediately!'

Although known at the time as 'the man who paints elephants', it was an epithet that David didn't always appreciate. As he told Sue Lawley during his second appearance on *Desert Island Discs* in 1991 (see Chapter 11) 'It's like an actor being on television's *EastEnders* and only being known for that.'

* * *

*A successful return (eventually!)*
Politics were to make things difficult for David when planning his next return to a continent for which, in the relatively short time he had previously been there, he had developed a great affection. At the time there were many successful independence movements in Africa which, arguably, reached their peak in 1960 – a year that saw some seventeen African countries gain their independence. Such actions were to prove disastrous for the young David, who had made serious plans for a painting tour which had included the Sahara and the jungles of East and West Africa, all of which came to naught as a result of the difficulties in travelling. The plan was, in typical Shepherd fashion, an ambitious one, as not only had he hoped to go through newly independent countries, he had also intended taking Avril and their eldest (and at the time, only) daughter, aged two-and-a-half. Despite its eventual aborted outcome, in April 1960 the trip was still being considered a feasible proposition and in an issue dated the 18th of that month, the *Evening Standard* newspaper featured an article outlining David's intentions. It began with the banner headline and subtitle 'OFF TO THE JUNGLES Go the artist, the artist's wife, the baby and a powder-blue van':

David Shepherd, 29-year-old artist from Frensham, Surrey, has converted a delivery van into a mobile studio, in which he plans to take his wife Avril, aged 25 and baby daughter on a painting tour … He will paint the scenes and tribesmen he sees on the way, and plans to hold an exhibition of his paintings in Nairobi at the end of the trek.

'The basis of my studio traveller, as I have called it, is a normal 30 cwt Commer delivery van which cost me £875,' he said. 'The conversion on it has cost more than £1000. I have had it specially insulated and installed a gas cooker. It has been slightly lengthened to accommodate my canvases and painting materials and we have put in a special storage space for a good supply of tinned baby goods. Our own luggage will be the minimum possible.'

Mrs. Shepherd added: 'Two pairs of slacks, a dress and several drip-dry shirts look like being as much as I shall be allowed.'

The front seat of the van has been altered so that it will convert into a 'cot'-style bed for the baby, and Mr. and Mrs. Shepherd will sleep on a convertible double bunk inside the van. The outside of the van is painted powder blue and slate. The inside is pale blue and acid yellow. 'From my experience of a short tour of North Africa I think those are the best colours to live with for 18 months in the African climate,' said Mr. Shepherd.

The back of the van opens right out with an awning and most of the time the family plan to live outdoors. 'To save space I am arranging for a number of canvases to be sent on ahead to check points where I can pick them up en route,' he said. 'I hope to sell a number of paintings on the way to help with expenses ... It would be mad to plan to take a wife and young baby on a trip like this if you were not properly organised, and that means sure of having enough money,' he said. 'In some of the places I have visited before and in others I plan to visit this time they have rarely seen a white man at all, let alone a painter.'

## A more successful trip

Despite being thwarted by the unrest in the Sahara, later in 1960, invited by the C-in-C, British Forces, Arabian Peninsula, David eventually travelled to Aden on an aircraft painting assignment. According to a magazine interview David gave in 1974, he showed his paintings to the RAF station commanders there, but 'They did not want them. They were fed up with paintings of aircraft. Too much like work. So while waiting for a Comet to fly me home I painted a local scene and this they liked.' The 'local scene' David mentioned depicted some Arab dhows and was entitled *Slave Island*. David had also talked of this particular painting in an earlier interview in 1964 (for *Animals* magazine, published in America) in which he commented that it had resulted in a total of sixty-three local residents commissioning him to paint pictures for them. From there, the RAF flew David to Kenya where his exploits and subsequent artwork was to make him ever more successful:

I did my first wildlife painting in Kenya. I'd gone out there as an aircraft artist but the station commander at Eastleigh, near Nairobi, wanted a couple of wildlife pictures for the Officers' Mess. Until then I'd never thought about painting animals, but I had a go. My first attempt was a rhino chasing an RAF plane off a landing strip [*Twin Pioneer*]. They bought it [and a follow-up one of a zebra], I returned home and took another painting of zebras along to Rowland Ward's gallery in London, at that time run by Aylmer Tryon.

The picture sold within a week, although, as he admitted later, Tryon had not held out much hope of it ever doing so. Soon after this, David departed on another mainly military painting assignment to the Far East. Aylmer Tryon, meanwhile, had started his own gallery in London and eventually arranged for an exhibition of David's animal paintings to be held on the premises in October 1962. This first collaboration was an overwhelming success, far greater than either man had ever envisaged. Thirty-five of the pictures were sold in the first half-hour and the remaining ten had achieved red dots by the end of the first week.

## Close encounters

David was to regularly visit Africa from thereon. In his 1971 appearance on *Desert Island Discs* (see Chapter 11) he told interviewer Roy Plomley that he went twice a year as 'you can only get the atmosphere by going yourself'. Initially the trips were to gather subject matter for his paintings but, increasingly, the painting and conservation work combined and in some cases, overlapped. In his book *An Artist in Africa* (1969) David was to comment that he always felt depressed when leaving Africa as he never knew what state the wildlife would be in on his return. At such a tremendously important period of his life, it is perhaps no surprise that Africa featured so heavily in *The Man Who Loves Giants*, a television programme that was first broadcast on Christmas Day 1971 (see Chapter 11).

The programme's compilation was not as straightforward as it could have been. During the filming of a part of the African sequences, the director and producer thought it would be a good idea to try a few camera shots of David walking up close to some elephants and painting them. It was a ridiculous plan and one which, to anyone's knowledge, had never ever been previously attempted. Nevertheless, undaunted by that fact, and after some discussion regarding the logistics, David and the film crew were joined by the head game warden and Rolf Rohwer, a professional hunter who was to become a great personal friend of David. A decade or so later, David recalled the attempt with great amusement – which, one would suppose, could only be done in hindsight and knowing one had lived to tell the tale.

We all piled into a couple of Land Rovers and off we went into the bush. I was in the back of the second Land Rover with everything ready – telescopic legs of the easel already stretched out, all my colours squeezed out around the edge of the palette, and brushes at the ready. Coming round the corner, we saw an elephant about a mile away under a tree, sleepily flapping its ears to keep itself cool in the heat of the midday sun …

We stopped both vehicles and hid them in the bushes … We walked as quietly as ghosts. I was carrying my easel above my head. If I hadn't, the legs would have got caught up in the bushes and the elephant would have heard the jangle of the brushes and bottles knocking each other. If a group of tourists had come round the corner at that moment … they would have seen twelve people in a long line, just like the old pack trains, carrying large items of mechanical equipment, from cameras to easels, all walking up to an unsuspecting elephant. It worked. We got to within sixty paces, when by sign language, Rolf … indicated that I had gone close enough. I could see her eyelashes. It was so hysterically funny; the only sound the elephant might hear would be my giggling.

The next thing I remember was Rolf suddenly yelling to me, 'Leave your easel and run!' It all happened so quickly. I seem to remember three or four tons of extremely angry cow elephant suddenly turning towards me. I dropped my palette, turned round, nearly knocked my wife over, and we all started belting back to the vehicles as fast as we could. I looked over my shoulder and saw the elephant charging flat-out for Rolf, straight past my easel.

Game wardens all react in different ways in situations like this … Rolf believes in shouting. He is gifted with a very fine deep bass voice. However, it was not the resonance of his voice echoing throughout the bush that stopped the elephant in her tracks, it was the obscenity of his language! I am totally convinced that that cow elephant spoke perfect English. I swear to this day that I saw her stop in astonishment and blink her eyes in disgust at the torrent of abuse thrown at her …

* * *

## An unwelcome intruder

Several of David's African elephant paintings feature one or more animals, ears flapping, looking ready to charge the artist, seemingly an unwelcome intruder in their territory. However, appearances can be deceptive – as David once explained:

Although his size may suggest the contrary, the African elephant is one of the most benevolent and gentle of animals … I have been out with game wardens into the African bush on countless occasions and, in order to get good sketching material, we have induced the famous 'mock charge' – usually by banging on the doors of the safari wagon.

The display begins … the head goes up, and with tusks up and ears extended, the elephant 'tilts' from side to side; this is the signal that invariably precedes the headlong rush, accompanied by a spine chilling shriek, towards the person so rudely disturbing his privacy.

The elephant will invariably, and hopefully, stop a few yards from the vehicle …!

* * *

*Family time in Africa*
'When we were old enough' – according to Melinda, 'we had the most amazing trips to Africa (almost always away from the

touristy places) and were privileged to see wildlife in the most amazing settings.' Mandy recalls that when she was around nine years of age, her father persuaded British Caledonian airlines to swap six airfares for a painting – and that was the beginning of family holidays in Africa. Their first safari was into the Kruger National Park where David bought huge bags of oranges at the gate every morning but, as Mandy reminisces, 'He never really did explain whether they were for us or the wildlife … but both kids and elephants loved them!'

On one occasion in Zambia's wonderful Mwamba Camp, supper was dramatically interrupted when a hippo charged right through the 'boma', sending everything flying as the entire Shepherd family tried to hide behind the fridge! On a walking safari with the legendary Norman Carr, the family once spotted eleven black rhino in one day – 'Incredible considering that within the next two decades during the catastrophic poaching wars, Luangwa lost 90 per cent of its elephants and all of its indigenous black rhinos … We were so lucky,' remarks Mandy.

Melanie's memories of the same trip are equally vivid: 'Our very first safari … was with Everard Read, Dad's South African gallery agent and great family friend. We visited a private farm and then Dad drove Mum and the four of us into the Kruger National Park where we saw amazing wildlife for the very first time … We spent most summers for the next few years going to Zambia… [and] stayed with two families in Lusaka – the Barclays (five girls) and the Millers (five boys) all exactly the same ages as us – so you can imagine the fun we had. We spent most of the time in Zambia's famous South Luangwa National Park at the Valley of the Elephants …'

Before the family holidays with the children ever began, at the outset of Avril's first trip to Africa with David they were met by Tuffy Marshall who worked for the Kenya Wildlife Department and who had a long association with David and Daphne Sheldrick and the Sheldrick Wildlife Trust. Avril remembered that she was so excited to meet him and how delighted she was by the gift he gave her at their first meeting – a huge blown-out ostrich egg which she treasured. David's 1969 book *An Artist in*

*Africa* (published in association with Alymer Tryon and the Tryon Gallery – see earlier in this chapter) was, appropriately enough, dedicated to both Tuffy and Avril.

The love of Africa and its delights are now being experienced by the third generation. All of the grandchildren have fallen under its spell and are frequent visitors, both for pleasure and conservation purposes. As an extremely successful artist in her own right, granddaughter Emily obviously loves Africa as much as did her grandfather: 'I have always felt Africa was more my home than anywhere else. I want to be close to the animals I love. I am still searching for a place to set down my roots, and this keeps me learning and moving across the continent where I have been able to see the wild and also paint in peace.'

* * *

## Eggs for breakfast

After an overnight stay as guests of Zambian president Kenneth Kaunda in the presidential residence, the Shepherd girls didn't seem to be overawed by their surroundings and mainly remember the breakfast they were offered – a seemingly endless array of eggs cooked in every conceivable way imaginable. Puzzled by the quantity, it was only later that they realised that there was method in the madness of the presidential kitchen staff: apparently, any food that remained uneaten was a standard 'perk' of the household staff and by quite literally, 'over-egging' the pudding, they could all be sure of plentiful and excellent fare once the guests had left the table.

* * *

## *African hunting and conservation*

People he met in Africa very easily became good friends of David and the family. Rolf Rohwer (mentioned elsewhere in this chapter) is a case in point. Always against animal hunting of any kind, it was somewhat unlikely that David and professional 'big-game' hunter Rolf could ever have anything in common but, despite their seemingly poles-apart differences, they nevertheless developed a close friendship over the years, regularly visiting one another's homes – and being VIP guests at the weddings of their respective children. David was also Rolf's best man at his wedding to Carole. In the introduction to Rolf's book *Campfire Tales* published in 2012 (and for which Mandy Shepherd provided the illustrations) David wrote of their first meeting:

I didn't know what to expect when we landed at the airstrip in our beloved Luangwa Valley National Park in Zambia. Walking towards us was a tall, dark, and very handsome young American, welcoming with a beaming smile. Rolf Rohwer was just twenty-two. His first words to me were:

'Let's go game viewing.'

'Where's the Land Rover?' I asked.

'I haven't got one. That's my transport,' Rolf said as he pointed toward a rather strange-looking object with a wheel on each corner and what turned out to be a little 'putt-putt' engine in front.

It was a Haflinger. It looked like a box without a lid. One frail armchair was in the back to welcome me. I began to have serious misgivings when I realised that the chair was not even fastened to the floor. I wondered what would happen if we should be confronted by an elephant and tried to escape. I could just picture us flying across the potholed roads of the Luangwa Valley, taking into the air, and landing with a bump. This was the first of many wonderful experiences I shared with Rolf Rohwer over many, many years.

Perhaps the fact that Rolf was also a qualified wildlife biologist and a founder member of the original Zambian Safaris helped establish their relationship. There were, however, certain points made by Rolf on which David could never be persuaded. Modern thinking now has it that certain types of big-game hunting can be beneficial to conservation (hunters happy to pay for the privilege of culling certain animals – old, infirm or whatever – the money from which is reabsorbed into the local African community as an incentive

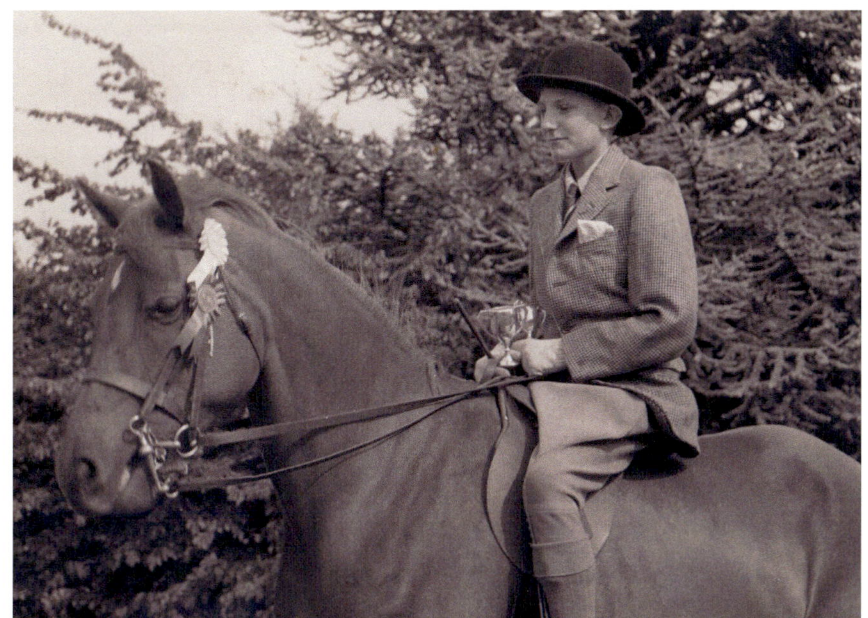

*Above:* David was a proficient rider in his childhood – and had the cups to prove it!

*Right:* David (crouched in white makintosh) and interested passers-by looking at his *Crewe Works from Life* painting exhibited on the Victoria Embankment.

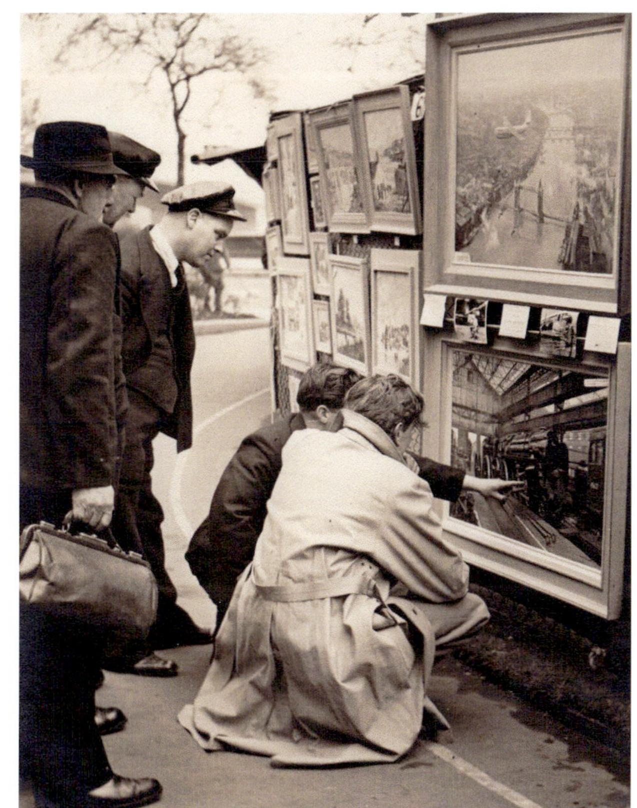

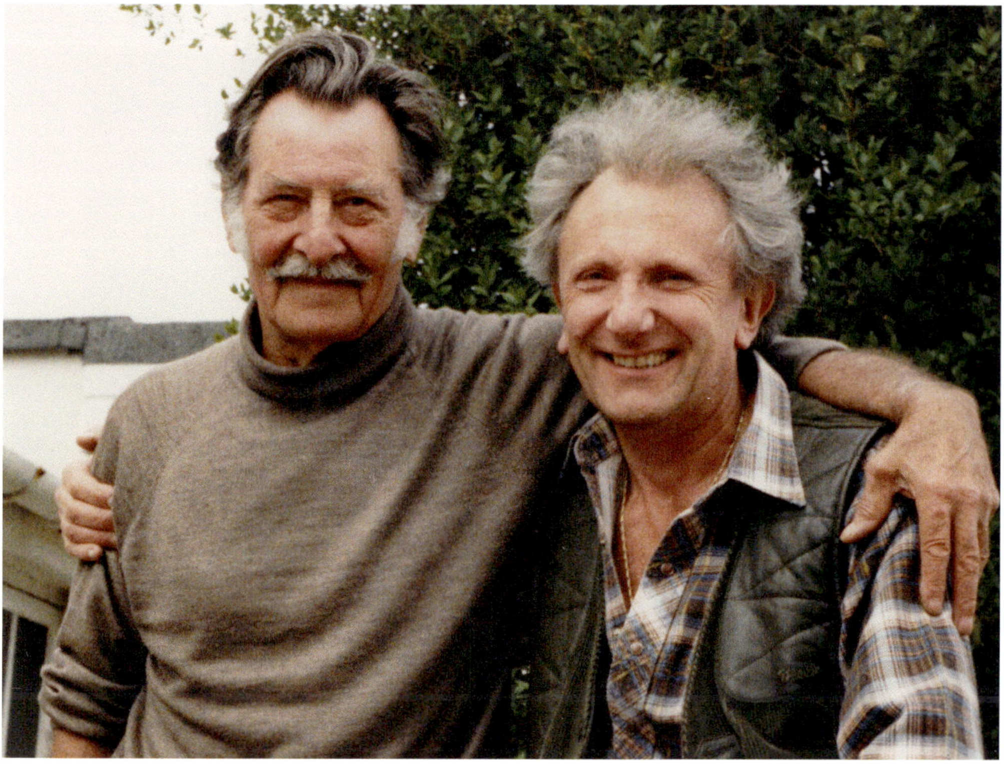

The marine and portrait artist Robin Goodwin was David's tutor and the two became lifelong friends.

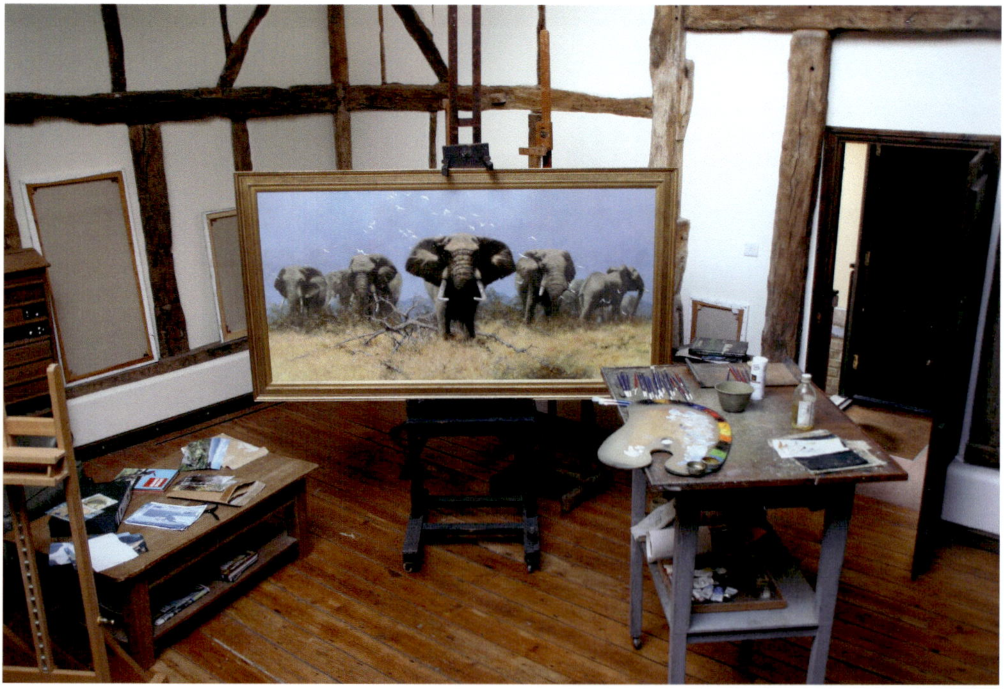

Inside David's studio at Brooklands – with *Just Elephants* on the easel.

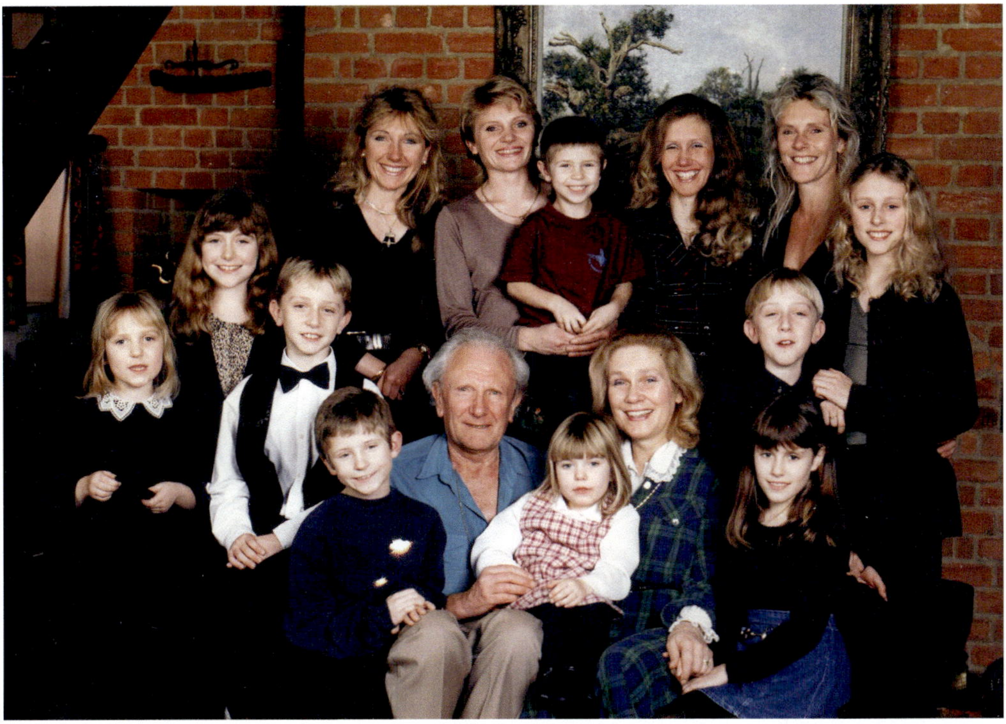

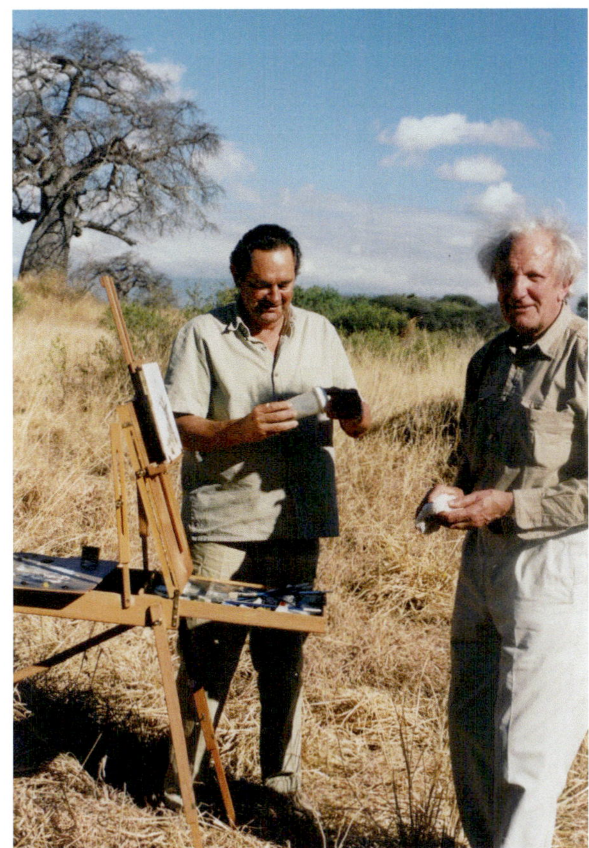

*Above:* David, Avril, daughters (from left, back row) Mandy, Wendy, Melinda and Melanie, together with all nine grandchildren, 1996.

*Right:* Game ranger and great family friend Rolf Rohwer and David out in Africa.

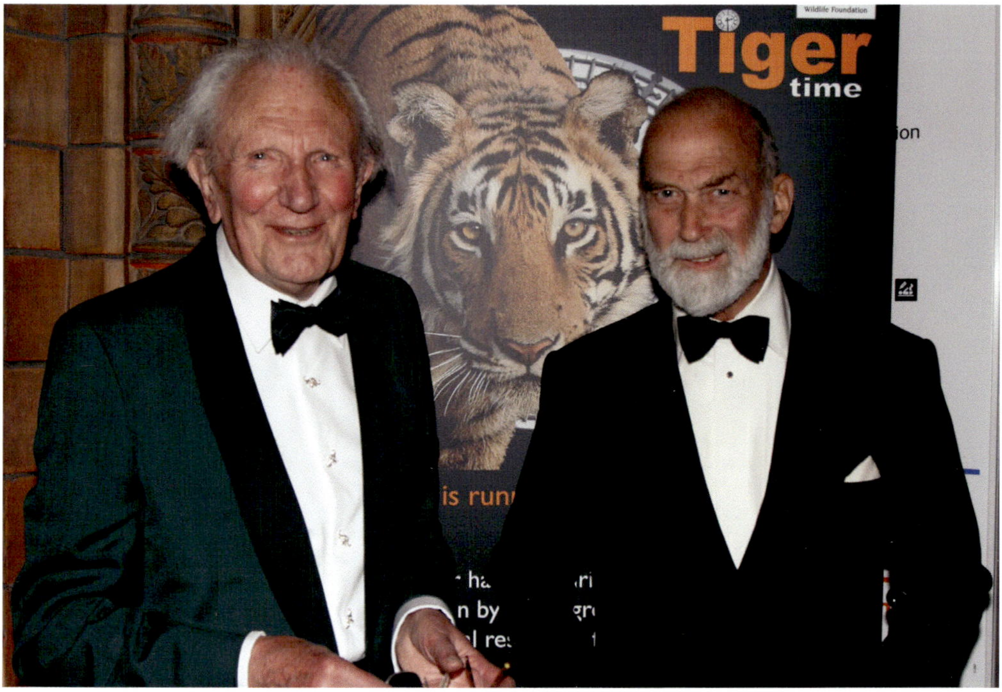

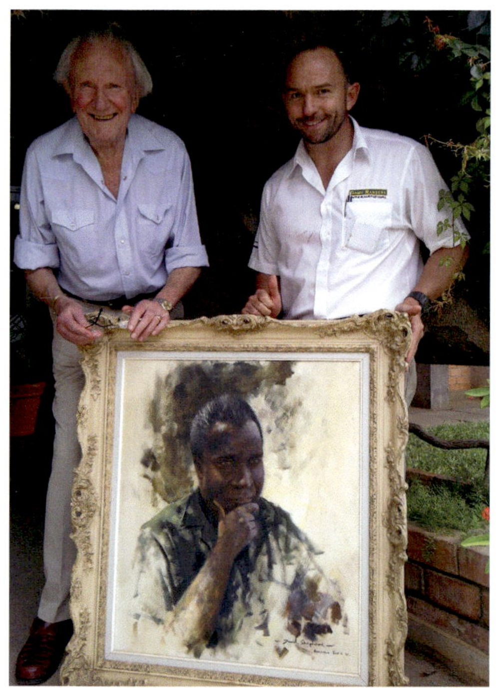

*Above:* David and HRH Prince Michael of Kent, past patron of the DSWF and friend of the family.

*Below left:* David and Sport Beattie, founder member of Game Rangers International and family friend, with David's portrait of Dr Kenneth Kaunda, ex-president of Zambia.

*Below right:* David sketching his beloved elephants on their home turf.

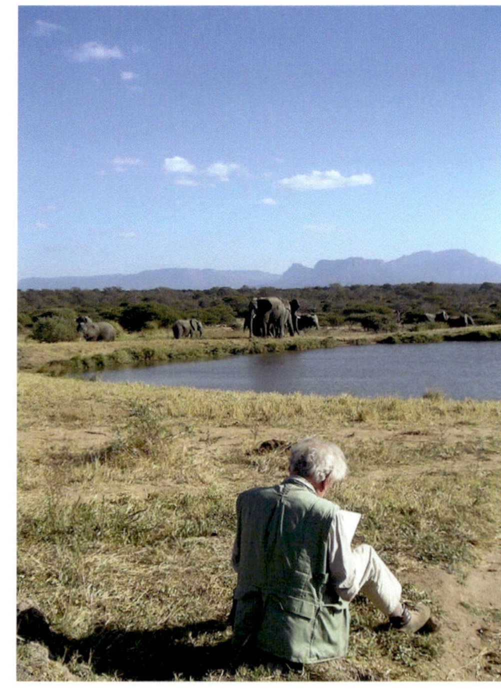

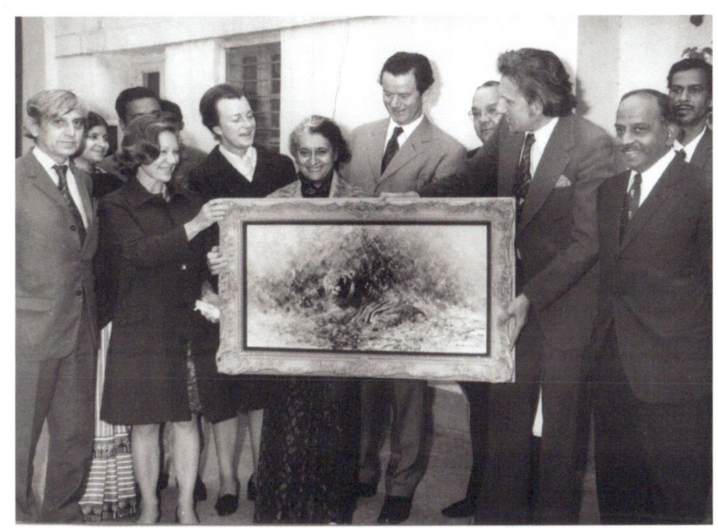

*Right:* Members of the Maasai and Johnathan Scott, zoologist and presenter of television's *Big Cat Diary* watching David at work.

*Right:* Presenting a tiger painting to India's president Indira Gandhi during fundraising for Operation Tiger.

*Below:* Four-legged residents and their rangers at the Lilaya Elephant Orphanage, a joint project with Game Rangers International and the DSWF.

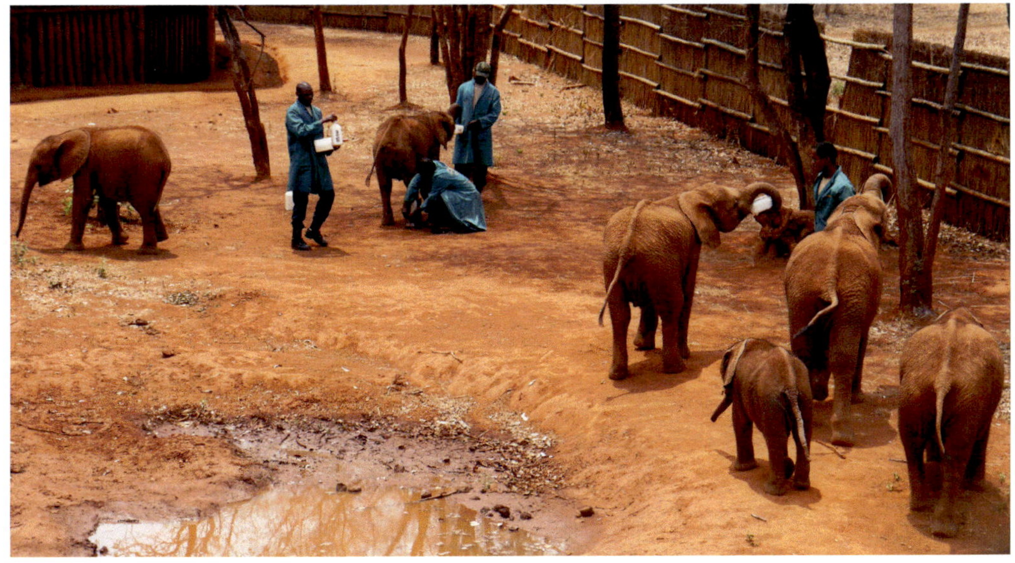

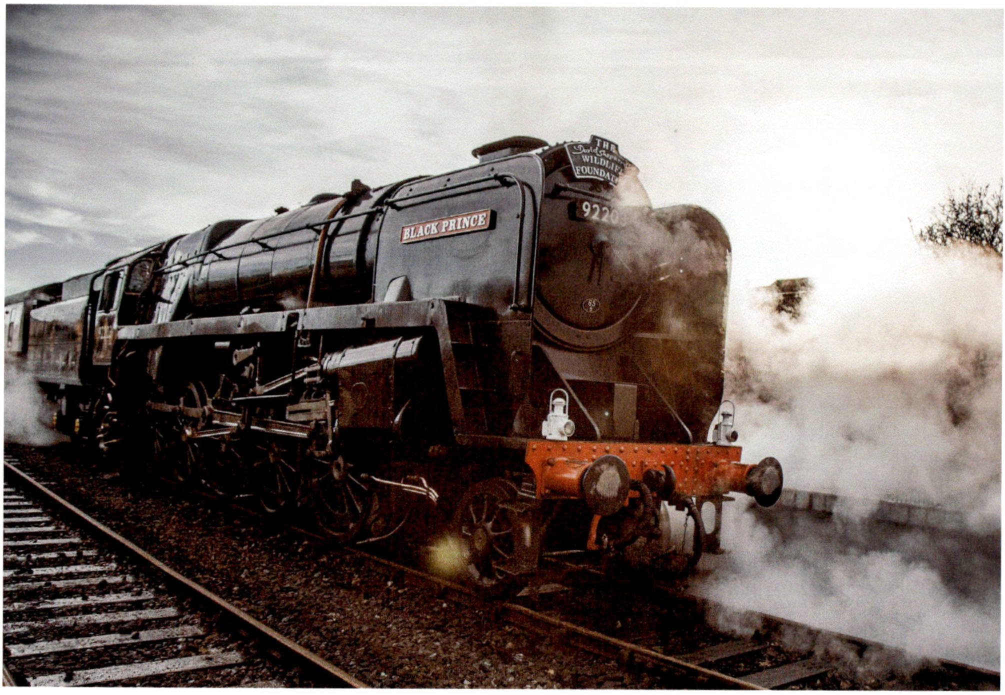

*Black Prince* – David's 'fifth daughter'. (Photo: Elliot Hobson)

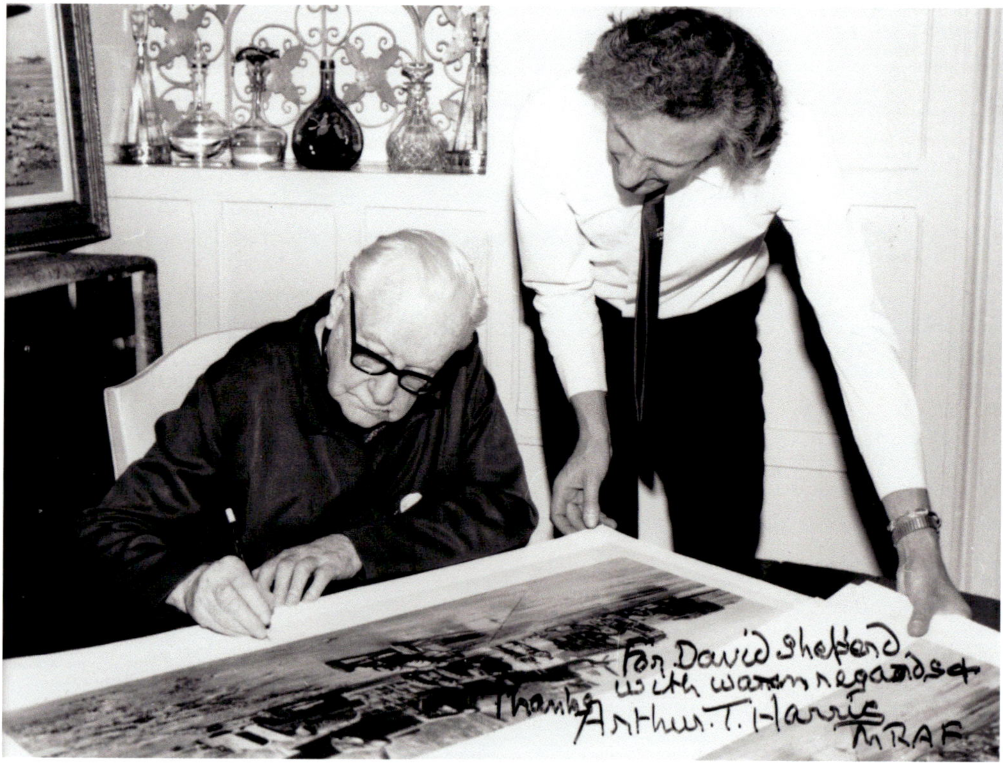

Sir Arthur 'Bomber' Harris signing limited edition prints of *Winter '43, Somewhere in England* as David looks on.

David and
Squadron Leader Al
Pinner; ex-Harrier
and Spitfire pilot
for the Battle of
Britain Memorial
Flight between
2003 and 2009,
with *Elephants at
Amboseli* painted
especially by David
to raise funds for
the BBMF.

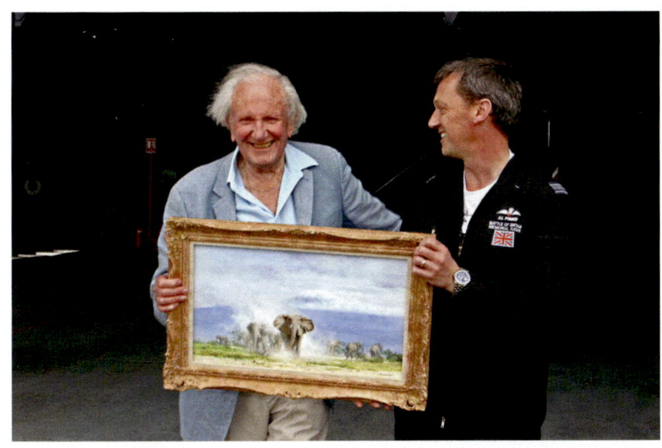

David and
*Christ on the
Battlefield* – the
one painting for
which he always
said he'd like to be
remembered.

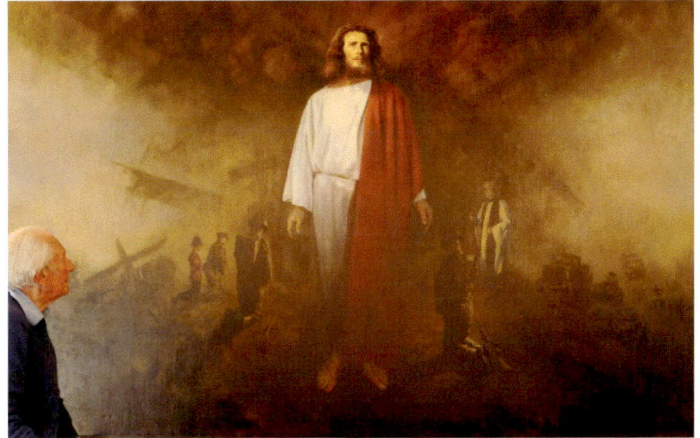

Making reference
sketches on the
deck of HMS *Ark
Royal*.

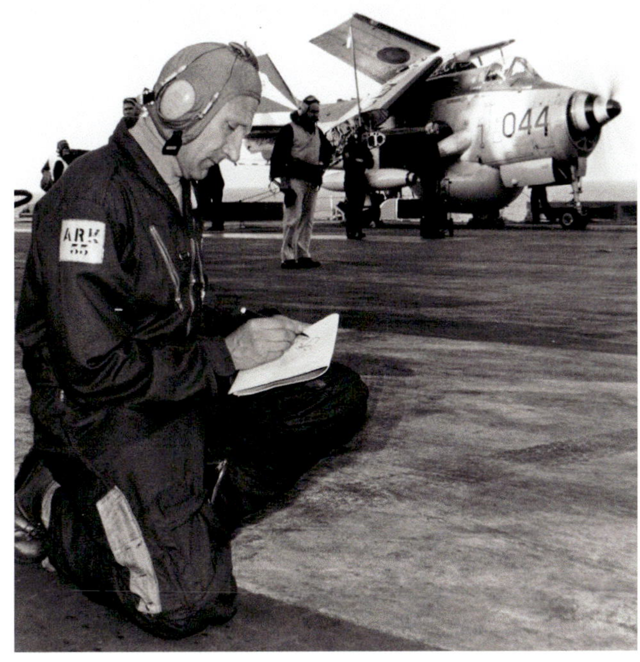

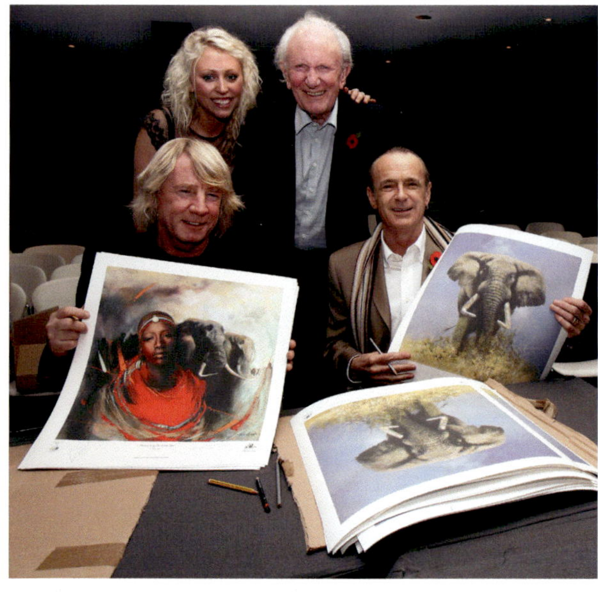

Emily Lamb and David fundraising for the Foundation with Status Quo band members the late Rick Parfitt and Francis Rossi.

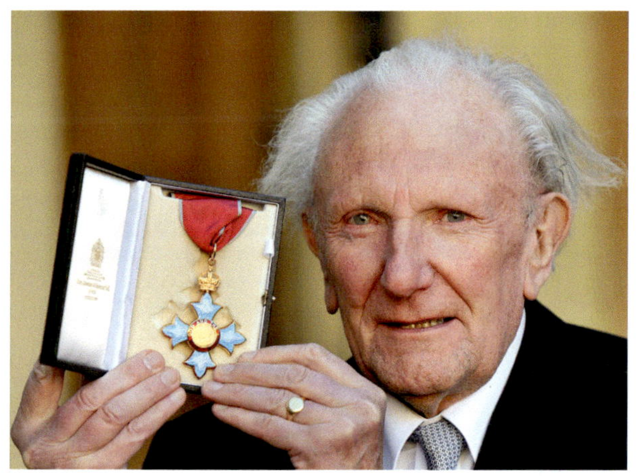

David after being presented with his CBE by HRH Prince Charles.

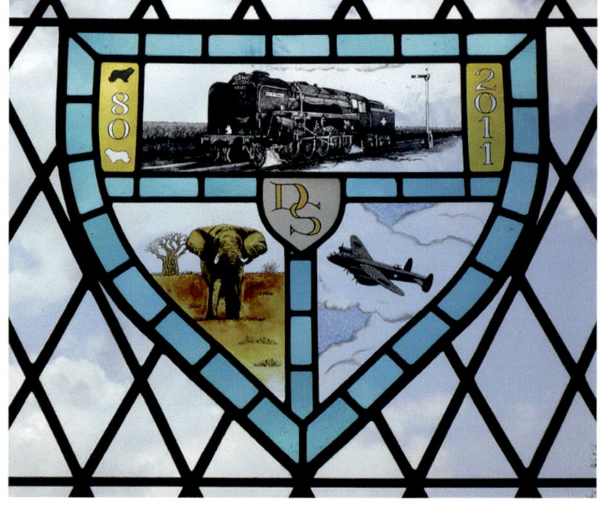

For David's eightieth birthday, Avril gifted him a coat-of-arms in a stained-glass window. It depicted three of his great loves, *Black Prince*, elephants and a Spitfire.

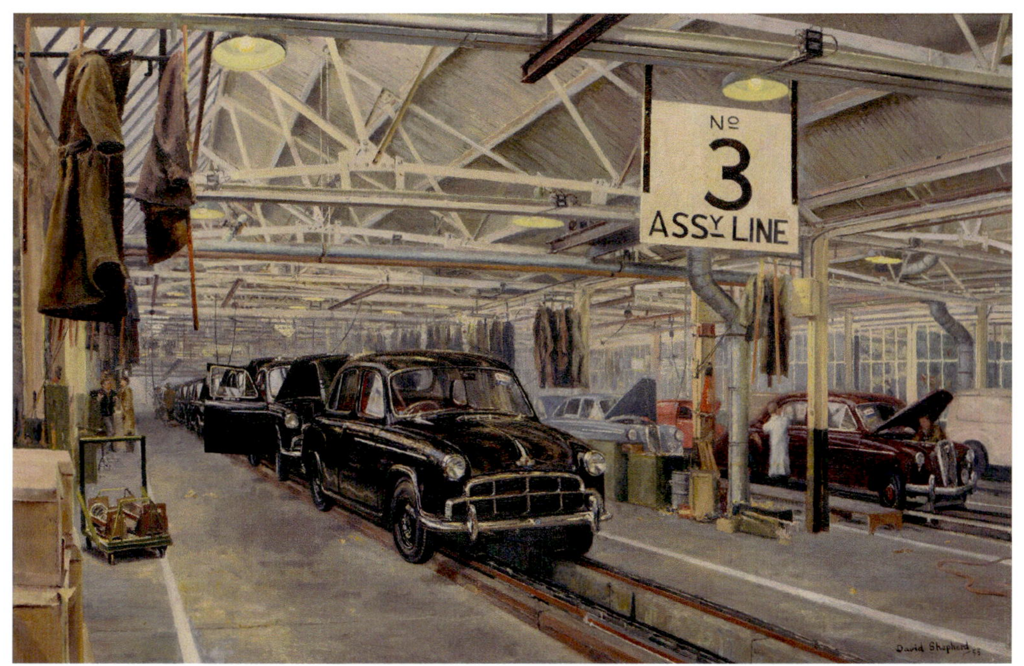

Several of David's earlier paintings featured artwork of car factories and industry. *The Morris Oxford No. 3 Assembly Line, Cowley*, dated 1955.

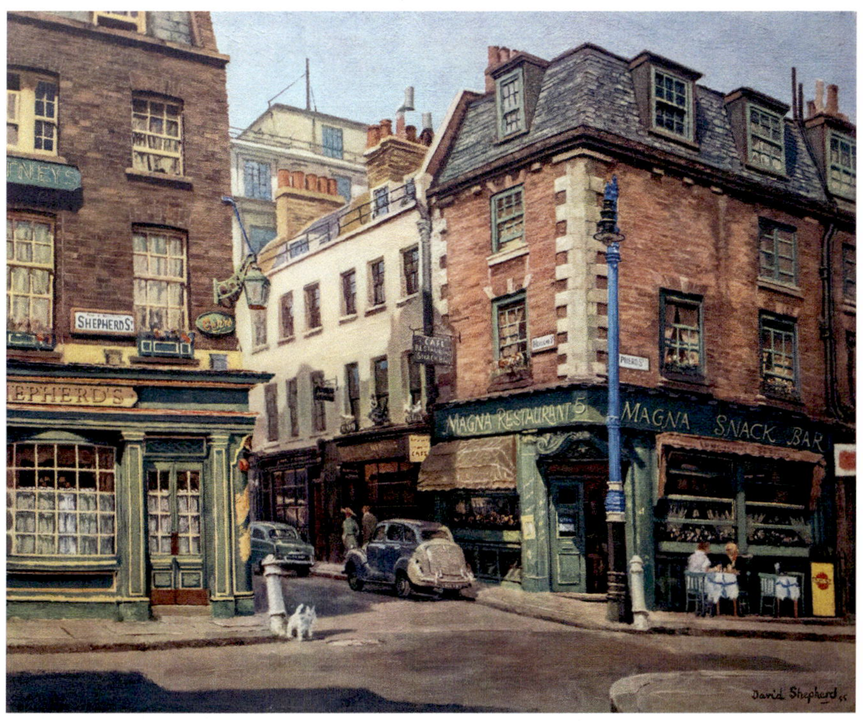

*Shepherd Street, Mayfair.* In the 1950s, David painted several pictures of London streets.

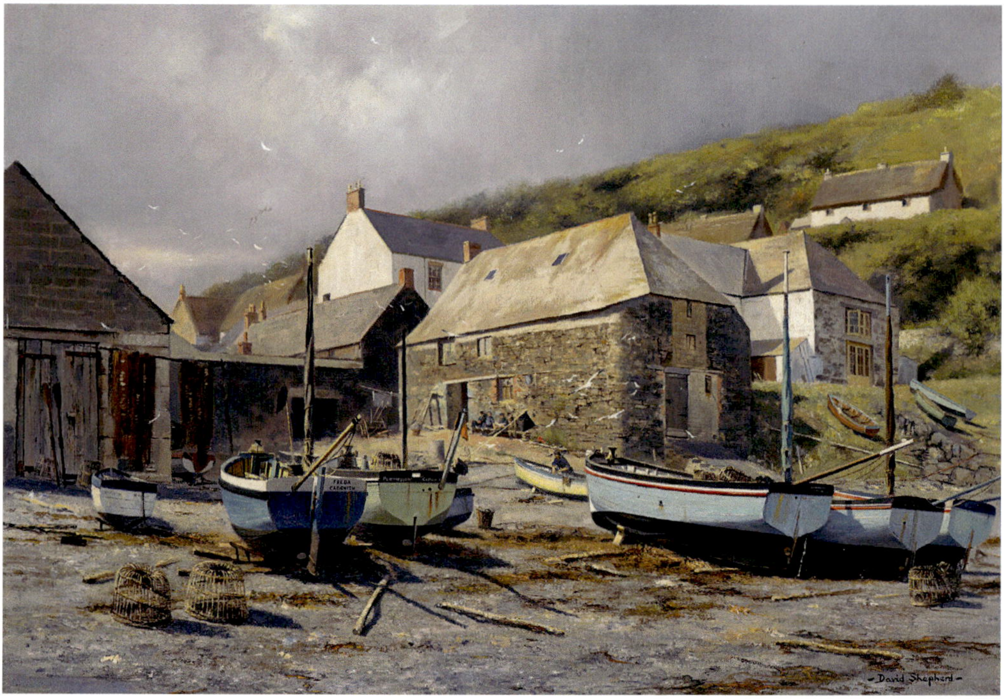

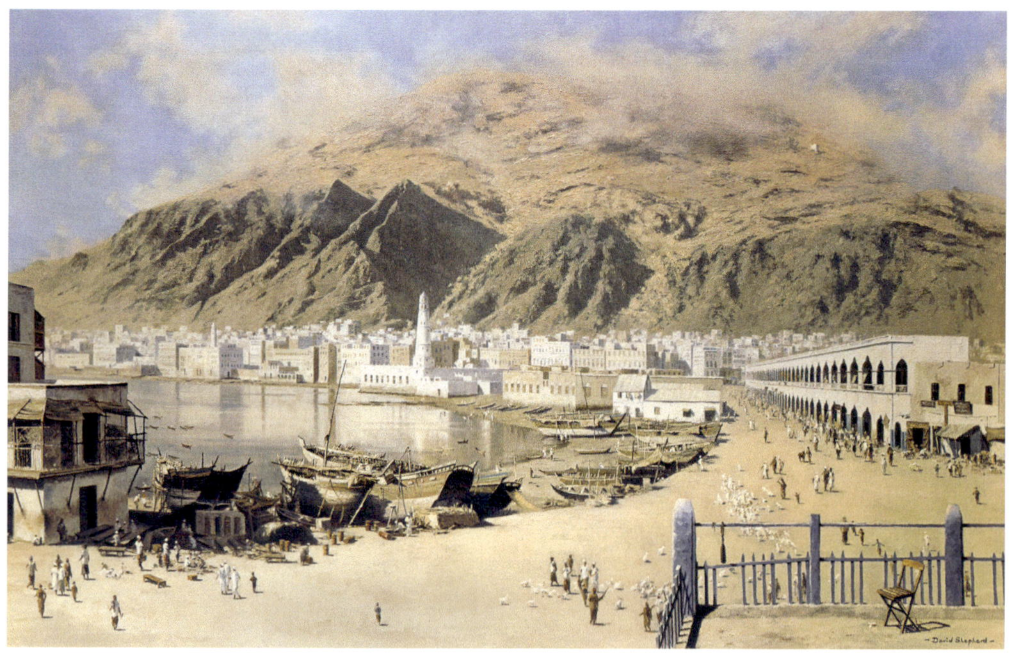

*Cadgwith Cove.*

*Mukalla*, Aden 1960. 'I sold it [the painting] for £250 and immediately regretted it. Then Christie's told me the painting was up for sale, so I bought it back, only to be disappointed because it was the wrong one; I had forgotten that I'd actually painted two versions; it was only about two-thirds of the size of the one I wanted, so I got the canvas extended on the left and painted in what I had expected to get from the other painting.'

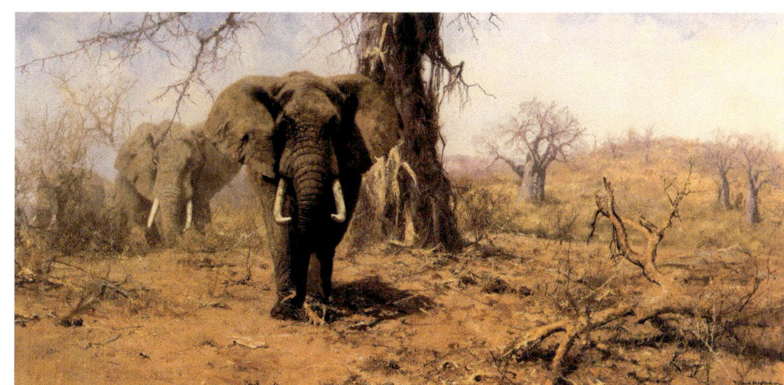

*The Land of the Baobab Trees*.

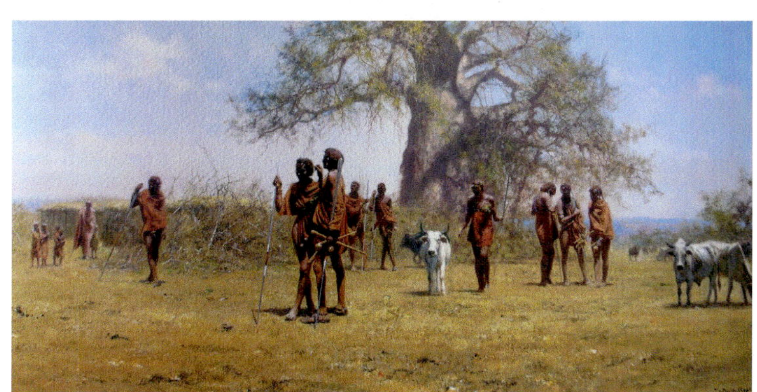

*The Maasai*: 'I had to negotiate with the chief about what I was allowed to photograph and how much I would pay. The rate was two warriors for one hour for £10.'

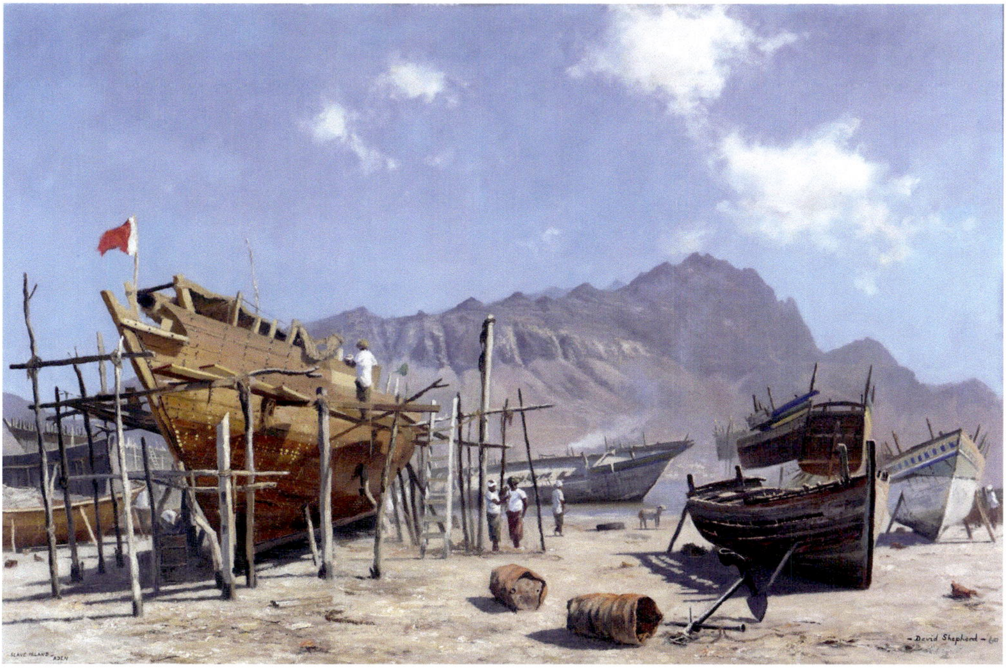

*Slave Island* – 'This painting changed my life. It was on the strength of it that the RAF in Aden offered me a trip down to Kenya with them…'

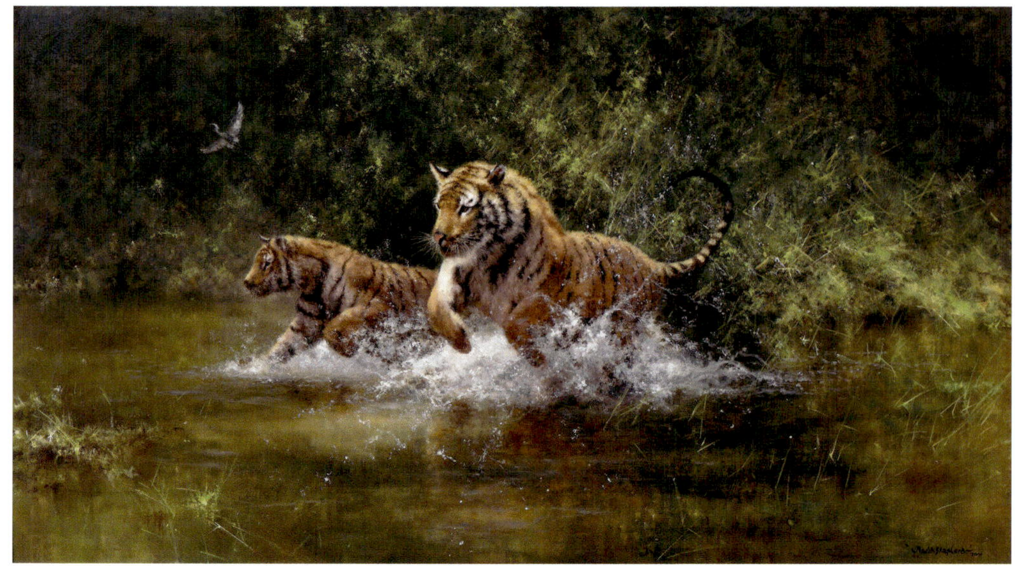

*Above: Indian Summer* – '...when one is lucky enough to see [tigers] in the wild ... particularly when ... diving into water, [it] is a sight that is with one forever.'

*Below left: Elephant and Egrets.*

*Below right: Up a Gum Tree – Koalas.*

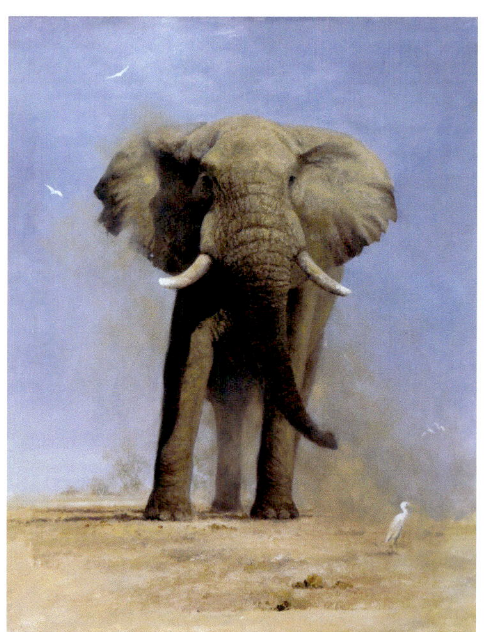

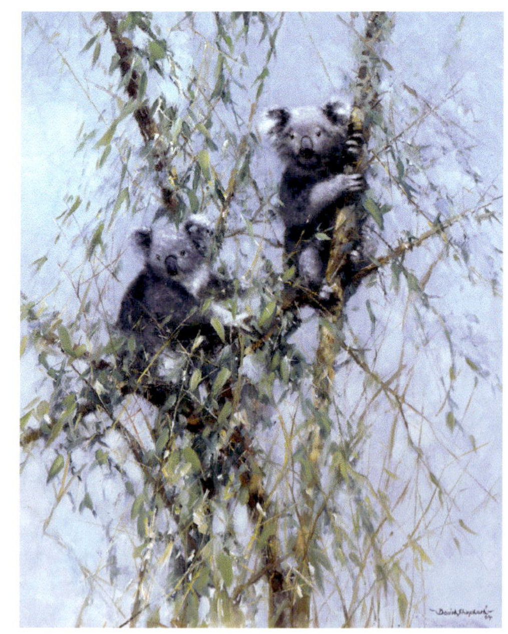

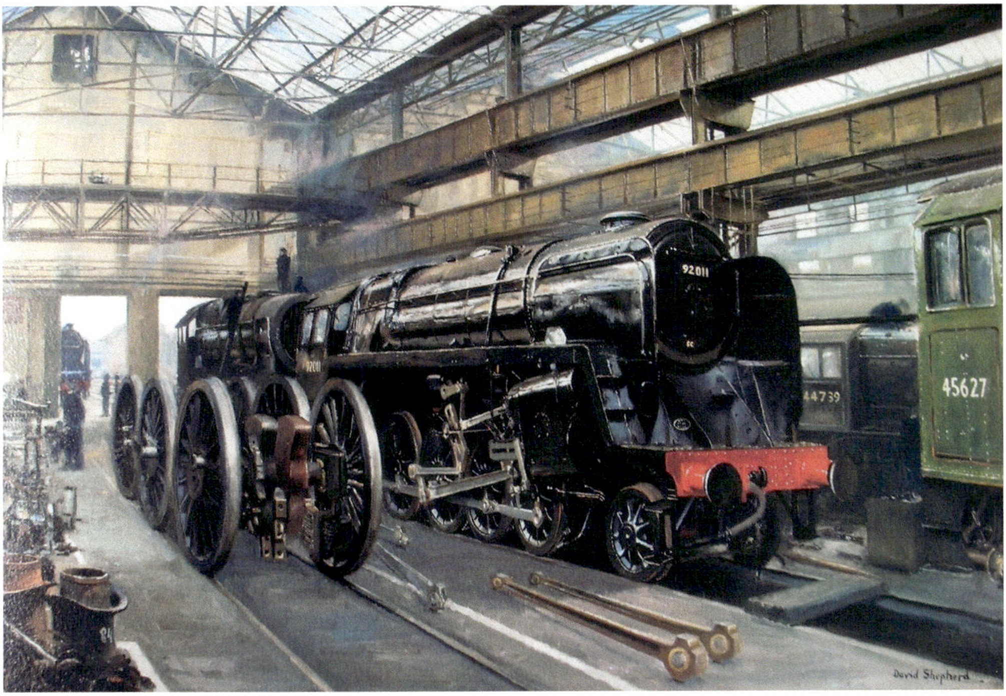

*Crewe Works from Life, a Standard 9F No. 92011.*

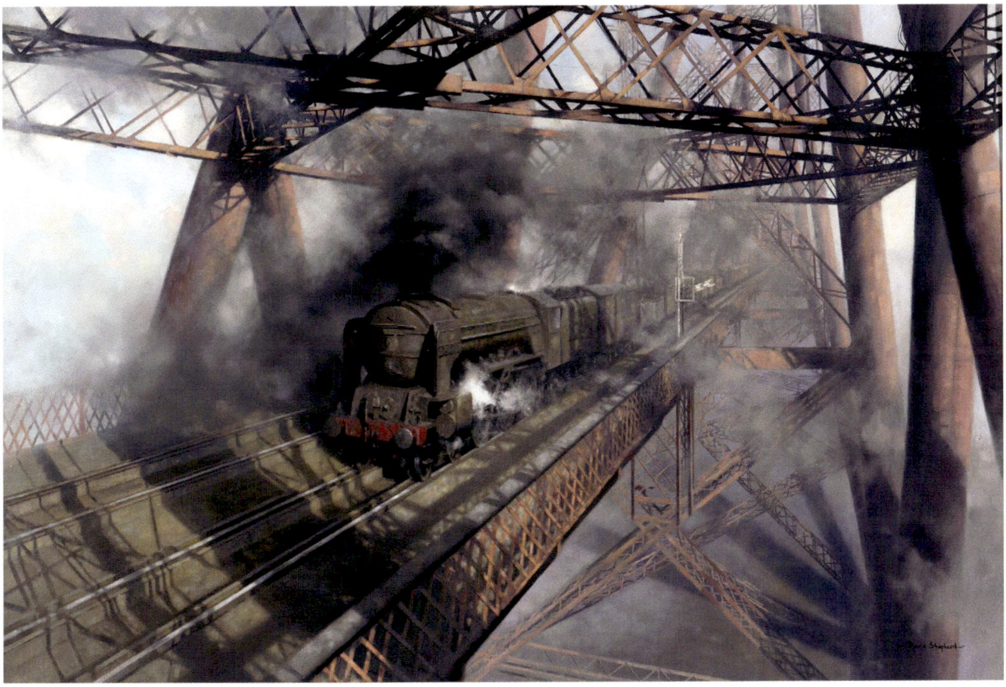

*Forth Bridge.*

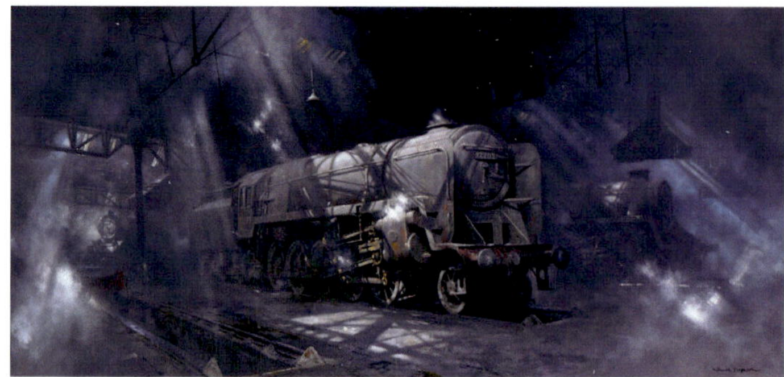

Variously titled *Black Prince*, or *On Shed – As We Remember Them in the Last Days of Steam*.

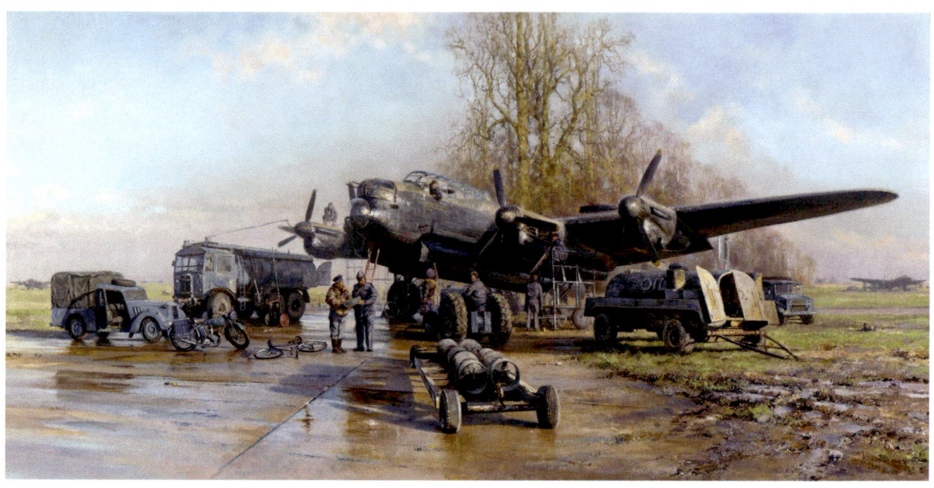

*Winter of '43, Somewhere in England* – painted in 1977 and, like *The Immortal Hero*, was intended to raise funds for the RAF Benevolent Fund. Some copies of the print were signed by Arthur 'Bomber' Harris and Barnes Wallis, inventor of the 'bouncing bomb'.

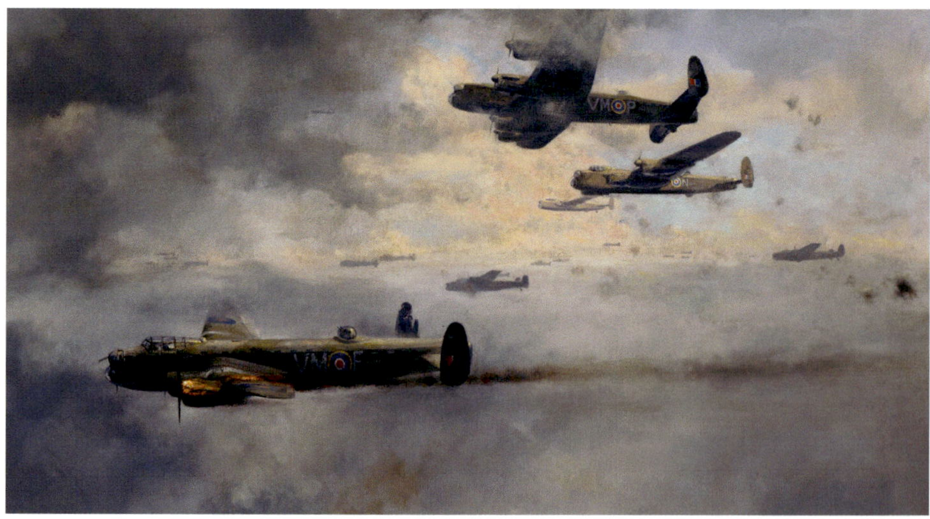

*F for Freddie did not Return* – a tribute to the men of Bomber Command, 55,573 of whom made the ultimate sacrifice for their country.

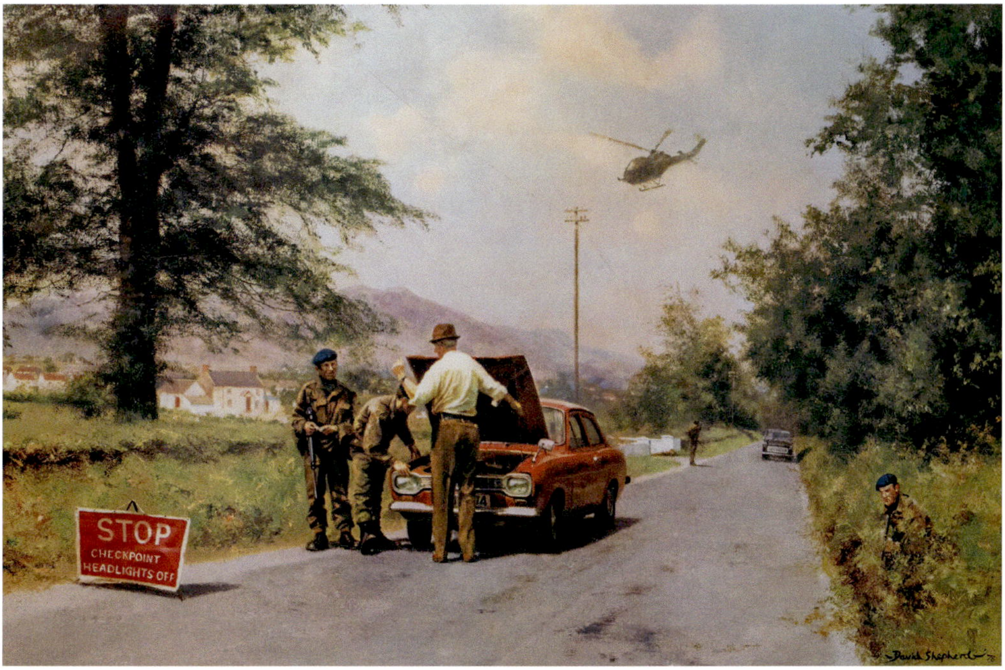

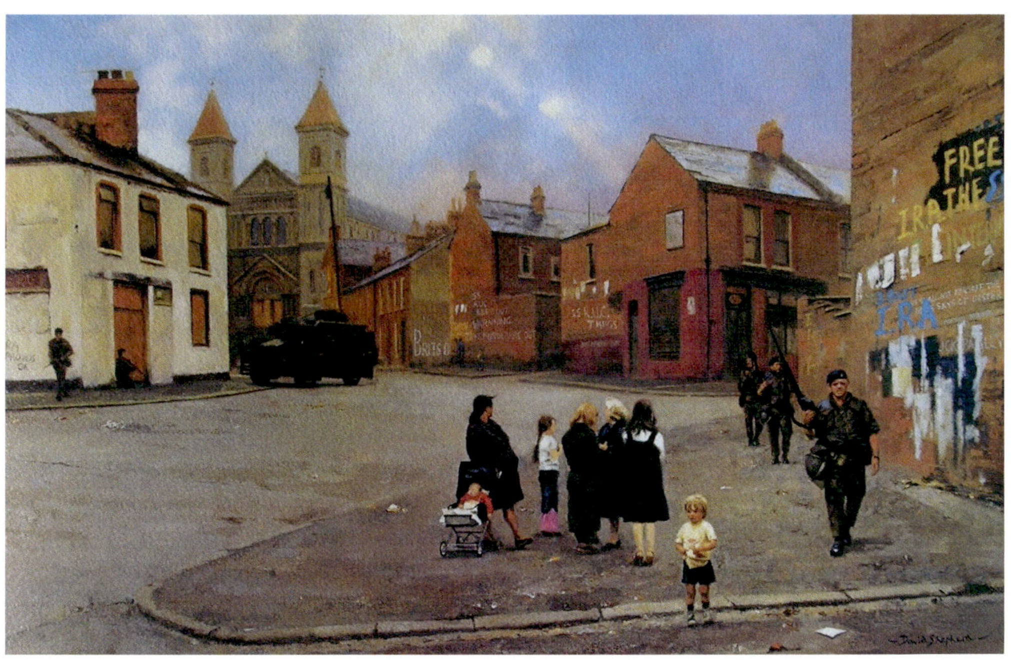


*Checkpoint at Forkhill* – an army patrol during The Troubles in Northern Ireland.

*Ardoyne Patrol* – commissioned to paint in Northern Ireland and seeing how The Troubles affected the lives of all the people living there was, according to David, a 'very humbling experience.'

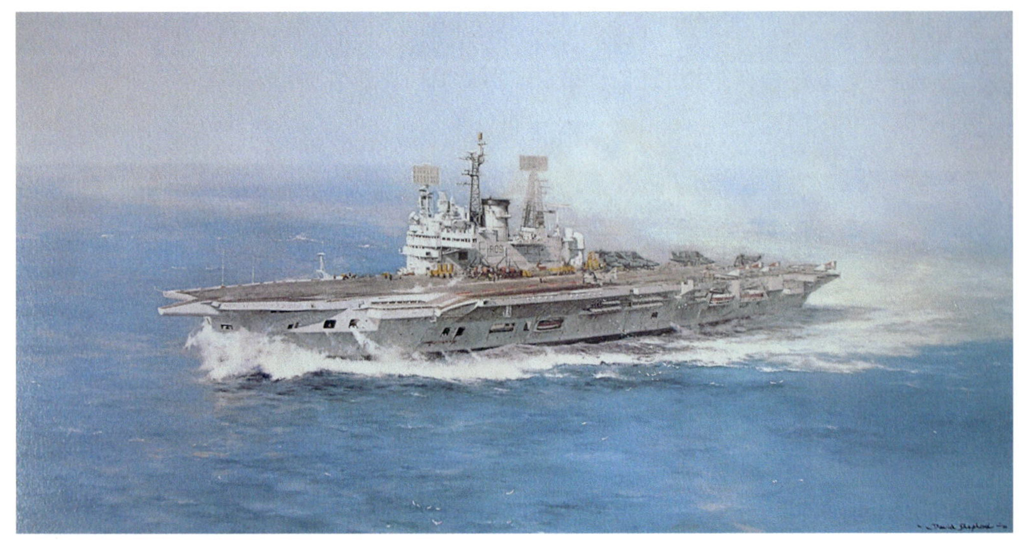

*The Ark, Turning Into Wind.*

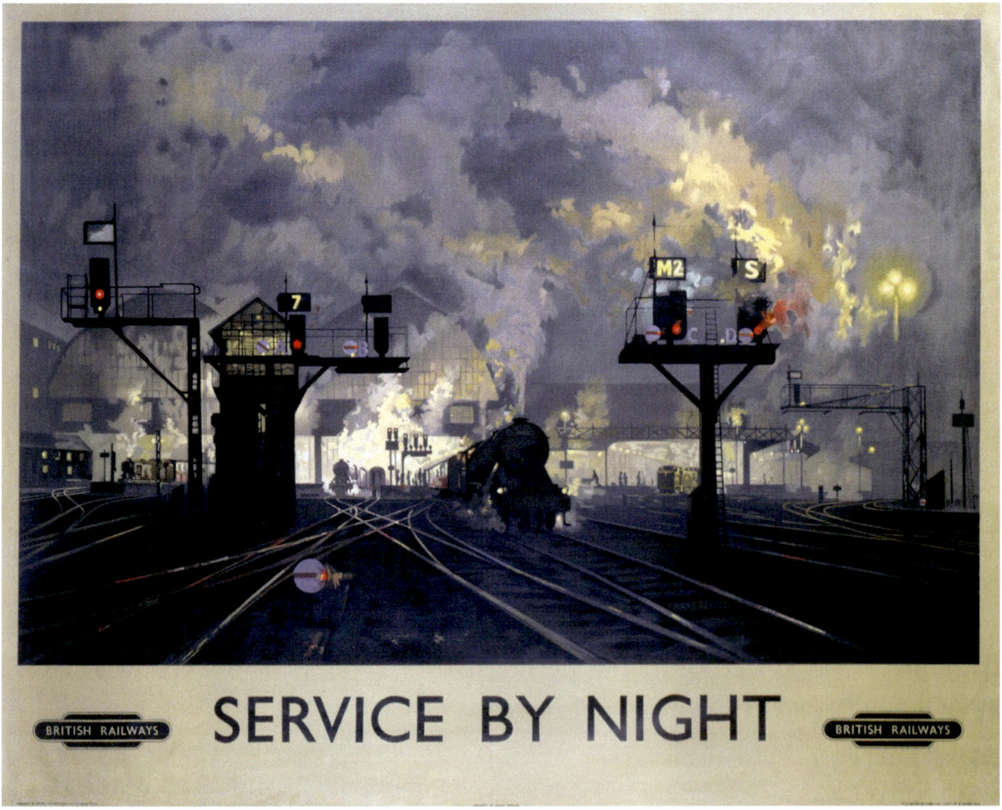

*Service by Night* – a painting of David's which famously appeared on British Rail posters during the 1950s.

to protect against poachers) but, despite all argument, Rolf could never, by his own admission, get David to come anywhere close to his way of thinking. Although over the many years they knew one another, there might have been the need to agree to disagree, in the introduction to *Campfire Tales* David admitted that 'Rolf was an internationally respected hunter with an impeccable record.'

* * *

## Lovely eyes and long eyelashes!

Despite being arguably best-known for his paintings of elephants, rhinos and cheetahs, not much African wildlife was absent from David's countless depictions of the country he so loved. Some were, however, by his own admission, easier to paint than others:

> Giraffe are almost impossible to paint because whoever designed them really made a mistake! There are many problems with painting them but I have found that painting their head first with their lovely eyes and long eyelashes was always a good start. The problem that followed was to tackle the shape of the rest of the animal which to me has always seemed very ungainly!

* * *

### *The rescue of two relics*

Although more appropriate for other parts of this biography – where they have been covered in greater detail – the acquisition of two steam locomotives in Africa does, however, deserve brief mention in this section. For those keenly interested in the steam locomotive side of David's life, one could do no better than get hold of a copy of his book *A Brush With Steam* published by David & Charles in 1983. This, recounting a little of the African side of things, forms just a part:

> I first went to Zambia in 1964. I was invited to paint twelve wildlife paintings for the new government ... I made many new friends on

that first visit and we didn't just talk about wildlife. It seemed that they all knew about my other passion in life. They said that I must get myself down, as soon as possible, to Livingstone, where I would find the terminal of a most remarkable, antiquated, railway system, a great part of which apparently dated from the early part of the century. It was called the Zambezi Sawmills Railway.

Three years later, on my second visit to the country, I decided to make the journey. On the border where Zambia meets Zimbabwe, on the great Zambezi River, at the majestic and awe-inspiring Victoria Falls, I found elephants and steam engines in profusion … I was determined to look at the steam shed. After all, what railway enthusiast just out from England, where steam was in its death throes, could resist such a temptation? … The shed master took a long hard look at me. It seemed that some sort of recognition was slowly dawning … The magic of steam knows no boundaries. We were immediately engaged in animated conversation. He knew all about me buying *Black Prince* and *The Green Knight* from BR …

In 1970 I returned once more to the Zambezi Sawmills Railway. This time, the BBC were with me and we were making *The Man Who Loves Giants* [see Chapter 11]. They wanted to include a shot of me driving one of the ancient Class 7s up and down the yard at Livingstone …

While we had been filming the short sequence … the BBC had become quite captivated by everything they saw [and] decided that it would be worth coming back to Zambia with me, to tell the whole story. The result was a half-hour television documentary, *Last Train to Mulobezi* [see Chapter 11]. By the time we arrived to make the film … the logging operation with steam trains had in fact ceased [but] when the company heard that we were coming to film … [a] complete train [pulled by engine No. 993] was laid on, with the attendant railway gangs to cut and fell trees as and when we required … the film crew obtained some marvellous footage in the steam 'graveyard' at Mulobezi …

Seeing all those old engines [potentially] being dumped in the bush was too much for me. I had become very fond of No. 993 … She had performed so well as the forest engine throughout the TV film, I asked if I could have her. They said yes!

> Not content with this one locomotive ... I asked if I could also have the ... main-line locomotive [No. 156] in the film. She was in full working order and they sold her to me for £100. I can only assume that as there was very little demand for scrap in Zambia, they thought that they were probably getting the best of the deal.

Separate to this was the acquisition of a third steam locomotive (No. 3052) in the early 1990s and a part of her story is told in Chapter 9.

## An emotional reunion

On one of David's last-ever visits to Africa, he was accompanied by Sue Rose, his PA. Sue recollects David being treated like royalty by everyone he met, from all those at the Lilayi Elephant Nursery on the outskirts of Lusaka (and with which the DSWF and Game Rangers International are heavily involved – see Chapter 8) to guests at the annual Elephant Ball organised by Chris Miller – one of the five brothers with whom the Shepherd girls regularly played during their early family visits to Africa. Held in a huge marquee, the event raised important funds, not least due to the fact that David donated an original painting to be auctioned.

From Lusaka David and Sue went on to Livingstone – 375 km (233 miles) as the crow flies – where David was guest of honour at a black-tie event held in the dining carriages of a steam engine as it ran along the 15 km (nine miles) of the refurbished Mulobezi railway line towards the Mosi-oa-Tunya National Park. The park is home to elephants, white rhino, buffalo, giraffe, zebra, hartebeest, bushbuck, impala, warthogs, baboons and monkeys and so was an appropriate destination for a man who had done so much to help conserve many species via his artwork and lifetime of fundraising. Not only that but the carriages were pulled by the steam locomotive No. 156, aka *Mulobezi Princess*, the second of the two engines acquired by David way back in the early 1970s (see above and Chapter 9). Nowadays organised by the Royal Livingstone Hotel and run by Chris Tett at Bushtracks Africa together with Rovos Rail, the excursion is known as

*The Royal Livingstone Express* and is considered 'a culinary journey of a lifetime'. Again organised as a fundraiser for wildlife, Sue Rose recalls that David was delighted by the trip – and that 'The railway track went out into the bush. At the end of the line, all the guests got off, the locomotive was turned around and all the guests got back on again! As the engine rumbled along, many of the children from the villages ran alongside laughing and cheering and helped make it a truly magical experience.'

For the last day of David's visit, it had been arranged that David should once again meet his old friend and fellow conservationist Kenneth Kaunda. David and Sue were driven miles through rough territory until reaching Kaunda's home where several generations of the ex-president's family had also assembled. The reunion was extremely emotional and the two old friends chatted away for an hour or more before it was time for David to take his leave. It seemed that both knew it was likely to be their last-ever meeting (David was just into his eighties, Kaunda his nineties). As David settled into the seat of the car where he was a passenger for the drive back to the airport, he heard a tap on the window and turned to see 'KK' standing there. As he wound down the window, the one-time all-powerful Zambia leader began singing, as Sue described it, 'in a frail little voice', the song made famous by Gracie Fields:

> Wish me luck as you wave me goodbye
> Cheerio, here I go, on my way
> Wish me luck as you wave me goodbye
> Not a tear, but a cheer, make it gay
> Give me a smile I can keep all the while
> In my heart while I'm away
> Till we meet once again, you and I
> Wish me luck as you wave me goodbye

A tearful David joined in. 'It was so poignant,' remembers Sue. 'He [David] talked about it for months afterwards.'

8

# WILDLIFE MATTERS

'With a few brushstrokes he has achieved more for animal conservation than anyone else has ever managed.' So wrote a certain Michael Glasspool offering condolences at David's death in September 2017 – and he was right; throughout most if not all of his adult life, David had put his artistic skills to their best possible use, and through his paintings raised several million pounds to benefit wildlife, both abroad and in the UK. A fact not realised by many is that he was long active in British conservation, supporting amongst others, the likes of artist Gordon Beningfield and the Butterfly Conservation and also broadcaster and author Robin Page and The Countryside Restoration Trust (CRT). Robin well remembers his first meeting with David:

In May 1998, I had to give an address at St Alban's Cathedral at the thanksgiving service for my closest friend Gordon Beningfield. It was tough ... the huge building was packed and I can still hear 'The Lark Ascending' by Vaughan Williams played on that wonderful organ – the acoustics were perfect – the mood was perfect. The whole afternoon was seen through a mist of tears – but afterwards a tall man came up to me who I had never met before: 'Thank you,' he said. 'I was a good friend of Gordon.' It was David Shepherd, and within two years he had followed Gordon by becoming Patron of The Countryside Restoration Trust – a post he filled with distinction and enthusiasm ...

## Concern for the British countryside

During the get-rich-quick days of agriculture in the 1980s, in the interests of 'efficiency' and in order to accommodate ever-larger machinery, hedges were frequently grubbed out – much to the detriment of the countryside's flora and fauna. It was of great concern to David who, in the very early 1990s, had this to say:

> In our own sceptred isle, we are still ripping out 4,800 km (3,000 miles) of hedgerow every year. Since I became a conservationist, therefore, nearly 161,000 km (100,000 miles) of hedgerow have disappeared under the blades of the bulldozer. It is incredibly stupid and short-sighted. There are areas of Suffolk and Norfolk which resemble the Canadian prairies. As far as the eye can see, one is confronted with a featureless landscape of cornfield ... Because there are no hedgerows to contain the top soil, much of it is blown into the North Sea and lost forever. Some English hedgerows are hundreds of years old, and once a hedgerow is ripped out, it can take generations to regrow – a conservationist once pointed out to me that 'every foot of an English hedgerow is a miniature national park'.

Fortunately, in the intervening years, there has been a greater awareness of the importance of hedgerows – and David lived to see many reinstated by landowners, farmers, gamekeepers and assorted conservation and restoration groups such as the CRT, all of which has helped recreate smaller fields and more diverse farming similar to that which David portrayed in many of his early rural paintings. His limited edition prints also include the likes of water voles, harvest mice and red squirrels, the future of which – although much brighter than say, thirty years ago – still remain of concern in some areas of Britain. Making the public aware of any animal species' plight by means of his paintings is something that David did throughout most of his life and so these depictions of some of Britain's smaller mammals have been of great importance in raising that awareness. Jean Wildman of the British Wildlife Centre in Lingfield (see also the Foreword by Dame Judi Dench and David Mills) comments that, 'he was a very good friend [to the Centre] and we appreciated his visits; he had a great love of animal life and was fascinated in particular by our red squirrels and little harvest mice, a great contrast to the magnificent creatures he was usually associated with and painted'.

## Where it all began

Before even embarking on his job-seeking trip to Africa in 1950, David had begun collecting books all about that particular continent, including those written by Victorian explorers and even acknowledged great writers such as Ernest Hemingway who were, reading their words, seemingly intent on big-game hunting with no thought whatsoever for conservation. Looking back through some of those books in later life, their attitude worried David:

> It seems to me that those early pioneers butchered everything that walked, crawled or flew. If it moved, you shot it. 'Saw five rhino today, downed four of the brutes with five shots.' What sickening terminology! I suppose the only justification for their behaviour was that in those days there was such an abundance of game that they never gave a thought to what they were doing.

However, although we are nowadays very scathing of the type of big-game hunting of the past as David described, the sickening (and illegal) poaching of elephants and rhinos for their tusks and horns today is arguably responsible for more deaths in a few months than Hemingway and the hunters before him were ever likely to have killed in a lifetime of big-game hunting.

The idea of African conservation in general began – according to E. B. Worthington writing in 1950 for the first-ever issue of *Oryx – The International Journal of Conservation* – at the beginning of the twentieth century as a result of concerns for Africa's wildlife. The creation of the Society for the Preservation of the Wild Fauna of the Empire in 1903 arose as part of that concern and one of its foremost members, E. N. Buxton, was moved to comment at the time that 'the great game fields' of East Africa, the 'Kilimanjaro Plateau' and the Sudan, had seen a massive depletion of wildlife numbers at the hands of reckless and 'unsporting' European hunters.

By 1950, hunting regulations and game reserves had been created across parts of East Africa, but even so there were worries regarding independence, economic development and population growth as it might affect wildlife. Mervyn Cowie, Director of the Kenya National Parks during the 1950s, was of the opinion that 'Africa is the last stronghold of wild nature and today is surging under the various forces of human achievement.' It was, then, into this sphere of thinking that David was to initially approach Cowie for a job as a game warden in 1950 (see Chapter 7) and, a decade later, to witness human-instigated atrocities that would begin his crusade for wildlife conservation.

## Unforgettable sights

Whilst David's love of Africa and its wildlife began very early on in life, it wasn't until when invited out there in 1960 in order to complete an art commission for the RAF that his interest in conservation really took hold. It wasn't a pretty introduction to the idea either – as David frequently explained in his many talks and magazine interviews – such as this, entitled 'Eco hero: The Wildlife Artist', which appeared in a *Telegraph* magazine in 2008:

I became a conservationist on the same trip, in one dramatic moment. I was driving around the Serengeti in a Land Rover with a warden, and there were so many vultures in the sky; he knew there was something wrong. We came across a waterhole into which battery acid had been poured, and found 255 dead zebra. You never forget a sight like that.

In the original version of David's autobiography *The Man Who Loves Giants* (published in 1975) David tells a slightly different story and recounts that it was Myles Turner, senior game warden in the Serengeti National Park who, in a letter to David, wrote: 'Found 255 zebra dead around a waterhole last week' and then went on to describe the terrible scene where countless carcasses of other animals too – giraffe, impala, gazelle and hyena – were lying. The waterhole had indeed been poisoned and in *The Man Who Loves Giants*, David explained by whom and for what reason:

> The Asian who had perpetrated this revolting crime – he was caught soon afterwards – had obviously considered it more practical and cheaper to poison the water than go out shooting zebra. He wanted their skins to sell on the black market. The fact that all the other animals died as well did not concern him.

Sadly, David was to experience many more horrific moments, both at first hand and via the stories of others – most of them because of the cruelty of poaching gangs:

> Many years ago, I was driving around the Tsavo Park with David Sheldrick and we came across an elephant hobbling along the road, suffering untold agonies from suppurating wounds caused by the automatic weapons of a gang ... I was incapable of controlling my feelings; I wept tears in the back of that Land Rover, tears of anger, disgust and frustration that anybody could sink to the depths of that depravity and do that to such a gentle and benevolent animal – for money.

Such experiences did, however, strengthen his determination to help enable local governments and like-minded individuals to do something towards preventing poaching – or at least to make things difficult for those determined to do so. Nevertheless, not all his efforts concentrated on the eradication of poaching gangs and were instead to prove beneficial to species which, whilst not necessarily directly killed for money, nevertheless suffered due to human intervention and local fear that too many of a certain type would interfere with their farming and livestock, and maybe even threaten the lives of their families.

## Tiger Fire

The alarming demise in the numbers of Indian tigers led David to paint on their behalf. In the early 1970s, their population had dropped to near 1,000 – and for a variety of reasons. There was, of course, the old traditional 'sport' of tiger shooting made famous by the writings of the likes of big-game hunters such as Jim Corbett, but perhaps most consistent was the poaching and persecution by local people. Poaching was (and is still) carried out to supply the demand for traditional 'medicines' in China, whilst native livestock owners were in fear of their animals being killed by tigers. Added to this was the pressure placed on the tigers' natural habitat by a rapidly increasing human population. Some fifty years on, a major effort to establish reserves and increase protection of the animals (in part led by the DSWF) has undoubtedly resulted in tiger numbers increasing, but so too is the human population and that means reduction of prey, threats to the isolation of the tiger habitat and continuing direct human-tiger conflict.

Although the Foundation's efforts have had far reaching and positive consequences for the tigers and people of Ranthambore (where a school and hospital nowadays exist and continue to serve the people thanks to the support of the DSWF and others) more importantly a donation in 2003/4 helped unearth one of the continent's most efficient poaching gangs which had, by that time, decimated half the tiger population in Ranthambore and all the ones in Sariska.

David's quest to save the tigers had, however, begun some three decades earlier. 'Project Tiger' was a conservation programme launched in 1973 by the Indian government during Indira Gandhi's premiership. David's personal involvement was – as with Zambia – initially through the World Wildlife Fund (WWF) who, at the same time, launched 'Operation Tiger'.

To aid funds, David painted a tiger picture called *Tiger Fire* (an indirect allusion to William Blake's words 'Tiger, tiger burning bright/In the forests of the night') in ten days and it was decided to run off a limited edition of 850 prints, each to be sold for £150. It was a format that was to prove successful in several other fundraising enterprises for which David was responsible over the years. All the printing and publishing was done at cost and the art trade took quite a number of copies and sold them at no profit to themselves. There was an extra incentive for the buyers of the prints in that one carried a lucky number, the owner of which was to be gifted the original painting once a draw had taken place (Prince Bernhard of the Netherlands eventually drew the lucky number out of the hat). The whole of the print edition sold in just six weeks and David's initiative had helped raise over £127,000 – a tremendous amount for the time. There is, though, as with much of David's life, a story behind the painting!

Even with funds, contacts and the ability to go and see wildlife in its natural habitat in order to collate the information, photos and necessary material required to put together a realistic painting, things are not necessarily easy. After several abortive attempts to see tigers in the wild – and with still no personally obtained quick sketches and photographs from which to work, David had no option but to call upon the services of his friend John Aspinall, founder of both Howletts Zoo and Port Lympne Wildlife Animal Park in Kent. In the 1960s/early 1970s, John's zoo near Canterbury was famed for its tigers and so it seemed an obvious place to go for research material. David, in his usual gung-ho fashion – and after being reassured that a tiger named Zharif was safe – went into his enclosure:

> As I entered and the iron gate clanged shut behind me, the noise woke Zharif up. He came bounding towards me like an express train and I stood there feeling rather foolish. I looked round to ask the keeper what I should do. To my dismay and slight surprise, I saw that he was outside the enclosure and I was on my own on the inside. All I managed to hear him say was, 'Just stand still and let him get to know you.' I didn't have time to find out precisely what this meant because the rapidly approaching Zharif was getting bigger by the second. The enormous animal skidded to a halt, and the first thing he did was rub his head up and down my legs, mewing like a domestic cat. He came up to my waist; tigers are big animals. He then rolled over on the ground with his legs in the air and allowed me to rub his vast white tummy…

Whilst a tiger that acted like a domestic cat rather than a jungle animal was infinitely preferable in such a situation, the fact that, for the *Tiger Fire* painting, a beast which reacted a little more ferociously and showed a snarling grimace was more what David was after and so, once out of the enclosure, some tactical teasing of Zharif eventually persuaded him to show his wild side and, with no further incidents ensuing, David took the required photos and made the necessary sketches before returning to his studio to embark upon the painting.

As a result of *Tiger Fire*'s success and in a wish to help further with the plight of the Indian tiger, David was to be responsible for a second tiger painting donated directly to Prime Minister Gandhi but, rather than use Zharif as his model for a second time, it was decided to return to India and to see if he could have more luck in tracking down a wild one than he had on his initial visit. He headed towards the north of Lucknow, almost to the borders of Nepal, to 'Tiger Haven' where lived Billy Arjan Singh who was, as David described him, 'a man striving almost alone … to save a tiny pocket of indigenous forest habitat in which a handful of tigers [were] fighting what might be their last battle'. With a little help from his host, he was to see his first ever truly wild tiger which was, for a variety of reasons, 'an unforgettable experience':

There had been two kills the previous night ... a tiny platform was built in a tree, right over one of the kills. It was agreed that I would sit up in the platform for three hours and ... Billy walked me for a mile along the forest track to the tree ... As darkness fell, the forest came alive, and my nerves began to fray at the edges; in fact I don't think I have ever been more frightened in my life. There was no moon, and there I was completely alone up a tree in the jungle – and tigers climb trees!

My host had given me a flashlight. 'You won't hear the tiger come – but you'll know when he's on the kill. He'll get into a frightful temper when he finds that it is tied up with ropes, and he'll try to drag it into the undergrowth. Give him ten minutes to settle and then shine the light at him. But he may be gone in a flash, and then that's all you'll see of him. Good luck.'

With my heart pounding in anticipation, there was all of a sudden a tremendous commotion below the tree and I knew the tiger had arrived ... scarcely daring to breathe I carefully raised the torch to rest it on my other arm and pressed the button. There, right in the arc of light, was a huge male Bengal tiger. Far from bounding away, he casually looked up with his eyes catching the flashlight like diamonds and then calmly went on eating. The time was 6.50 p.m., and I had the button of the torch pressed until 7.30 p.m. They were possibly the most exciting forty minutes I ever had, but I felt sad. I was seeing a tiger in the wild for the first and possibly the last time.

## Zambia: poachers and helicopters

Working alongside Zambia's president, Dr Kenneth Kaunda, David was responsible for initiating and supporting a wide range of projects beneficial to the country's wildlife, including the purchase of an anti-poaching helicopter (subsequently named

'Melinda' after his eldest daughter). It was in the days before the DSWF had been formed and David was therefore conducting most of his fundraising on behalf of the WWF. As David explained at the time:

> It is sincerely the greatest thrill of my life that I can raise money for wildlife so easily … I am a compulsive painter and have to paint every day; but no one wants to paint all the time for the benefit of the government via taxation, so it is simply a case of diverting the proceeds in another direction. It is infinitely more satisfying to donate the paintings to the World Wildlife Fund, so that the rhinos or the tigers are the ones to benefit.

In the late 1960s, the political situation in Zambia was an interesting one. By definition a dictator, President Kaunda was in the perfect position to push through eco-friendly legislation, control the government policy agenda with regards to wildlife conservation and, as Commander-in-Chief of the country's armed forces, was even able to instruct his soldiers to combat any poaching by armed gangs. On one particular occasion – as American political scientist Clark C. Gibson described when writing a résumé of *Wildlife Policy in Zambia*, 'Hundreds of Zambian army troops, supported by dozens of military vehicles and three helicopters, made a wide sweep through villages in the Luangwa Valley to make arrests, and confiscate weapons and wildlife products.'

Despite all that – and Kaunda's constant campaign against those determined to illegally take elephant ivory and rhinoceros horn (whilst most possibly think of elephant ivory as being the most sought-after commodity, rhino horn was actually the most lucrative, the price for which on the international market exceeded ivory by a factor of ten) his efforts only proved partially successful in curbing the poaching epidemic that was currently sweeping through the country. It was then an almost impossible task to contemplate when David and the president first joined forces, and it says much for the determination of both men (and subsequently other outside conservation organisations) that, over the years, they were actually able to make great inroads towards stopping the trade in parts of endangered species – a trade sadly second only to the international trade in narcotics.

*Fundraising for 'Melinda', the Bell Jet Ranger helicopter*
In the first edition of *The Man Who Loves Giants*, David explained why combatting poaching could be best done via means of helicopter surveillance:

> ... light aeroplanes are no good for this purpose because if a band of poachers is sighted they cannot land. So, through the World Wildlife Fund's British National Appeal, I took on the project of [providing] a five-seater Bell Jet Ranger. Anything smaller than a five-seater would have been inadequate, for the African rangers using the machine would be at considerable risk if only one or two of them went after a poaching gang.

Fundraising was, as has previously been established, best done by the sale of David's paintings and at the time one of the best places to do that was at the biennial conferences of the American-based Mzuri Wildlife Foundation (MWF) held alternately at Lake Tahoe, Reno and San Francisco – so off went five of David's paintings. It was 1970 and the host for that particular year's conference was Lake Tahoe, on the border of California and Nevada.

The MWF began life as the Mzuri Safari Club in 1958 ('Mzuri' – pronounced 'umm-zure' – is the Swahili word for 'good') but changed to its current name in 1969. It immediately began building an international reputation and was fanatically supported by politicians, professional big-game hunters, wildlife conservationists and, most importantly, well-known celebrities and royalty. Bing Crosby, American presidents Ronald Reagan and Gerald Ford, Rhodesian Prime Minister Ian Smith, the 8th Duke of Wellington, Lord (Patrick) Litchfield, Joy Adamson (of *Born Free* fame) and astronaut Wally Schirra were all conference attendees in their time.

The biennial gatherings were, therefore, high profile – a profile heightened even further by the fact that the MWF recruited some of the world's leading wildlife artists to display their work at each conference – as a result of which, these exhibitions soon became known as 'the most spectacular showing of wildlife artwork ever assembled under one roof'. It was, then, the ideal venue at which to sell David's paintings in aid of a helicopter. Even HRH the Duke of Edinburgh, wished David good luck with the fundraising. In a letter dated October 1970, he wrote:

> I hope your excursion to Lake Tahoe is a resounding success. Indeed I hope it resounds all the way to Zambia in the form of a helicopter for the protection of wildlife.
>
> I have little doubt that your generosity in painting and presenting five pictures will be matched by the competitive and well-known generosity of the Mzuri Safari Club [sic].
>
> At this moment in the long history of the world nothing could be more important than to remind people to take care of this fragile planet of ours and of all the living things which share it with us.
>
> Good luck and congratulations to the lucky ones who end up with your pictures.
>
> Philip

The success for which Prince Philip had hoped was astounding. David remembered that 'In an hour we raised enough money [£50,000] to buy that beautiful machine.' The support and assistance of royalty and those well known to the general public undoubtedly helps with such ventures. Virginia McKenna (actress and star of the film *Born Free*, who, with her husband Bill Travers, founded Zoo Check – later to become the Born Free Foundation) also played a leading role in David's Zambian fundraising adventures and when the day came for the helicopter to begin its journey to Zambia, it did so via Winkworth Farm where it landed on the lawn with David and Miss World as passengers – undoubtedly fabulous publicity for the project and the raising of awareness regarding the state of wildlife in Zambia! David's daughter Melanie remembers that 'The photocall included Mum (with green hair and hot pants) Dad, the four of us [daughters], Virginia [McKenna] and Bill Travers, the 1969 Miss World, Eva Rueber-Staier, and the Zambian High Commissioner to London.'

***

## Rhino911

In early 2018, the DSWF announced a new partnership with Rhino911 – a rapid response helicopter unit focused on providing lifesaving aid to rhinos that have fallen victim to poaching (DSWF funding goes directly towards the maintenance and flying costs). As with the Bell Ranger helicopter which David's artistic and fundraising efforts helped purchase almost half a century before, the helicopters of Rhino911, piloted by volunteers with the aid of support teams, cover vast areas of difficult, otherwise unreachable terrain. The speed of their response means that poaching is made more difficult for the perpetrators, and their presence has helped in making arrests, saving rhino lives or, in the unfortunate event of being too late and a parent animal killed, the rescue and successful upbringing of orphaned calves.

***

### *Shibula the black rhino*
In 1989, a black rhinoceros (who was eventually given the name of Shibula – meaning 'wild lady') was captured in Namibia and transported to Lisbon Zoo in Portugal as a mate for their animal of the same species. Sadly, the male subsequently died and Shibula was noticed 'languishing alone in her concrete cage' by Anthony Hall-Martin of the National Parks Board of South Africa. With funds raised through Lagamed (a 'green' pharmaceutical company based in Johannesburg) plus David and his charitable foundation, she was eventually transported back to

South Africa where, with the invaluable assistance of the Parks Board, she was reacclimatised to the wild as part of an ongoing project. As Cobus Raath, the National Parks veterinary surgeon who accompanied Shibula on her journey to Africa pointed out at the time, '[She] will be incorporated into a breeding programme and will make a greater contribution to rhino conservation than ever would have been the case, educating and entertaining people in Europe.'

In addition to direct financial help from the DSWF, David further assisted the project in its aim to buy more land – and thus extend the breeding area – by painting a portrait of Shibula and appearing on South African television whilst meeting and sketching her for the first time. Shibula herself was also given massive media coverage when, in 1994, having successfully adapted to being back in the wild, she made history by becoming the first of her kind ever to be re-released and mate with a wild bull. Their liaison produced a calf named Dundagos (meaning 'we have achieved') and Shibula has since given birth to a further five calves.

## A Vision in Black and White

In tandem with the Shibula project and with the assistance of other interested parties, David and the DSWF embarked upon another project to expand the Mountain Zebra National Park in the Eastern Cape Province. The aim was not only to secure the long-term future of the last remaining 700–1,000 Cape Mountain zebra, but also to create a park large enough to reintroduce endangered mammals such as cheetah and black rhino, in addition to benefiting the local people through the development of tourism potential. At the beginning of the two-phase venture, the land available measured just 6,500 hectares (16,000 acres) and, in order to increase it – by the purchase of adjoining farmland – some serious fundraising was required. Once more David's artistic ability was put to good use and he painted several pictures, including one of the zebras themselves. Through the sales of *A Vision in Black and White* and others, sufficient funds were raised for a series of project phases and with the support of sponsors and the South African public, by 2001 the park had extended to over 20,000 hectares (49,500 acres). With its rich diverse vegetation, it is nowadays home to not only the Cape Mountain zebra and black rhino, but also to the likes of springbok, hartebeest, wildebeest and mountain reedbuck. No wonder then, that David considered this ongoing and extremely ambitious project to be one of, if not the greatest of his personal successes.

## Game Rangers International

A further feather in David's capful of wildlife and conservation achievements must be his involvement with Game Rangers International (GRI) which he helped set up a decade before his death and which is today, quite possibly the most effective conservation project with the highest strike rate against poachers anywhere on the African continent.

GRI works alongside the Department of National Parks and Wildlife (DNPW) in order to help protect Zambian wildlife and is particularly active in Kafue National Park, the largest national park in Zambia, covering an area of about 22,400 square km – similar in size to Wales – and home to over fifty-five different species of mammal. Originally founded to empower rangers and local communities to conserve nature, the DSWF further supports not only that aim but also the 'community outreach' working with schools, clinics, women's groups and wider communities in order to increase the awareness of the huge problem of wildlife crime and inspire better management of natural resources. A third aspect concerns financial assistance and involvement in the Elephant Orphanage Project and rehabilitation programme. The latter is intended to provide a safe sanctuary for abandoned elephant calves, often victims of poaching and human conflict. At the Lilayi nursery, young elephants under the age of two are cared for by a team of locally employed and trained keepers before being moved to the Kafue National Park where they are introduced to older orphaned elephants and, from a designated release site, can spend most of their time browsing freely in the National Park with minimal human contact.

***

## What's in a name?

Not long after David died in 2017, an orphan elephant was rescued and taken into the Lilayi nursery and, in honour of David, named Mulisani (meaning 'Shepherd' in the local language).

In September 2019, to commemorate both the second anniversary of David's death and DSWF's thirty-fifth year, Game Rangers International decided to name a week-old wild elephant calf born to Chamilandu (the project's first-ever female orphan) 'Mutaanzi David' – Mutaanzi meaning 'first born' – with the second name being included in honour of the man whose life's work had helped give Chamilandu a second chance and thus enabled this particular calf to exist.

The choice of name was particularly significant to both the DSWF and the Shepherd family due to that fact that, by coincidence or maybe even a spiritual connection, Chamilandu was mated on 19 September 2017 – the date on which David died.

***

The Lilayi elephant nursery is situated on the farm and property of the Miller family located in southern Lusaka, on two hectares of land donated to GRI by the Millers, long-time friends of David's. It is a friendship that began over fifty years ago when David and Avril first met Peter and Annette Miller and has continued via their five sons, particularly Chris, the eldest, and the Shepherd daughters, especially Melanie and Mandy.

Sport Beattie, a founder member of GRI, knew David well on both a personal and professional level. After an army career and during a period spent in the UK, he became a volunteer for the DSWF and would often drive David to various fundraising events – sometimes only after good-natured and light-hearted argument as David would always much prefer to drive himself. Appropriately enough, Sport was the first recipient of the 'David Shepherd Conservation Award' which was launched at the Wildlife Ball in November 2017. Created in order to recognise the 'dedication, bravery and hard work' from the DSWF's portfolio of supported conservation projects across Africa and Asia, that Sport should be honoured in such a way was one of David's last wishes.

## The David Shepherd Wildlife Foundation

Once voted by a BBC poll as being one of the most effective and popular wildlife charities in Britain, what is now the David Shepherd Wildlife Foundation, created by David in 1984 was, at its outset, referred to as the David Shepherd Charitable Foundation. Its main aim has always been to save critically endangered mammals in their wild habitat and benefit the local people who share their environment. And therein lies the reason for the eventual name change in 1992 as, despite it still being a relatively young organisation, such was the Foundation's profile that the office became inundated with requests for grants for a whole range of issues such as butterflies, churches and steam engines. In essence, the all-encompassing name didn't do what it said on the tin – so a change was agreed in order that it reflected more of the actual project work they supported. As David wrote in the first-ever issue of *Wildlife Matters* magazine in the autumn of that year:

> I believe that over the short life of the Foundation, we have been spreading our resources too thinly. We have been associating ourselves with a great many national and international conservation issues which, important though they are, have not really been appropriate to a charity carrying my name. We therefore decided to concentrate on those major endangered species which I am known to paint. We still of course intend to concentrate on education, bringing conservation awareness to young people which is of such importance.

I am convinced that with this change of direction we are returning much more to the original concept of the Foundation; a small charity with a specific focus, Endangered Mammals. I also believe that with this aim, those … who so generously support us financially can feel that … money is going where it should – to help emergency and specific issues.

## Royal patronage

The Foundation was fortunate in having royal patronage in the form of HRH Prince Michael of Kent who, commenting on the change of name, gave it his unstinted support:

As David has already outlined, the Foundation has recently changed its focus to concentrate on the major endangered mammals with which he himself is associated as an artist and conservationist. I have every confidence that this small, highly successful charity will grow from strength to strength and continue to provide funds and stimulate awareness for our vanishing wildlife. Times are hard for us all, but for the wildlife of this world conditions are even worse.

It was, though, HRH Prince Bernhard of the Netherlands who first proposed that David should set up his own charitable foundation. Prince Bernhard was the founder-president of the World Wildlife Fund and David had been producing a great deal of artwork to donate towards their fundraising. During conversation, Bernhard suggested that whilst David's work had undoubtedly created thousands of pounds for the WWF, he nevertheless, had no say in where the money he had raised through his paintings was allocated. Therefore, argued the prince, would it not be better for David to set up his own charity in order that he could control where the money was spent? As Bernhard opined in the Foundation's initial brochure:

David Shepherd is in the unique position through his paintings to raise large sums of money for the conservation of wildlife and the habitat. It seems to me wholly appropriate, therefore, that he should have his own charitable foundation to coordinate his charitable activities and maximise this potential.

*From small beginnings …*
From little acorns do mighty oaks grow and, in this instance, charity most certainly began at home as the initial office of the Foundation was at Winkworth Farm where it slotted (sometimes uncomfortably) between slices of family life and David's work. The confusion of post brought daily by Royal Mail eventually led to the use of a Post Office (PO) Box for all Foundation communication and to the eventual employment of a full-time worker. Eventually, however, such was the success that the office was moved to nearby Smithbrook Kilns – a premises-to-rent development that was created from the derelict remains of the old brickworks, seven miles south of Guildford on the A281 to Horsham – and, having subsequently outgrown the space available there, in 2012 went on to premises at Kings Road, Shalford, near Guildford.

* * *

**To repay in fair measure**
One of the earliest publicity posters for the charity – one declaring it to be 'The David Shepherd Charitable Foundation' – showed David's painting, *Tiger Fire* (the subject of the 'model' for this particular painting is discussed elsewhere in this chapter) and the name of the foundation had the subheading of 'For the Conservation of Wildlife and the Habitat'. A quote by David at the bottom of the poster stated: 'The greatest thrill of my life now is to be able to repay in fair measure the debt I owe to the animals I paint, and which have brought me such success in life.'

* * *

*A dedicated following*
Over the years the Foundation has had many influential followers, supporters and ambassadors, both official and unofficial. The list

reads like a *Who's Who* of film stars, actors, musicians and sports personalities, amongst them the likes of Dame Judi Dench, Rula Lenska, Ricky Gervais, Dame Vera Lynn, Dame Joanna Lumley, Brian Blessed, Sir Michael Parkinson, Sir Roger Moore, Jeremy Irons, Angelica Huston, Stephen Fry, Brian May, Gary Lineker and David Gower. Zoologist, environmental activist, writer, television and radio presenter Mark Carwardine has been a long-time supporter as have Saba Douglas-Hamilton, elephant expert, conservationist and presenter, and wildlife film-maker Simon King. Of the DSWF, Saba is a great admirer: 'I like their attitude and the fact that they put their money where their mouth is and I've seen the kind of effect they have on the ground.' Simon says: 'It [the DSWF] punches well above its weight and, as a consequence, is having a dramatic and direct impact on conservation.'

## A few examples of DSWF projects and successes

- Funding countless illegal wildlife trade investigations across southern Africa and helping fund the establishment and operations of Africa's first-ever task force set up to fight wildlife crime across borders, now operating out of its headquarters in Kenya.
- Supporting the ongoing campaign to release moon bears kept in Asia's 'bile farms'.
- Making strong representations at global debates and in decision-making at CITES (the Convention on International Trade in Endangered Species).
- Almost on the eve of Rwanda's Civil War, David and Avril had been visiting Diane Fossey (of *Gorillas in the Mist* fame) to discuss the parlous state of the country's gorilla population and had to evacuate quickly when it became apparent that unrest was inevitable. Subsequently, the DSWF raised emergency funding to help safeguard the remaining mountain gorillas.
- An active involvement in the snow leopard project in Mongolia.
- Providing grants to train and equip forest guards patrolling India's Sundarbans Tiger Reserve – and, in 2008, a similar

project protecting Gir National Park, home to the last few hundred surviving Asiatic lions.

- Supporting key tiger populations across Russia and Thailand, helping ensure their survival in some of the world's most important and remote habitats.
- The Painted Dog Project in Zimbabwe.
- Pangolins in Uganda.
- Chimpanzees in Guinea.
- The Rapid Action Project of the Wildlife Trust of India – to help address the fact that wildlife in India is impacted by innumerable threats (from natural endemics or anthropological pressures) which more often than not, require an urgent response.

## Wildlife Matters – *the magazine*

*Wildlife Matters* is published twice-yearly (spring and autumn) and is sent out to all members of the DSWF. The first-ever edition was published in autumn 1992 and featured re-homing zoo-kept black rhino Shibula back into the wild (see earlier). The spring issues for 2005, 2006, 2007 and 2008 all came out in a format more practical and informative than illustrative (more as a newspaper than a magazine) but, apart from these, all have been highly polished, perfectly illustrated and much enjoyed by the supporters of the Foundation. Each covers important wildlife issues, ongoing projects and the opportunity to purchase merchandise, David Shepherd prints and paintings and much else likely to be of interest to its typical reader. Most crucially, it profiles upcoming fundraising events and reports on the success of those that have recently taken place. For instance, the autumn 2008 issue carried an account of the inaugural Wildlife Artist of the Year exhibition held at the Mall Galleries in London.

## *Wildlife Artist of the Year*

The first-ever Wildlife Artist of the Year competition had as its subtitle, 'the art of conservation'. Describing its function, Melanie, then CEO of the Foundation said, 'Art has always been a mainstay of our fundraising work at DSWF … [and] this is a great platform for showcasing new artists and a wonderful way to raise funds and awareness.' Of the exhibition and quality of over eighty shortlisted works of art, including sculptures, watercolours, acrylics and oils, David considered that 'The broad spectrum and variety of styles made it a hugely interesting and stimulating collection ...' Entrant Nicholas Osborne recalls, 'It was David's passion and amazing artwork which inspired me to enter my drawing for the first Wildlife Artist of the Year ... I was very fortunate to be selected and my picture sold on the preview evening. I was so happy knowing that the money raised would be used in the best possible way for conservation.' Since its inception, the competition has attracted more than 10,000 entries and has raised more than £1.2 million to help fund the Foundation's projects. Alan Titchmarsh and David Gower were amongst the well-known faces involved with the first event in 2008, and in the intervening years many other celebrities have stepped onto the platform to present awards to the winners and show their support of David's passion for wildlife and its conservation.

* * *

## Knowing nothing about wildlife

For one considered such a great conservationist, in a newspaper interview, David once made what at first sight may seem to be an extraordinary admission when he claimed to know nothing about wildlife – but then qualified the comment by saying that he knew nothing 'in the sense of how much a cheetah eats in a week – and I'm not interested. What I'm interested in is raising money to stop poaching so that our great-grandchildren can see tigers and rhinos in the wild'.

* * *

*Conservation parallels – like father, like daughter*
Despite being forever passionate about animals, there was never any real intention that David's third daughter Melanie

should ever follow in his footsteps when it came to active wildlife conservation. However, after a gap year in Africa, she returned home and very quickly became interested in the work of her father's Foundation. Possibly not running at maximum efficiency when it came to organisation and fundraising, Melanie and Mark Carwardine (see above and other chapters – also the *Ode To David Shepherd*) looked into the possibility of making improvements – and so began an involvement which lasted twenty-six years, the majority of which as the Foundation's CEO. 'Having been brought up with a father who was driven by an energetic passion for wildlife and the environment, it was hard not to get involved,' says Melanie '... Dad and I worked brilliantly together ... we understood each other ... [but] Dad was a loose cannon and his enthusiasm had to be restrained at times!'

### So much achieved

A list of just a few of the DSWF successes and achievements, plus ongoing support to other specific wildlife charities, has been previously itemised but it is, however, important to realise that they are mere examples of the many projects funded as a result of David's initial vision when he created the Foundation back in 1984. Other organisations have equal cause to be grateful, just one of which is headed by Michael Keigwin:

> In early 2000, I was desperately trying to find support for southern Queen Elizabeth National Park – trying to attract support to a region and an elephant population that was less known and under serious threat. Twenty years later and the wonderful David Shepherd Wildlife Foundation has enabled the Uganda Conservation Foundation (UCF) that I founded in 2001, to steadily achieve more and more. I've been mentored and supported, guided and pushed ... to help the Uganda Wildlife Authority to succeed ... Over the years so much has been achieved and it is gratifying to say the recovery of Murchison Falls National Park is real and wildlife numbers are bouncing back quickly. Yet another legacy of David's.

Suzy Fox of the UCF says that:

> David has changed the lives of many people in Uganda ... [There are] several ranger posts and a new Uganda Wildlife Authority veterinary lab that would have not been possible without the contributions of the DSWF... We are also personally grateful to the many donations of art by David and family members that helped us raise funds over the years.

## *Doing what felt right*

The Freeland Foundation is an international NGO headquartered in Bangkok. Its overall mission statement is a huge one: 'To protect vulnerable people and wildlife from organised crime and corruption, while revitalising ecosystems and communities for a more secure world. Our vision is a world free of wildlife trafficking and human slavery.' Steve Galster, Freeland's director, is of the firm opinion that some of their success is undoubtedly down to David's personal involvement and to the support of the DSWF:

> He trusted us and put his art, passion and faith into our cause like a good loyal friend. And it paid off. Because of the support from David and his amazing family and staff, we have managed to save tigers, rhinos, elephants and big cats, while also making the life of rangers and other wildlife protectors safer. While wildlife crime continues, we've managed to slow it down by disrupting some of the world's biggest criminal gangs, while helping poachers become protectors. And that was because David and his organisation were willing to support our new approaches when others didn't dare. He knew what felt right and he just did it.

In an interview with Natural World Safaris, David explained how he knew what felt right – and why he did it:

> It is only through collective efforts that we can drive change. From careful consideration of what we consume – from the food we eat

and the items we buy – to providing financial and physical support for conservation (by donating or volunteering) we can all help to make a difference. Being optimistic about the successes we can collectively create is vital too.

Like many, I admire David Attenborough for introducing so many people to the natural world through film and television. Education is at the heart of protecting the natural world ... The natural world is too precious and too beautiful to lose. Without wildlife and wild spaces the world would be a bleak place. We must protect it.

9

# RAILWAY MANIA – A FULL HEAD OF STEAM

Among the various initials David was allowed to include at the end of his name, was 'FGRA' – Fellow of the Guild of Railway Artists – and he was one of only a very few permitted to use such post-nominals. Nevertheless, his numerous and extremely atmospheric railway paintings were not always treated with such respect and honour, and David recollected (with some amusement) that he had once sold a painting of the paint-shops at Swindon to British Railways for £60 'and it was last seen hanging in their cafeteria in Swindon, covered in fish and chip grease'.

Well known as both a wildlife and railway artist, it was through the financial success of his paintings that David was able to buy two giant steam locomotives from British Rail and become founder of the East Somerset Railway, a registered charity, which also helps raise funds for wildlife conservation as well as ensuring the well-being of railway preservation.

David's creation of the East Somerset Railway began as a result of him paying a visit to the derelict station at Cranmore – some three years after his abortive attempt to establish a 'heritage' railway at Liss in Hampshire (see later). Discovered almost by accident, as fellow railway enthusiast Mike Palmer drove David around Somerset (Mike's widow Gill has an original painting of a Jinty engine at Cranmore given by David as a way of a 'thank you') it was, like many others, a victim of Dr Richard Beeching's advice to the government of the time that many rural branch lines should be closed in the interests of economy and efficiency.

Excited rather than depressed by what he saw, David realised that the site had the potential to become home to a thriving heritage railway and in typical gung-ho Shepherd style, set about turning his vision into a reality by giving much of his time and using a great deal of his money in building a new engine shed and workshop (unique in that it was a copy of traditional Victorian railway buildings), station building, ticket office, gift shop and café. Various vintage items of railway 'furniture' from other areas of Britain were also incorporated – including the original Victorian footbridge and road crossing gates from Chilworth station, Surrey, which were bought by David for the combined sum of £15 and which were transported on low-loader trucks to Somerset, for re-use on the railway.

## A not inconsiderable task

Transportation of a great iron bridge and a set of railway crossing gates is not, by any stretch of the imagination, an easy task. It was, however, made slightly easier by David having contacts in all the right places. At the time, British Road Services had a depot at nearby Shalford, the manager of which also happened to be a member of the recently formed East Somerset Railway. David went to see him:

'John, I've got a problem. I've gone and bought that footbridge just up the line from here. I've got to take it away at midnight tomorrow, and I am desperate.' As I spoke, John must have noticed me looking longingly out of his office at a number of enormous British Road Services low-loaders doing nothing in particular, in his yard. 'OK, David, we will see what we can do for you.'

I arrived at the scene at 11 p.m. the next night. BR had instructed its men to cut the bridge in as few places as possible. They were marvellous; I think they were as pleased as I was to know that ... the bridge would see a new lease of life. At a few minutes to midnight, two low-loaders arrived and the bridge sections were carefully loaded aboard for transport the next morning to Godalming, to Charterhouse School, where, because one of the masters was an enthusiast, the bridge was given a temporary home on the edge of their playing fields ... Unfortunately, after a few months, I got a little note from the school asking me to remove the bridge as it was beginning to interfere with cricket matches!

The bridge was later taken down to Cranmore but, as if that wasn't enough, David subsequently heard of a part of the old London and South Western station at Ash Vale that was due to be demolished – and he wanted it:

We made contact with the demolition contractors and BR, and they told us that provided we didn't get in their way, we could take whatever we wanted, free of charge. We would have to dismantle the canopy ourselves ... and remove it during the night, between the last train and the first one in the morning, when the electric current was turned off.

I still had my Bedford three-tonner and we certainly made good use of it. Several of us participated in the exercise and very large quantities of valuable and reusable material was rescued. It all had to be transported back to Winkworth and this meant many journeys in the lorry back and forth while everybody else was asleep ...

## Exploring the boundaries

Realising that, in order to be able to do all that David and his fellow railway enthusiasts envisaged in the way of expanding the East Somerset Railway, extra land had to be purchased so as to be able to create sufficient space for the engine shed and sidings, David approached the relative authorities: 'I learnt so much about human nature in those early days,' he recalled. 'For instance, while negotiating to buy the one and a half acres of land for the shed from Amey Roadstone Corporation, the BR chap turned up with an old vellum map – the stuff you make lampshades from – inscribed "Great Western Railway". It was the only one they had – I don't think they knew they owned Cranmore! We were digging around in the nettles trying to find the boundary between BR's and ARC's land, which these two grown men were arguing about. I thought it all seemed a bit crazy.'

Such difficulties notwithstanding, once up and running, the East Somerset Railway very quickly became a huge success and at one point was home to *Black Prince* (No. 92203) and *Green Knight* (No. 75029) two Standard 9F class locomotives purchased by David from British Rail for a combined price of £5,000 in 1967 – a very significant year as far as he was concerned. Apart from anything else, his art exhibition in New York that year had, quite literally, sold out overnight and the profits from it allowed David to pick up the phone and ask British Railways if he could buy the two engines. The year was significant in other ways too as it pushed David more and more towards painting steam locomotives and their environment before they disappeared forever. In the introduction to *An Artist Among the Ashes – A photographic record at the very end of Southern Region steam* (published by Noodle Books in 2012) David wrote:

It was early in 1967 that I realised that steam was going and going very fast, to the scrapyards. For my part, I was therefore painting in my studio all day and then, at every opportunity, collecting up my oil paints and camera and dashing off to the nearest steam shed, Guildford and other sheds to record something of the emotional last months. In some cases, I only managed a few brushstrokes before the locomotive was taken away ...

All the photographs and sketches were simply providing me with invaluable material to be used in creating major works such as *Black Five Country* to be painted in the comfort of my studio. When working in the steam sheds, I was not interested in accuracy and detail. It was simply a question of trying to record atmosphere through my camera lens and my palette. Atmosphere to me meant little nuances such as the gorgeous colour of a pool of oil on the floor catching the sunlight. I was fascinated by shafts of sunlight coming through a shed roof encrusted with soot, firing irons hanging on a hook, an old steam engine crane such as that at Fratton, all adding up to a scene of degradation but with an atmosphere tinged with sadness ...

Many people have asked me why I always paint such sad railway paintings. It is simply because I believe that a locomotive covered with grime with sad messages chalked on the smokebox, 'Farewell old friend', mean so much more than a clean locomotive, of which there were very few in those days at the end of steam.

It was then, almost inevitable that David would become so actively involved with the preservation and restoration of both locomotives and derelict railway stations – and in doing all he could to encourage those with perhaps only a casual interest to become involved, or at least visit heritage railways in the hope that they would capture at least some of the romantic atmosphere of the great age of steam which, for many, has only ever been witnessed in evocative classic films such as *Brief Encounter* and, of course, *The Railway Children*. The romance of it all did, however, need to be tempered with practicality and David was quick to realise that, in order to be successful, a venue such as the East Somerset would also be required to provide all the amenities required and expected by the public. As he once remarked: 'Clean toilets are just as important to visitors as the engines they have come to see.'

In the early days, David's two steam locos at Cranmore (on the old Cheddar Valley line through to Witham Friary, Shepton Mallet and beyond) were joined by one owned in partnership with Lord Montagu of Beaulieu, and these in turn, by a further five small engines, several railway coaches and goods wagons. Permission had to be sought to trade under the name of the East Somerset Railway (the original having opened in 1858 and then becoming part of the Great Western Railway in 1874) but it was important to David that the new venture should retain much of its old tradition and status. In an article for the Diners Club *Signature* magazine, written back in 1974, David is quoted as saying:

> Steam locomotives are worth preserving. I believe passionately that although they belong perhaps to a more romantic and leisurely age, this fact alone surely justifies their preservation. Steam locomotives should be kept in working order for the enjoyment and enlightenment of young people growing up in a modern world which does not bother as much as it should about the great inventions of the past.

## *Nostalgia and the artist*

In order to create authentic-looking paintings, any artist has to understand their subject and to spend time with them. David certainly did that with the wildlife he portrayed, and also with the engines and sheds in which they were housed. In order to convey the age of steam before it quickly began to disappear in the 1960s, he was diligent in spending as much time as he could accumulating photographs and sketches. It was frequently dusty work, especially at Guildford, his local station, where space was always at a premium for the engines and it was sometimes necessary for the ashes from the firebox to be raked out inside the shed.

Towards the end of steam, there was no attempt to keep sheds and their surroundings tidy and engines were stripped where they stood, leaving all manner of debris to amass. David found it heartbreaking: 'I knew only too well the dedication and indeed love that loco men, drivers and fitters showed towards the engines … Such was the amount of emotion generated … at Nine Elms that some of the engine men actually raised enough money to save their engine *Blackmoor Vale*.'

Comparing a diesel shed to a steam shed, David remarked that whilst a diesel shed could make him feel physically sick, the smells from one where steam locomotives lived and almost literally breathed, smelt wonderfully of a mixture of dirt, soot, steam, hot oil and smoke. Whilst sight and sound could be recorded by many means, the smell of a steam engine shed was impossible to capture yet somehow, in paintings such as *Over the Forth* (a steam locomotive travelling over the Victorian-built Forth railway bridge and its '148 acres of steelwork, 17 tons of paint and 4,200 tons of rivets') and *On Shed – As We Remember In The Last Days Of Steam*, he managed it – and managed it extremely well.

There was also always the urge for the artist to see under the dirt and grime of a locomotive and expose its original livery. Quite often David would do so with the nearest thing to hand – his handkerchief, a fact which no doubt made him very unpopular at home when they came to be added to the household washing! Talking of which, a knotted handkerchief was often preferred by some drivers as being more practical than the standard issue cap and, at least according to David, it was 'seen by some as being more attractive to female passengers ...'

## Artistic licence

One of David's most well known and easily recognisable paintings from that era was *Nine Elms – The Last Hours*. In his book, *The Man and His Paintings* (1985) the artist captions his painting thus:

> In the half-demolished shed, it's the end of the line for 73155 and she now stands forlorn and rusting. Merchant Navy 35030 is in steam for the last time – she has just run the final steam train into Waterloo and together, chalked with corny but sincere slogans of affection, they await their last journey, hauled by diesel to the breaker's yard and the cutter's torch.

That is not, however, the end of the story. Geoff Burch, who worked on the steam locomotives into the 1960s, is a railway historian of note and has written several books on the subject. During his working life, he had become familiar with '73155' and, when he first saw David's painting, scratched his head in bewilderment as he knew that she couldn't have been available for the artist to sketch and paint at Nine Elms during her 'last hours' and that David must have employed some artistic licence. As Geoff subsequently wrote in one of his books in the hugely successful *Rambling Railwayman* trilogy under a photograph of the aforementioned engine:

> The interesting thing about BR Standard Class 5MT 73155 standing idle with her rods off is that the locomotive failed at Basingstoke on the 18th June 1967. According to the foreman's log book, on the 29th June 1967, Driver Stan Harms was booked to tow the locomotive back to Guildford for repair utilising 1550hp Type 3 'Crompton' diesel-electric locomotive D6500, arriving at Guildford loco at 19.10. The connecting rods on 73155 would have been removed beforehand to ensure the pistons and valve gear remained inoperative as there wouldn't be any lubrication without the engine being in steam.
>
> The locomotive was subsequently repaired and re-entered service for the remainder of steam working on the Southern ... I was the fireman on this locomotive on July 9th 1967; the final journey being to Salisbury to await its fate with the cutter's torch at Barry, South Wales.

## Black Prince *and* Green Knight

David's love affair with *Black Prince* (built in 1959) began with the locomotive's purchase in 1967. To describe his association with the engine as being a 'love affair' is not too strong as, in the 1971 BBC Radio 4 recording of *Desert Island Discs*, David chose *Black Prince* (along with canvases and oil paints) as his luxury item with which he would most like to be cast away.

Like its owner, this particular locomotive has since become something of a celebrity amongst railway enthusiasts and is even a record holder. In 1982 it hauled the heaviest train ('train' being the carriages/wagons to which it is connected) ever by a steam locomotive in Britain, pulling an incredible '2,178 ton' train at the Foster Yeoman – one of Europe's largest independent quarrying and asphalt companies, now part of Aggregate Industries – quarry in Somerset.

During its life with David, *Black Prince* has variously been kept at the Longmoor Military Railway in Hampshire, with a short stint at Eastleigh, various heritage railways (including the East Somerset) – and finally – the North Norfolk Railway (NNR). Julian Birley is a former NNR chairman. On David's death in 2017, Julian wrote that it was 'the end of an era' and that David was:

A great man who will forever be credited as one of this country's greatest pioneers of railway preservation. And in so doing brought pleasure to hundreds of thousands of people … David first brought his beloved *Black Prince* to Norfolk over ten years ago. He loved the railway and the staff and volunteers loved him … The arrival of the *Black Prince* was a turning point in the railway's fortunes. With David's support and the immense popularity of both him and the engine, visitors came from all over the country to see them … *Black Prince* will always be known as David Shepherd's engine and for many years to come she will welcome visitors to north Norfolk never forgetting that had it not been for David, the country would have been deprived of a wonderful example of British engineering at its best.

Talking with Julian in 2020, he struck a more personal note regarding his friendship with David and their mutual love of steam:

Whatever time we arrived in Norfolk even after a four-hour drive David would insist on going straight to the shed to see his beloved engine. This I found to be very moving. It was usually about ten o'clock at night, everyone had gone home. The duty night fitter would be quietly pottering about and we would walk down through the dimly lit shed and there at the end waiting for her next turn of duty the next morning would be this massive monster of an engine: *Black Prince*. Nearly seventy feet long, thirteen feet high and weighing 140 tons. Sitting there quietly, a fire warming the heart of her, David would approach her with all the same love he had for his daughters. He always referred to her as his fifth daughter. The affection he had for this engine was palpable. To David a steam locomotive was the closest mechanical thing to a living creature, it had a heart; it had a personality and flowing through its pipes like veins and arteries was steam instead of blood. Cut a pipe they would bleed steam.

David saw so many aspects of life from working with the Services to meeting royalty from all over the world but I think he was never happier than when he was sitting on the footplate of *Black Prince* after a day's running, after all the staff had gone home, when she was still warm, still alive and with a cup of tea in his hands he would close his eyes think of the old days.

## Green Knight

*Green Knight* (sometimes referred to as *The Green Knight*) was actually bought slightly ahead of *Black Prince* from British Railways, but both were purchased for the combined sum of £5,000 (£3,000 for David's pride and joy – his 'fifth daughter' – and £2,000 for *Green Knight*). She is now at the North Yorkshire Moors heritage railway and their website (www.nymr.co.uk) contains all the necessary information:

Essentially a tender version of the Standard 4 Tank like 80135 and 80136, the 4-6-0 version of the British Railways Standard 4 design was intended for general passenger and freight use on lines where the usual 'Black Five' and similar locomotives would be too large or heavy. Eighty examples were built between 1951 and 1957 and were allocated to the London Midland, Western and Southern regions.

75029 was built in 1954 and was decidedly mobile during her service life, being allocated to depots across the Western region including Reading, Oxford and Swindon, with a stint in Wales at Machynlleth and Croes Newydd sheds in the early to mid-sixties. It was withdrawn from service in August 1967 when it was bought by artist, David Shepherd, several years later it finally made its way the NYMR in October, 1998.

Painted in British Railways' Brunswick Green livery used on passenger engines, 'The Green Knight' has been a stalwart of the North Yorkshire Moors Railway, including being passed to work to Whitby and Battersby on the national network. A crack in the firebox was identified in 2015 and she is currently awaiting attention.

Neither *Black Prince* nor *Green Knight* had monikers in service and they were christened by David purely and simply because he liked the names. After leaving British Rail's ownership – and before the acquisition of the Cranmore site – they were driven under their own steam to the Longmoor Military Railway in Hampshire, and when that closed they spent a further two years in a siding next to BR's Eastleigh locomotive depot, at a rent of £20 per week. Such arrangements were, however, far from ideal but, as David remarked in the August 1986 issue of *Somerset & Avon Life*, 'Because the siding was surrounded by electrified third rails we didn't have any problems with vandalism – there's nothing like a few thousand volts to keep vandals away!'

## A military railway and militant opposition

*Black Prince*, whilst at the Longmoor Military Railway (built by the Royal Engineers at the turn of the twentieth century in order to train soldiers in the technicalities of railway construction and operation) was located in one of the last bastions of steam in the south of England. After the LMR closed – a ceremonial last day of operation being held on 31 October 1969 – David, along with friends under the group name of the Association of Liss Enginemen, attempted to establish a heritage railway at nearby Liss. The residents there (as David described them: '"real" people with the railway on their doorstep') were keen and supported their application because, as the chairman of the parish council at the time is on record as saying, the community would 'benefit from the recreational and the educational points of view ...'

Those in nearby Liss Forest (upon whom the proposed venture would barely have any impact) were, on the other hand, incensed and some quite spirited opposition ensued. As David's widow, Avril, recalled, 'They were quite a nasty group, worried about the influx of people and the possibility that they would clog the roads with traffic.'

Bearing in mind the fact that not all that far away was the army garrison church of St George, containing the huge painting of *Christ in the Battlefield* painted by David as a background to the altar (see Chapter 10) as a result of which, David already had an affinity and association with the area, it seems like Nimbyism (Not in My Back Yard) of the worst kind. No matter, the Liss Forest Residents Association were up in arms in protest and the parish council there held public meetings, at which one spiteful householder asked David, 'Why don't you just go back to your painting, for which you appear to have at least have a modicum of talent?' As David was to later write:

Letters started flying to the local papers and a hate campaign began in earnest. As the conflict gathered momentum, and the news spread further afield, the circulation of the *Hampshire Chronicle* and the *Petersfield Post* must have gone up by leaps and bounds. People love to read about controversy. The letter pages seemed to be filled each week with a forest of abuse, of me and everything that I stood for.

There were utterly absurd letters … They complained that the peace and quiet … would be shattered … and that … children would be in danger of being struck down by 'hissing, clanking, smoke-belching monsters' [quoted precisely from one letter to the *Petersfield Post*] as they ran 'unchecked through level crossings setting the countryside ablaze'.

On another occasion, when *Black Prince*, in steam and on a run out from Longmoor to Liss Forest, had temporarily caused an unfortunate delay at a level crossing, an irate woman driving a Mini got out from her vehicle and told all assembled to 'move that bloody thing or else I'm going to ram it'. Mini cars might have been British-built at the time but it's doubtful whether even the best quality vehicular engineering would have made much of a dent in a steam loco of that weight and measurement!

All in all, it was a bizarre reaction, given the fact that nowadays heritage railways are so popular and that there are many who would undoubtedly love to have steam locomotives running nearby. After all, even back then it's not as if the locals were not unused to public interest in the area as, at various times of its life, the nearby Longmoor railway had been used as the location for a number of high-profile films, including *The Lady Vanishes* (1938), *The Inn of the Sixth Happiness* (1958), *The Great St Trinian's Train Robbery* (1966), and *Chitty Chitty Bang Bang* (1968), as well as *Young Winston* (1972).

* * *

## Railway Ramblers president

Today, parts of the military railway line are accessible to walkers, many of whom are those that enjoy a ramble down memory lane and who also have a love of the golden age of steam.

David was, for several years, the president of the Railway Ramblers – an organisation formed in 1978 when Nigel Willis, the club's founder member, placed a small ad in *The Railway Magazine* asking if there were other individuals in the UK who were interested in accompanying him on walks along abandoned railways. The response was far greater than Nigel had expected and, as a result, he decided to form a club. As its website (www. railwayramblers.org.uk) explains, 'The club's main purpose is to bring together groups of like-minded people to explore old railways, but it has also done much to encourage the preservation of old railway lines as footpaths and cycleways. As most railway enthusiasts know, Dr Beeching and his successors axed about 8,000 miles of railways within the UK, but thanks to the efforts of local authorities and Sustrans (the charity behind the National Cycle Network) over 2,500 miles of this discarded network have been brought back into use as public walks and cycle trails.'

***

## Young Winston

Just before it was intended to move *Black Prince* from Longmoor in the early 1970s, she became a film star. Through his association with wildlife and conservation, David had long known (Sir) David Attenborough but it was to be at Longmoor where David first met his brother, film director (Sir) Richard 'Dickie' Attenborough. The film-maker was working on *Young Winston* for Columbia Pictures and they were looking for a suitable location to film a steam engine sequence for their epic of the early life of Winston Churchill. *Black Prince* was, with a little cosmetic modification, to be used as a South African locomotive and it was arranged that she would be in steam for the best part of a week. Columbia Pictures paid £250 a day for her contribution, but there was, according to David, very little profit: 'The coal had to be paid for, and there had to be some recompense for the volunteers who had taken time off from their work to service and drive her and to attend to the other diverse railway tasks when required.' The whole business was, nevertheless, a great experience for David who found several parts of the filming to be extremely amusing. As he was later to write in *A Brush with Steam*:

> Because of her speed and the weight of the train behind her, *Black Prince* could hardly be expected to stop immediately she was out of camera range. Throughout the filming period we had a walkie-talkie apparatus on her footplate; this little gadget enabled Arthur, who was driving the *Prince*, to keep in contact with the film crew up the hill ... We kept getting rather strange messages from the [film] crew as we stormed past them ... 'Why on earth can't you stop sooner? ... You're wasting precious time and film.' They seemed to expect us to stop on a sixpence once we were out of

their view. This so exasperated Arthur at the end of one particularly fast and long run that he grabbed the intercom and ... shouted into it: 'What the bloody hell do you think we've got, a f ... ing wheelbarrow?'

I was all the time making a colour film record of the filming of the great epic, and a number of people who have seen my humble effort have said that mine is better than the film itself! It certainly includes some extremely funny episodes ...

On one of our runs they decided to take some film from the train ... with Simon Ward [playing the part of Winston Churchill] leaping from the wagon as the train was moving, and making his escape to freedom. This necessitated building a platform out from the side of the wagon on which they placed the multi-thousand-pound Panavision camera. On to this small projection crowded a quite astonishing number of people, all of whom were apparently required to operate the one camera. To our astonishment, and it wasn't our job to tell them, it had not occurred to anyone in the film unit to do a slow dummy run first to make sure that the projection would clear any telegraph poles or any other obstructions along the side of the line. The order was given to start, the train stormed down the hill and, sure enough, the whole platform hit an obstruction – hard. The camera, Richard Attenborough and attendant personnel were all sent flying in different directions ... Fortunately no one was hurt, but Richard Attenborough was clearly shaken.

## The Zambezi Sawmills Railway

The November 1974 issue of *Signature*, the magazine of the Diners Club Ltd, carried a feature on David written by Frederick Radford. Given the title 'Man on the Move', bearing in mind David's dynamism, it could not have been more appropriate. Radford was stunned by his interviewee's enthusiasm and verbosity:

No interviewer need leave David Shepherd's company short of material. The words pour out. 'Must hurry. Got a lot to do. Off to Zambia in the morning to collect two 100-ton locos, made in Glasgow in 1896 and 1920. I'm bringing them back by sea – bloody expensive too.'

As it turned out, transporting those two locomotives back to the UK was not quite as simple as David had made it appear in the magazine interview.

Initially constructed to carry timber from Mulobezi to Livingstone in the southern province of Zambia, when the country was known as Northern Rhodesia, the railway ceased working in the early 1970s. David was eventually to acquire two of its locomotives, plus a passenger sleeper carriage, the story of which was chronicled in *Last Train to Mulobezi*, a 1976 BBC Television documentary (see Chapter 11).

While the initial intention was to bring both locomotives and the carriage back to Great Britain, in the event, only the passenger sleeping car and one of the engines made it back (the other, the *Mulobezi Princess* No. 156, was fully restored and remains at Livingstone where she nowadays runs dining-car tourists from the Royal Livingstone Hotel – see also Chapter 7).

The one which eventually returned to England originally had the number 390 and was built in 1896 by Sharp, Stewart & Co. in Glasgow as part of an order for six engines for the Cape Government Railway. In 1910 the Cape Government Railway was absorbed into South Africa Railways and it was renumbered SAR 993. Zambezi Sawmills Railway took it over in 1971 and it remained operating on their lines until that railway ceased operations in 1973.

In an inventory compiled at the time, a note mentioned that 'This engine is ... wood-burning [but] can easily be reconverted to coal – in full working order – excellent condition and repainted – with approx. fifteen tons of spares.' The sleeping car was described as being 'forty years old in immaculate condition – clerestory roofed – Ornamental balcony ends – wood body – complete with green leather bunks, wash basins. All fittings, mosquito net blinds, sun blinds, etc.'

Logistics, both political and financial, made things difficult – getting locomotive and carriage back to Britain involved a long and complicated route. A letter to David from the office of the Chief Mechanical Engineer at Bulawayo dated 23 September 1974 observed: 'It appears you are contemplating quite a project in moving these old locomotives on their own wheels over some 1,650 miles of rail from Livingstone to Cape Town and then on to the UK!' Politically things were not easy either and, as ever, officialdom reared its ugly head. The chief mechanical engineer's letter went on to inform David that 'Before the locomotives can be moved onto our lines, or the South African Railways lines at Mafeking, there are a few points which you should have checked ...' A list of requirements followed and the tone of the correspondence suggested a slapped wrist for David and a difficult journey ahead in more ways than one!

However, in typical Shepherd style, no problem was insurmountable and, with the financial assistance of millionaire Jack Hayward, locomotive No. 993, together with the sleeping car, eventually arrived at Salford Docks, Manchester, where they were unloaded over the two days of 25 and 25 March 1975. As an aside, Jack Hayward's connection to David is an interesting one: both had gone to Stowe School, although at different times, and both had a love of all things British. Known by many as 'Union Jack' because of his patriotism, Hayward's entry in *Who's Who* declared his interests as 'promoting British endeavours, mainly in sport ... protecting the British landscape, keeping all things bright, beautiful and British.' His influence obviously rubbed off on David and made him love all things British even more than he had previous to their acquaintance – to the extent of creating an intense dislike of foreign-built cars: as did Hayward who banned non-British vehicles from his estate in Sussex and refused to drink French wine or mineral water!

After the locomotive and sleeping car arrived in England, their first port of call was to the Whipsnade and Umfolozi Light Railway in Bedfordshire (see below). Over the following years it was moved to the East Somerset Railway and then arrived at the

British Empire and Commonwealth Museum at Bristol in 2003. A year later, locomotive and carriage were donated to the National Railway Museum, and between the years 2008 and 2012 was cosmetically restored and put on display at Shildon Locomotion – a part of the Science Museum Group.

## Side-valves on the rails

Viewers of *Last Train to Mulobezi* (see Chapter 11) witnessed the extraordinary sight of a Ford Eight car being push-started by a steam locomotive. It was, however, no ordinary Ford motor as it was without tyres and instead ran on wheel rims along the railway tracks of the Zambezi Sawmills Railway (ZSR) where it had been used for many years as an inspection buggy or trolley. Since the 1930s, a motley collection of old cars (usually ancient Fords) had been used as platelayer's trolleys to get around the sawmills railway and, if a train was due to be approaching from the opposite direction, the car was simply lifted off the tracks in order to allow the train to pass!

Conversions of side-valve cars to run in such a way had been carried out at various times in order to provide low-cost rail inspection trollies. The ZSR had used a whole selection of side-valve vehicles, some rebuilt with railway running gear and axles, others simply fitted with flanged rail wheels bolted to the existing hubs. Of course, when David discovered one such vehicle whilst involved with his efforts to bring back the two locomotives to Britain, he became typically excited about getting hold of something similar – and, in 1976, persuaded the Ford Motor Company, based in Essex, to give him a 1938 7Y Ford. It was superficially restored and soldiers of the 27 Command Workshops REME at Warminster made a set of rail wheels. Once completed, the replica ZSR trolley was officially handed over to David by Sir Terence Beckett, then chairman of Ford, and went on static outdoor exhibition alongside the returned Sawmills locomotive at Whipsnade Zoo.

The handover of the car and the grand opening of the 'Zambesi Sawmills Railway Exhibition' at Whipsnade, took place on

6 August 1976. Alongside Sir Terence Beckett representing the Ford Motor Company was His Excellency L. H. Shamoya, High Commissioner of the Republic of Zambia. The opening was timed for 11.00 a.m. – and was followed half an hour later by a '… steam train ride through the zoo's rhino enclosure'!

Obviously fuelled with enthusiasm, at some point David located an old Model T Ford rail-car which had been used to run on the Shrewsbury branch line as an inspection trolley but sadly, further correspondence on the matter is missing from family archives and general research has failed to find out more. The fate of the 1938 Ford immediately after its time at Whipsnade is however, documented and it went on show at a transport museum in Bristol.

## Avril – *African queen of the tracks*

Entrepreneur Wilfred Mole reputedly has the largest collection of narrow-gauge steam locomotives in the world and dedicates much of his huge organic commercial farm in South Africa to housing them, along with many vintage tractors, military vehicles and aircraft. Wilfred's unique collection became the basis of what is now known as the Sandstone Heritage Trust and is home to *Avril,* a 15F Class locomotive, originally in David's ownership. How it came to be so is typical of David and his enthusiastic nature:

I was being interviewed on South African television, on the *Breakfast Show*. My interviewer knew that I was potty about steam engines, so he said, 'David, get a plug in about wanting a 15F – someone may be listening.' Someone was. Shortly after the programme, South African Railways rang up the television studios: 'What's this about David Shepherd wanting a 15F?' That was when the project was born. It was agreed that if I painted a picture of one, they would give me a fully restored 15F Class locomotive.

It was a most marvellous ceremony. Three hundred people were on the platform at Kimberley Station. When I made my speech (difficult because I was getting excited) I knew what was going to happen. Behind me was … No[.] 3052, fully restored and in a fresh gleaming coat of paint … After my speech, she stormed into the station and the engine was handed over to me. We rode off down the line and had a lovely time …

When the engine was handed over to David in 1991, he had every intention of bringing *Avril* (as he was to name steam locomotive No. 3052) back to the UK and had, according to correspondence dated around that time, obviously been in contact with various shipping companies with a view to getting a 'steam engine and tender' from 'Durban to Cranmore'. One quote included: 'Durban handling, Durban heavy lift, Durban floating crane (up to three hours loading) sea-freight quay Durban to UK port, UK terminal handling, UK mobile crane, two specially adapted vehicles to transport locomotive and tender to Cranmore, customs clearance … TOTAL CNF [Cost, No insurance, Freight] CRANMORE £30,650.00'. Although this appears to be a far lower price than any others quoted, in the absence of a sponsor, *Avril* was to remain in South Africa – and eventually, in the very capable care of Wilfred Mole and the Sandstone Heritage Trust. Wilf Mole takes up the story in more detail:

In 1991 after a brief allocation to Millsite depot in Krugersdorp, 3052 was selected as the engine to be presented to David Shepherd by Spoornet in exchange for an original painting by the artist, in fact of the locomotive itself. The presentation took place on Kimberley Station by Dr Anton Moolman and 3052 hauled a short train southwards from Kimberley. [For various reasons – see above.] David was not in a position to move the locomotive to England … and decided to leave the locomotive in South Africa where it could be used. After some time at Kimberley and in Germiston depot it was moved to Hilton in KwaZulu-Natal where it saw occasional use but was generally unsuited for the lines in the area. It was eventually moved to the Umgeni Steam Railway depot at Mason's Mill in Pietermaritzburg where it stood out of use.

In 2002 Sandstone Heritage Trust funded repairs for the loco to be steamed to coincide with a visit by David and his wife Avril to South Africa. On November 3rd 2003, 3052, complete with a three-year boiler certificate, hauled a special train from Mason's Mill to Cato Ridge and back. Excited by the prospect of 3052 being in steam again David asked Sandstone to take custody of the locomotive in the hope that it could be used on the Bloemfontein to Bethlehem line while being based at Ficksburg. Some months later in April 2003, number 3052 was prepared and steamed and hauled in light steam from Mason's Mill to Bethlehem from where it steamed under its own power to Ficksburg. In 2006 it was steamed specially for a visit by David Shepherd to Sandstone.

Unfortunately continued usage of 3052 on the line was not practical and in 2007 it was moved to Reefsteamers [a non-profit-making South African steam railway organisation run by volunteers] in Germiston ... and the locomotive was donated to Sandstone in May 2011 [since when] it has been used frequently on local and longer distance tour trains before being staged with various defects in 2009. [She] underwent major repairs, including re tubing the boiler, prior to its return to service in 2016 ... [when] 'Avril' ... was loaned to Friends of the Rail in Pretoria.

After a derailment on the Cullinan branch in March 2017 [she] has now returned to Reefsteamers in Germiston. [The locomotive] is in working order but currently out of service as the boiler certificate has expired but this may be reinstated for an international tour to South Africa in June 2020.

Some wonderful film footage of David and Avril taken during the presentation and naming ceremony can also be found on YouTube (Keywords: David Shepherd/and/No. 3052).

***

*Personal recollections from Patrick Ackerman*
Patrick Ackerman first met David in 2003 when he (David) visited Sandstone Estates where Patrick worked in the steam

heritage division and was involved in the restoration of one of the ex-Beira Railways locomotives. He remembers David as being 'captivating' when he joined Patrick on the footplate of the engine as they took a trip around the railway system – with David taking to the regulator in order to drive in fine style and then enjoying a 'braai' (barbeque) in the steam shed with the engine simmering gently in the background.

In 2008, the two met again when David joined Reefsteamers and participated in a trip to Ficksburg, the train of which was hauled by *Avril*. However, Patrick's favourite image of that particular trip was when: '[David] lovingly repaired a print of his painting *Nine Elms* with a pencil in the mess room at the Reefsteamers depot ...'

* * *

## *On the right track for fundraising*

As with so many things that David did and enterprises (madcap, eccentric or not) with which he involved himself, much was to benefit steam locomotive preservation and, of course, wildlife conservation. On many occasions, the two were interchangeable. In 1989, in Omaha USA, at a fundraising event organised by the Union Pacific Railroad – and in honour of David – the company put in steam No. 8444, a locomotive of a type that will be familiar to those who enjoy Western films and are of an age to have enjoyed the *Casey Jones* series on children's television. David was, of course, delighted:

> They steamed it in from Cheyenne, stopped some twenty miles short of Omaha in case 'I might like to drive her the rest of the way into the city.' I needed no persuading, hopped into the cab which seemed to be the size of an average-sized bedroom and, excited beyond belief, steamed into the town. That evening we had a black-tie reception in the recently-restored 1930s vintage Union Pacific Railroad station in Omaha and then some 300 people were transported to the waiting train. No. 8444 was in full steam under

the floodlights with eight vintage coaches behind her and, walking up a red carpet with the State Governor, we boarded the train for a sumptuous dinner whilst we stormed out into the countryside. We took over $30,000 off the passengers and I cannot imagine a more exciting way to raise money for wildlife than that.

In the UK, the various heritage railways and museums associated with David (and on which *Black Prince* had been kept in steam before finally moving to the North Norfolk Railway) frequently organised charitable events to boost charity coffers. Several chat shows (see Chapter 11) have been held at the North Norfolk Railway (NNR) and all have been well supported by steam locomotive and wildlife lovers in equal measure. Through the invitation of David, other charities, such as the Battle of Britain Memorial Trust, have also benefited from visits to one or other of the various railways with which he was connected. As well as fundraising, they were inevitably great fun for all who attended, particularly when David himself was in full flow and giving one of his exuberant, infectious and amusing talks with, as frequently happened on the NNR platform at Sheringham, the giant *Black Prince* gently steaming away on the rails behind him.

# FLYING HIGH – AEROPLANES AND A MILITARY CONNECTION

'I paint aeroplanes. Or should I be called an aviation artist. I prefer the term "painter" but however I describe myself, people usually take me for the chap who works on a ladder with a spray-gun and paints "BOAC" along the fuselage.'

David Shepherd: *Shell Aviation News*, January 1959

Despite a career in which he was perhaps to become most famous for his paintings of elephants and steam engines, much of David's early work not only featured London street scenes, but also a larger than life portrait of Christ commissioned by the army for their church at the Bordon Garrison in Hampshire. It was though, initially, paintings of commercial planes that first filled most of his canvases in the 1950s. Such paintings were important, not only because of his long-standing love of them, but also because of the more practical fact that the sale of his work would, he hoped, help pay the bills. As he told Pamela Coleman, a reporter for *Express* newspapers in 1986:

Aviation became my passion in World War II, when as a young boy living in London I would stand in my pyjamas at the window at night watching the German aeroplanes caught in the searchlights …

After I finished my three-year training as an art student with Robin Goodwin, it seemed logical to specialise in painting aircraft. I spent a year at Heathrow … [and] was given a permit to go anywhere I wanted. I trundled round in my little ex-army pick-up truck with my canvases and easel in the back and painted Stratocruisers and Constellations and all those lovely old aeroplanes with propellers.

It was a very friendly place and I was fortified by endless mugs of strong tea handed out by the chaps who worked in the hangars. They thought I was mad and I was constantly being asked: 'Why don't you take a bloody photograph instead?'

All that was in the summer of 1953, a summer which, in the January 1959 issue of *Shell Aviation News*, David describes as being something of a 'milestone' in terms of experience and productivity:

The physical problems of painting at the airport were many and varied and wind was always the worst hazard … I used to put three bricks and a car jack on the platform of my folding easel and still the thing would shake like a jelly. Brushes would blow away. And then there were slipstreams. Just when I was engaged on a particularly detailed part of the picture when absolute rigidity of canvas, hand and palette was essential, somebody would start up an engine. The painting would either be sucked forward or blown backwards. I had to hang onto it for dear life to stop the whole thing taking off …

In those weeks, I did some ten paintings on the airport and in the hangars and was even known as the 'London Airport Artist'. Coachloads of trippers on conducted tours used to stop behind my easel [shades of his time painting out on the London streets with Robin Goodwin! See Chapter 2] and I used to hear a complete, if not always accurate, description of what I was doing over the microphone … I was even filmed for television as a result of my painting the scene before the departure of the London-New Zealand air race. I was painting the KLM DC.6A lined up with all the other entrants in the transport sections, taking the gamble that if it won, KLM would buy the painting. It did, and they did.

On other occasions, David gave away paintings to companies such as Vickers-Armstrong, Handley-Page and de Havilland, hoping that they would hang them in their boardrooms and he would get commissions as a result. Quite often the plan paid off: one of the first was from Vickers-Armstrong, who wanted a picture of a prototype Spitfire and a prototype Valiant V-bomber for their test pilot, Matt Summers. David was paid £25 for each.

It was, though, perhaps a painting of a Vickers Viscount during the period just before he and Avril married that David remembered best – as he explained in his 1985 book, *The Man and His Paintings*:

In 1955 Capital Airlines of Washington placed an order with Vickers Armstrong for seventy-five of the new Viscount turbo-prop airliner. This order was a great success story for the British aircraft industry ... and it was won in the face of the fiercest and often ruthless competition from America's own aviation industry. Capital Airlines had to have their representative stationed at Hurn Airport, near Bournemouth ... and my future wife was his personal secretary.

The American ferry crews used to come over at regular intervals to fly the brand-new aircraft to the United States ... Only a few seats were fitted into the aircraft before delivery and we used to watch some amusing scenes at Hurn. The ferry crews used to go into Bournemouth to visit the antique and junk shops; they purchased huge Victorian dressers and sideboards, and even street lamps, and all these were loaded into the aircraft.

Because [of Avril] ... I was able to get a lift on one of the aircraft going out to Washington and it was a fascinating journey. Before I left Hurn, I painted a picture of one of their Viscounts flying over Manhattan Island, hoping that if I showed it to Capital Airlines they might buy it. When I arrived in Washington with the painting, they did.

Throughout his life, David never missed out on any opportunity to fly in an aircraft, be it commercial, military or private. As an aviation artist, it was, he always maintained, absolutely essential to have first-hand experience of flying: 'not only to see for oneself cloud formations and effects from their own level, but also to get the "feel" of particular aircraft'. As he so frequently told anyone who might be interested in his painting a plane on their behalf, 'I can't possibly paint it at its best unless I fly in it.' Be that as it may, being up in the air most definitely appealed to his childhood enthusiasm, an enthusiasm that was to last all his life.

Jayne Le Cras, who worked alongside David fundraising in Guernsey (see Chapter 11) and her husband Steve Rogers, had a Beechcraft Baron 58 six-seater, and as an ongoing friendship developed as a result of the wildlife fundraising, the two would often take David in their plane. Jayne recollects that, even in his eighties, so great was David's readily apparent joy of flying, he would insist on taking the front passenger's place – which would, in essence, mean climbing up over the wing in order to get there. On such occasions, Jayne often looked forward to being able to talk with David about their mutual love of wildlife and conservation but more often it appears that it was conversation with pilot Steve about all things old – be they aeroplanes or steam locomotives – and Jayne was left, quite literally in the back seat, never able to get a word in edgeways!

Any wartime plane could equally grab David's attention, in particular, the Spitfires for which he and his brother Peter had helped raise funds during their childhood (see Chapter 2). Arguably, one of David's best-known aircraft paintings was of a Spitfire. *The Immortal Hero* went on to raise money for the Royal Air Force Benevolent Fund – a charity whose aim was to look after the families of those who served – and was originally hung in the Battle of Britain bar at RAF Kenley.

Very much an aircraft associated with the Second World War in most people's minds, a few Spitfires (there are nowadays only around fifty airworthy ones dotted around the world) have been preserved by aviation enthusiasts in the same way as David Shepherd helped to preserve steam locomotives. A chance meeting with Caroline Grace, who flies a two-seater (none were ever specifically built as two-seaters, but were converted from original Spitfires for use as 'trainer' aircraft) led to her flying over Brooklands Farm as part of family celebrations for David and Avril's Golden Wedding in 2007. For those standing next to David at the time, it was an emotional experience watching both the plane go overhead and David's face as his expressions alternated between boyish delight, awe and tears.

* * *

## It complements the lounge

A handwritten letter, undated year-wise, but likely to be mid-1950s, from J. A. McWonald, assistant commandant at London airport, thanks David for a painting of a Spitfire in the following fashion:

I returned home yesterday to behold your splendid picture. My wife and I are thrilled. That Spitfire is very much alive (nearly 3D wise) so much so it sent rather a shiver down my ageing spine. Well done – that's how it should be surely. The aircraft colour is admirable. I do congratulate you. The frame is ideal for my lounge décor ...

* * *

*Parson's Gallery – David's first 'aeronautical' exhibition, October 1955*

Although David had previously held an extremely successful relatively small exhibition of aircraft at Biddles, Guildford in 1954, it was at Parson's Gallery a year later where his

'First London Exhibition of Aeronautical, Industrial and Landscape Paintings' was held. Via their catalogue cover, readers were informed that 'Air Vice Marshal Sir John Cordingley, KCB, CBE, RAF (Retd) [Controller of the Royal Air Force Benevolent Fund] will introduce Sir Miles Thomas [Chairman of British Overseas Airways Corporation (BOAC)]'. In the catalogue introduction itself, Conservative politician (and owner of *Surrey Beeches* and *Westminster Square*: two early David Shepherd originals) Edwin 'Ted' Leather, MP, wrote the following:

David Shepherd, besides being my favourite young artist, has one of the most enquiring minds I know. He possesses real enthusiasm for his work, which to me as a business man is one of the essential qualities for success in any field. It certainly seems to be carrying him to success very quickly in his. Though my artistic friends will probably regard it as the crudest kind of philistinism, I also have the business man's natural liking for being in on the ground floor with a good thing! Just watching the value of my pictures rise gives me a peculiar pleasure! Finally, and I don't care if it *is* philistinism, although he paints an amazing range of pictures, I can understand them all – and I don't like pictures I cannot understand.

His insistence on working from life, regardless of the subject and conditions, in preference to relying on sketches, notes and imagination, enables him to record in paint the subtleties which only a sensitive eye can catch. I don't pretend to be an expert on art, but it seems clear that, as in politics, the hard way of doing things is usually the best in the end.... These aeroplanes are living things, not just hunks of machinery. He approaches everything with the same boundless enthusiasm and vigour, and his love of painting is such that he seems equally happy whether the subject is an aircraft works or a nude – he tells me 'It's all painting to me.' Not being an artist myself, I am in no position to know.

Edwin Leather was not the only politician to attend the official opening and view David's work. Always good with his publicity, David had invited many – and those such as John

Boyd-Carpenter, MP and Christopher Soames, MP, did so. Also invited was Winston Churchill, whose private secretary replied, 'Sir Winston is abroad just now for several weeks, and would therefore be unable to see the exhibition of your paintings next month. No doubt he would be most interested to see the catalogue, however, and I shall show him this on his return from France.' Also invited, and of interest due to his subsequent involvement in the trial of Christine Keeler, was John Profumo who responded saying, 'Unfortunately I won't be able to come to the actual opening, but I certainly look forward to the opportunity of visiting it during the period of its duration. You certainly couldn't have a better man than Miles Thomas to open it for you ... I do wish you every success.'

A success it was, with over twenty paintings sold at the gallery opening. It certainly gave credence to the fact that just twelve months previously, David's association with aircraft and his ability to paint them had been recognised by the committee of the Society of Aviation Artists (later to become the Guild of Aviation Artists) who had, on 2 July 1954, elected him a Member – possibly on the back of the Guildford exhibition held in April of that year, at which it was said that he had: 'brought something entirely new to the curiously unexploited field of art, aeronautical painting ...'

Interestingly, a fellow Member was Roy Cross (Cross had begun work as an illustrator in Fairey Aviation during the Second World War. Over the next thirty years, he progressed from line illustration, via colour artwork, to top-class advertising art for the aircraft industry) who, in *The Art of Roy Cross* (Crowood Press, 2019) is recorded as saying: 'I ... met a young David Shepherd, already a decent oil painter, who told me he was aiming to become another Terence Cuneo [see Chapter 6] ... he certainly achieved equal distinction.'

At the time, most examples of aviation art were considered to be somewhat poor in execution and even wrong in shape or detail. David thought this 'unbelievably crude' and 'unforgivable' and perhaps it was this realisation that led him to ensure that whatever he painted would be accurate; whether it be anatomically correct in the case of wildlife and portraits, or structurally and engineering-wise when it came to dealing with aircraft, steam locomotives and buildings. Apart from anything else, artistic licence notwithstanding, there were always critics ready to take delight in pointing out any errors.

* * *

## More courage than skill

It was obviously inevitable that David's life as a wildlife artist and conservationist would involve a great deal of flying and, as established earlier, he never tired of the thrill of it all and seemingly enjoyed all his aviation experiences, be they good or bad. One of his first trips to Kenya was in 1950:

> To see the sunrise over the desert and to land on the Nile in a Solent flying boat were experiences I shall never forget. Nor will I forget in a hurry being taken up in an ageing Tiger, from a dusty Kenya airstrip. My pilot was a woman who, I think, had more courage than skill; she said she needed practice 'to keep her eye in'. And the so-called airstrip suffered from an appalling rash of ant-heaps.

* * *

*Supporting Air Force charities*
The Royal Air Force Battle of Britain Memorial Flight (BBMF) operates from RAF Coningsby, a fighter base in Lincolnshire. Its mission is 'to maintain the priceless artefacts of our national heritage in airworthy condition in order to commemorate those who have fallen in the service of this country, to promote the modern-day Air Force and to inspire the future generations.' No wonder then, that its aims and objectives were so close to David's heart and that he would, throughout his later life, do all that he could to support them.

In 2009, he staged an exhibition and donated a painting (*Elephants at Amboseli*) to the Bomber Command Memorial Appeal which raised thousands through a nationwide raffle. It was, as David said, 'an important thing to do ... not least because, had the RAF not taken my work all those years ago, I might never have begun painting wildlife'. A year later, in December 2010, *Daily Express* reporter Paul Callan went to see David at Brooklands Farm – and wrote the following as a result:

> Two bombs lie deep in rich East Sussex earth, unmoved since they fell from a Heinkel 177 in the early hours of March 2, 1944. The German bomber, soon to crash after being hit, unleashed what remained of its lethal cargo over the neat village of Hammerwood near the Ashdown Forest.
>
> Today, almost seven decades later, those ... bombs have a ... relevance for the man who lives close to where they plummeted. He is distinguished wildlife artist and conservationist David Shepherd CBE, internationally known for his magnificent paintings of lions, tigers and elephants. The artist is also fascinated by the Second World War and has produced fine works showing the aircraft that took part in the conflict, including the Lancaster bomber.
>
> Appropriately in recent years he has put considerable energy and influence into the campaign to fund and erect a permanent memorial in London's Green Park honouring the 55,573 British and Commonwealth aircrew who died between 1939 and 1945.
>
> The campaign is gaining ground each day but the target sum of £5 million still has some way to go ... Shepherd is deeply dedicated to the campaign to raise money for the memorial. 'We owe them so much,' he said. 'It has taken nearly 70 years to express such gratitude for what they did ...'

## *Aviation parallels – like father, like daughter!*

In recent years, the DSWF have been involved in a four-day fundraising trip to Cyprus, which, as Kay Roudaut, long-time roadshow organiser and nowadays art liaison manager for the

Foundation (see Chapter 8) remembers, 'was great fun and David loved it'. As might be imagined, taking original paintings and trading stock is not an easy task and it was one that was only accomplished as a result of the army flying them out in airline containers. Prior to that, David had, however, a long and wonderful association with Cyprus and RAF Akrotiri; home of the Cyprus Operations Support Unit. It was an association that began in the early 1960s and remains today as a result of his artist daughter Mandy's involvement with the military. So much so that, when it became necessary to become a little more politically correct and rename 'The Ladies' Room' at Akrotiri, it was suggested that it be called 'The Shepherd Room' in recognition of both David and Mandy's long links with the base.

It is an interesting juxtaposition between father and daughter as Mandy began her career in art by firstly painting wildlife and then becoming a military artist, whilst David got his first major painting breaks as a result of his involvement with the RAF and then went on to paint the wildlife for which he was to become internationally famous. Although driven by her father's enthusiasm, Mandy has always forged her own connections but even so, there are parallels between the two artists. Take, for instance, the paintings of various scenes on the Falkland Islands which were commissioned by the military. David's were done from photographs whilst Mandy's were painted as a result of several visits there, initially to paint the wildlife. However, fate has a strange way of altering one's intended path as Mandy was to discover:

At no moment had I ever thought that my love and passion for wildlife and conservation would lead the way into the world of military art. How could I have known when I flew to the Falklands in January 1996 to write and illustrate a book [on wildlife] that my journey would open a window onto a world well beyond the realms of stunning landscape, fauna and flora of those beautiful South Atlantic islands.

Once on the Falklands and subsequently visiting various military mess rooms, it rather surprised Mandy to come across aircraft paintings of Buccaneers and Jaguars painted and signed by her father. But perhaps it is not so surprising as throughout his life, David had been commissioned to paint many aviation and military subjects not necessarily meant to have been seen by the general public and which were instead, intended exactly for such places. They are, however, important records of military history – an example of which can be seen in the 1971 BBC documentary *The Man Who Loves Giants* (see Chapter 11) where there is a sequence showing the refuelling of an aircraft in flight with David in the plane watching and frantically drawing sketches and taking notes.

*Not seen in public*
Although not always necessarily relevant to either the RAF or the military, many paintings which are connected to David's artistic life in the 1950s, occasionally appear from nowhere – of which there are no records, and of which the current Shepherd family have never previously been aware. John Bulmer, a friend of Mandy's with a long interest in David's work and with a long career in aviation, emailed in January 2020 with photos of two paintings of BEA Vickers Viscounts painted by David in 1953. John wrote, 'They probably haven't been seen in public for over 30 years … [and] the reason I am confident about that statement is that I found them in the BAE Systems archive at Farnborough yesterday!'

***

## Airborne Forces and the DSWF – a joint venture and royal support

The year 1990 was the fiftieth anniversary ('PARA 90') of the foundation of Airborne Forces – a division of the British Army that originally included the Parachute Regiment and battalions or units of other regiments, services and corps, and the SAS and Glider Pilots regiments. It also marked thirty years' work dedicated to wildlife conservation by David. Thus it seemed wholly appropriate that to tie in with both, the joint celebration be celebrated by a book of cartoons, an exhibition, and an auction embracing the two themes. All royalties from the book sales and all of the proceeds from the auction were split between the Airborne Forces Charities Development Trust and David's own wildlife foundation.

In the book's foreword, HRH Prince Charles, talked of the Airborne Forces having 'cared for members and their families since it was set up in 1942', and that 'The 1990s will bring its biggest task so far, to help the tens of thousands who served in The Second World War who are now entering their seventies and eighties.

'It is also splendid that this fund should be associated with the work of David Shepherd, who has personally raised well over a million pounds for wildlife and other charities. He has formed a charitable foundation to act as its own "rapid intervention force" to support wildlife and conservation projects. And this appeal is to support that Foundation too.'

* * *

*Creating an atmosphere*
Alongside the all-important issues of drawing, composition and light, creating 'atmosphere' in his paintings was essential to David. A nostalgic Second World War painting, *Winter of '43, Somewhere in England* has a somewhat casual atmospheric tension. Working on it in 1977 gave David the opportunity to return to aviation art – which he had almost totally neglected for several years:

I hope I have been able to evoke, in [this] painting, the memories and feelings which must still be fresh in the minds of ground and aircrew, now dispersed all over the world, and who flew 'Lancs' with the Royal Air Force during those momentous days of World War II. How many must still remember 'their' Lanc, at far-flung dispersals; a watery sun casting long shadows on a chill autumn evening; the leafless elms of a countryside 'somewhere in England; the wet runway and the mud; and all the untidy clutter of last-minute preparations before take-off; final adjustments to an engine – 'the revs were a bit low on the port inner over Essen, Fred – it's Cologne tonight, so get 'em right' – and the inevitable bicycles. I hope it is all there, that 'feeling' of those historic times.

David donated the earnings from the entire print edition of *Winter of '43* to the RAF Benevolent Fund, and in doing so raised £96,000 (a not inconsiderable sum in the 1970s) for the proposed extension to Princess Marina House, the RAF Benevolent Fund's convalescent and residential home at Rustington, Sussex. Both Sir Barnes Wallis (inventor of the ingenious 'bouncing bomb' used so effectively by the wartime 'Dambusters') and 'Bomber' Harris, C-in-C Bomber Command 1942–45, agreed to sign a limited number of prints after they had been purchased, for donations of a further £100 to the fund.

However, according to David, one of the best compliments he ever received was when someone told him that they could smell the atmosphere in a painting commissioned by the Green Howards. *Checkpoint at Forkhill* depicted some of the regiment on active duty at the time of The Troubles in Ireland and showed soldiers checking under the bonnet of a Ford Escort car, a helicopter overhead and, in the undergrowth of the right-hand verge, an armed soldier crouched down and looking ahead for possible attack. It was a very extraordinary scene on a very ordinary stretch of an Irish country road. As the complimentary observer remarked, 'The tension of the moment simply flowed through the artist's paint brush onto the canvas with such utter realism that it was possible to smell the sense of fear and the highly-charged feeling that anything could happen.'

### The military connection

The painting of *Christ on the Battlefield* for the reredos (an ornamental screen covering the wall at the back of an altar) at

St George's, the army garrison church at Bordon Camp, near Petersfield, Hampshire, is considered by many to be one of David's finest works. It is, without doubt, the one painting for which David always said he would like to be remembered. At 6 m (20 ft) by 2.5 m (8 ft) it's certainly one of his largest paintings and features possibly his most unusual subject matter.

David always said that the portrait (painted in the 1960s) despite him being neither religious nor an atheist, had always meant a great deal to him. Asked about the painting in an interview for the *Metro* conducted by Kieran Meeke in 2009, David mentioned that the commission was such an incredible undertaking for many reasons, including finding the correct model and costume. 'The challenge was terrifying because the money that was paid to me – though I got practically nothing for it – was raised through an appeal to those who had lost sons and fathers in Korea or the Second World War so I had a huge responsibility to get things right.'

Before all that, there was an enormous amount of research to be done due to the fact that all of the regiments which had been stationed at Bordon over the years had to be represented in the form of cameos surrounding the central figure. On the point of pose and dress, David loved that the military were very broadminded and had told him 'We don't want fat cherubs floating all over the place. We want a realistic portrayal of Christ as a man, which will bring the men into church. Nor do we want a lot of modern rubbish, squares and triangles, and all that stuff.'

With such an undoubtedly daunting challenge ahead, David was reluctant to make a start on the work until long after the commission had been agreed and in fact, left it so long that in the end, he had only three weeks in which to complete it before the date of the consecration service – and made himself 'ill with worry' in the process.

### The model and dress for Christ
An article in the *Farnham Herald* eventually solved the problem of a suitable model. They had heard of someone working for the

Forestry Commission based at Alice Holt who was known as 'Jesus' by everyone due to his long hair. His real name was David Winter and he was introduced to David by a journalist from the newspaper. When he took Winter to David's studio, it was, as the artist described it, 'Just like Christ walking into the room'. The would-be model had never been in an artist's studio before, but after chatting together, he agreed to sit for a small fee.

David Shepherd thought David Winter 'incredible' as a model. 'I painted him in five days. He stood absolutely still and as rigid as a rock … Sitting is hard enough without moving; standing is a lot harder. David stood on that dais while I painted his costume in one go, a session that lasted nearly five and a half hours.'

As far as the costume was concerned, David had in mind something similar to that worn in *The Robe*, a film starring Charlton Heston: as the artist described it, 'a simple white costume tied around the waist with a cord, and with a lovely rust-red robe of homespun material over his shoulder'. Finding such attire was not, however, as straightforward as one might think and after several fruitless and frustrating visits to several theatrical costumiers, Avril came to the rescue and agreed to make it. 'She and I we went up to London, walked into the first suitable store in Oxford Street, and there was all the material we needed, in a sale, on the front counter.'

### *'I just painted it!'*

David visited the portrait of Christ on several occasions whilst it was at Bordon and, as his last PA, Sue Rose, remembers: 'he would always be emotional' on seeing it again. Eric Birkett, then verger also recollects these visits and, on one occasion, the fact that David insisted on touching up small pieces of the painting before allowing the church to print off 250 copies intended to be sold for charitable purposes. The visits didn't all involve work though – as Eric was later to remark 'He had a great time at the church playing with my golden retriever, Brindle. I have photos of him rolling over the floor with [the dog] … It really showed how much he loved animals of any kind.'

In June 2015, St George's Garrison Church was decommissioned after a century of service, during half of which period David's painting had provided the backdrop to the altar. As Lawrence Tristram, warden of the church, said at the time, it was sad that the painting was having to be moved: 'It's a fantastic painting, you can actually get lost in it and have a reflection on everything.' It was subsequently transported to the Chaplaincy Centre Chapel of Saint George, MOD Lyneham, near Chippenham, Wiltshire and Sue took him to see it there – and noted that he was angry about the move as the painting had been in storage for a year and he was anxious about its well-being. Also, once it was eventually hung, he apparently didn't like the fact that it was in a modern church, and was also somewhat scathing about the lighting chosen!

Others thought differently and one of the chaplains at its new home believed that there was a huge amount of spiritual guidance behind the way it was painted and was persistent in asking David about the possible nuances and significance of almost every brushstroke. In the end, David was forced to say 'I just painted it' – a response which visibly disappointed his questioner!

Asked in the *Metro* interview whether he would ever consider anything similar, David's comment was, one would assume, somewhat tongue-in-cheek: 'I'd love to paint a crucifixion, which is an extraordinary thing to say, but it is a challenge … The trouble is, you can't find enough people who are prepared to be crucified [and you would] have to crucify the model to get the hang of the muscles in the hands.'

### Humbled

Whilst the painting of *Christ on the Battlefield* might be the one for which the artist would most like to be remembered, it was, according to his artist daughter Mandy, the scenes of the army in Northern Ireland at the height of the IRA bombings which changed his perspective of life and brought him back to basics. As an artist commissioned to record the scenes of daily life, 'It made him realise that, in that particular situation, he was just a tiny cog in a wheel of a world where people were actually always at risk of their lives.' He was, she says, 'humbled by Northern Ireland … he felt uncomfortable and nervous.' Of his depiction of *Ardoyne Patrol* – a scene in which mothers, children (including a baby in a pram) stand on a street corner whilst an army patrol walks behind them and, above their heads, on a wall behind them is IRA graffiti – David wrote the following:

When the Green Howards asked me to paint Northern Ireland, my first reaction was to decline. However, they asked for a painting to portray the day-to-day life of the foot soldier in such a setting and I thought this would be an interesting challenge so I was flown out to Belfast to see for myself. On my arrival it was decided that … I would have to be escorted by an army patrol. There was good reason for this. The Parachute Regiment, who would carry out the unenviable task of seeing that I did not do anything stupid, had obviously done their homework. They remembered my last visit to Aden [see below] when I did a painting for them and nearly got my head blown off …

The following day I walked into the Ardoyne from the Crumlin Road. This was an intensely Republican stronghold. I had my camera with me, and within minutes a group of women started spitting at me. It was not a particularly pleasant experience … [nor] was the torrent of filthy language and abuse. I tried to point out that I was an artist, trying to take photos for a painting. They were unconvinced; looking at the Parachute Regiment patrol and armoured personnel carrier behind me, one of the women said, 'If you were a f … artist you wouldn't need the f … Brits behind you; you're f … Special Branch'.

I wandered further down into the ghettos of the Ardoyne, and saw scenes of devastation and squalor the likes of which I had never experienced before; rows of gutted houses, with high fences down the middle if that particular street happened to be Catholic on one side and Protestant on the other … Yet, amongst all this awfulness, with the walls covered in obscene graffiti, I passed a house where, in the open doorway, a lady stood watching me. As I passed she said, 'Come in and have a cup of tea, dear?' ... This particular person was desperately trying to hang on to a thread of normality in a totally abnormal situation ...

## Aden, Checkpoint Golf – First Light

David's trip to Aden in 1967, was, like the streets of Northern Ireland a decade or so later, not necessarily the best place to be either as a serving soldier or a commissioned war artist. The Parachute Regiment had asked for a painting of Checkpoint Golf – a fortified position containing a sandbag observation post and a rooftop gun emplacement and, always enthusiastic and excitable and yet to savour the sobering experiences of Northern Ireland, David seemingly caused the officer in charge certain problems when it came to ensuring the artist's safety:

[W]henever anything of interest seemed to be happening down below, I would insist on jumping up onto the sandbags with my camera! One of the soldiers who happened to have a camera did, in fact, snap me taking my photos in a somewhat exposed position, with an exasperated officer imploring me to get down otherwise I would probably have had my head blown off ... I survived, more by good luck than anything else, and I think the painting has an extra realism about it because I was there. Three weeks later, we pulled out, and left Aden to its fate.

## Arnhem Bridge, 5pm, The Second Day

In September 1944, Operation Market Garden was intended to open a direct path for the Allied armies to circumvent the West Wall and threaten Germany's industrial Ruhr heartland. British, American and Polish airborne forces were ordered to assault and capture key bridges along the main highway leading through Holland, the Arnhem Bridge being the most distant of them all. Unfortunately, the Allies had gravely underestimated the strength of German forces in the area; so, when the airborne forces landed, they found themselves scattered amid an SS Panzer division. The various bridges thus became the fulcrum of the entire operation for both sides and Arnhem became legendary in the history of the Second World War.

No wonder then, that David was honoured to be asked by the 2nd Battalion of the Parachute Regiment to paint a scene of the bridge:

We decided right at the beginning that we would endeavour to portray an actual moment of the battle. We discovered that a RAF Mosquito had flown over the bridge just as a column of German trucks and tanks were coming over it, and had taken a photograph. This was on the second day, at five in the evening. The Germans didn't see the men of the 2nd Battalion dug in on the ramparts of the bridge and the whole column was 'brewed up'.

We enlarged the photo taken by the Mosquito and an amazing amount of detail came to life that had not previously been deciphered. For example, what had just been a blur turned out to be a knocked-out German truck below the bridge, so this detail went into the picture. I tried to portray those incredible hours where hand-to-hand fighting was taking place on and below the bridge, with the British on one side of the approach road and the Germans on the other.

Reprinted in many formats since its original publication in 1974, several editions of Cornelius Ryan's book *A Bridge Too Far* feature David's depiction of the scene at the bridge – as does the cover artwork of *Arnhem: The Furthest Bridge*, a video/DVD game for two players, produced in 2010.

## The Iranian Siege

Before describing the reasons why David was asked to depict the scene during the siege of the London Iranian Embassy between 30 April and 5 May 1980, it's necessary to explain a little of the background behind the incident that had most of the UK population glued to their radios and televisions waiting for the latest news update.

Margaret Thatcher was Prime Minister and William Whitelaw her Home Secretary when an Arab terrorist group took over the embassy and made various demands. Contingency plans following the 1972 Munich Olympics terrorist incident had seen the SAS made responsible for any armed response to a terrorist incident in the UK, so within hours of the hostages being taken, they were deployed from Hereford to the embassy at Princes Gate, South Kensington, in order to prepare for if the operation had to be resolved by force. They were stationed in the next door building together with the UK intelligence security services, MI6 and GCHQ. Together they began building a profile of the terrorists in order to understand the level of threat and danger to the hostages, until, on the sixth day of the siege, the SAS finally and successfully made an assault on the building as a result of a hostage having been executed by the terrorists.

In the past, the regiment had commissioned David to depict previous campaigns including Malaya in the 1950s and Operation Mirbat in Oman in the Dofar war – the original paintings of which hung in the officers' mess in Hereford – so, in keeping with previous commissions, it was logical that they would approach David in order to see if he would be willing to capture the events inside the Iranian Embassy as there was, for obvious reasons, no photographs or film of the events as they had unfolded inside.

David enthusiastically took on the commission, firstly travelling to Hereford to meet B Squadron in 1982 on their return from the Falkland Islands. Two further research meetings took place: one at Brampton House, a stately home in Herefordshire, which had a similar staircase to the one in the embassy and where they re-enacted the siege with David's youngest daughter Wendy playing the part of one of the hostages. Secondly, David visited the Iranian Embassy in a trip jointly organised by the Metropolitan Police and the regiment in order to see the interior of the badly damaged embassy – including the central staircase which was to become the setting for the painting, known as *16 Princes Gate – 5th May 1980 (The Final Scene as the Last of the*

*Terrorists are Dealt with and the Hostages are Safely Evacuated from the Embassy).*

### Unexpected consequences

The painting commission proved to have unexpected consequences for the Shepherd family. At the time of the commission, Major Graeme Lamb – now Lieutenant General (Rtd) Sir Graeme Lamb – was commanding B Squadron, having taken over on their return from the Falkland Islands, and David Juster was the senior troop commander who had also been in the Falklands and subsequently led one of the assault teams at the embassy siege itself. During the research necessary for the painting, both Graeme and Juster struck up a friendship with David, Avril and the rest of the Shepherd family: a friendship which eventually resulted in Graeme's marriage to their daughter Melanie in April 1984. After the ceremony at St Peter's Church, Hascombe (at which David Juster was Graeme's best man) the couple drove the short distance back to Winkworth Farm in an SAS 'Pink Panther' Land Rover. With the whole of B Squadron in attendance, there's no wonder that the wedding was a unique and riotous occasion!

### Walking With The Wounded

As their website (www.walkingwiththewounded.org.uk) explains: 'Established in 2010, Walking With The Wounded supports a pathway for vulnerable [military] veterans to re-integrate back into society and sustain their independence. At the heart of this journey is employment ... We recognise the inherent skills of our armed service personnel and want to complement these qualities, as well as provide support to transfer their skills into the civilian workplace. We offer assistance through our programmes to those ... who have been physically, mentally or socially disadvantaged by their service and assist them in sustaining their independence through new sustainable careers outside of the military. This includes providing support to homeless veterans and veterans in the Criminal Justice System, areas which are too often ignored.' It is an organisation supported by both Mandy and David, and in

2002 he donated a painting of an elephant charging through the African bush which raised a five-figure sum at auction.

As with the joint venture with Airborne Forces (see above) and as is so often the case with David's fundraising, the money was intended to assist both the military charity and wildlife and as such, helped fund a British armed forces expedition to Zambia to help wildlife conservation authorities in their battle against poachers. Known as Operation Helping Hand, thirty-eight Royal Electrical and Mechanical Engineers and RAF personnel took part, taking with them five Land Rovers (reconditioned by themselves) together with vehicle spares, for use by Zambian game wardens. At the time, but before the expedition took place, David was quoted as saying 'These men and women from REME and the RAF will save the wildlife authorities £100,000 in repair bills alone and that's money we can plough into wildlife conservation … In just two weeks they can repair thirty-eight vehicles, twenty radios, two boats, thirty-six weapons, two boreholes and countless other pieces of essential equipment.'

## In the navy

In 1978, David was commissioned to paint the aircraft carrier HMS *Ark Royal* on her final voyage, and to do so he travelled with her on an eight-day trip. As he told Sue Lawley on *Desert Island Discs* in 1999, 'It was marvellous being able to ask the captain to change the direction of the 50,000-ton ship just so that the sun and shadows were just right for the painting!'

*The Ark, Turning Into Wind* was commissioned by the Fleet Air Arm Museum at Yeovilton and a print run of the original painting went on to raise a considerable sum for the museum. The Royal Navy flew David out to Malta in order to join up with the ship on her way back to the scrapyard but, once on board, he in fact spent a great deal of the voyage above its decks in an air-sea rescue Wessex helicopter, the better to see an overall view. David was later to blame the experience for his 'inflated ego' which he said, was brought about by the power he, as a civilian, had on the ship's movements – and from a distance too:

It occurred to me that if the carrier swung a few degrees to starboard, this might inspire some further ideas for the painting. In radio contact with the captain via the helicopter pilot I asked, therefore, if he could turn just for me, and minutes later the great ship started to swing round. I got quite carried away by this and, by the end of five days, when the captain and I were on Christian name terms, I was well and truly playing with the *Ark Royal*. On one occasion the sun was in the wrong place and, as it was easier to move the ship than it was to move the sun, Captain Anson began turning to go all the way back to Malta … I duly apologised for all the trouble I had caused. 'Don't worry, David,' said the captain, 'it gave the navigator something to do, going home in a zigzag instead of a straight line.'

I I

# ROADSHOWS AND AUDIENCES

David liked nothing better than being centre of attention and in the limelight – and put it to good use. His charm and charisma wooed many an audience during his numerous roadshows and personal appearances around the country.

In the early days – and long before the time of social media – David needed to publicise himself in order to best sell his artwork. As his paintings, his interest in railway preservation and wildlife welfare became nationally and internationally known, he was increasingly in demand as a radio and television guest and personality (the word 'celebrity' was not used back then). He definitely used his profile to its best advantage – most certainly whenever and wherever the importance of the need for wildlife conservation was concerned – and much of his time was given over to public appearances that were likely to prove fundraisers.

Always approachable, in 2011 the organisers of an arts festival at nearby East Grinstead contacted David after another locally-based, well-known figure (the singer Peter Andre) who had initially agreed to open the event, had to cry off at short notice. Would David be able to take his place? Yes, fortunately he could and would be happy to do so. But what of a fee or something in exchange for his time? His reply was typical: '[Just] a chance to speak about the plight of wildlife and the work of the foundation and to display some brochures at the event somewhere.' The organisers were then delighted when not only did David turn up promptly, he 'stayed for several hours chatting with locals and even at one point, picking up a paintbrush to join in a group mural painting. He also agreed to come along a few days later to an art workshop we were delivering to local children and to which he turned up with his latest tiger painting ... he then went round the children looking at their work and giving encouragement and, as ever, talking to them about his beloved wildlife'.

## *Make them laugh!*

Any occasion, evening, daytime or even a whole weekend spent in David's company was likely to draw crowds. He had a huge following, many of whom would attend various functions with amazing regularity. Even though the format and many of the anecdotes remained exactly the same, no one seemed to mind – perhaps his greatest attribute being that he could engage with audiences at any level whether they be the 'ordinary person' (whoever that might be) royalty, lords and ladies or schoolchildren. He could also always, as the old show business adage has it, 'make them laugh', even at the expense of himself.

His ego notwithstanding, he was frequently self-deprecating: 'I often got confused with David Sheppard [who was the Bishop of Liverpool from 1975 to 1997]. The BBC used to ring me up and ask me onto their programmes to talk of ecclesiastical matters ...' In his chat shows he also regularly mentioned how his appearance on Thames Television's *This is Your Life* (see below) didn't go down well with everybody: 'When we'd finished, I heard one lady from the audience say to her friend, "You know Doris, I love this programme, but that was boring, I still don't know who the hell that was."'

Rotary Club dinners were always a good source of fundraising revenue. A tiny painting David once donated to a local charity raised £11,000 on one particular night. Unable to attend the event due to other commitments, he later discovered that the purchaser was a fruit and vegetable salesman with a market stall so, wanting to thank him for his generosity, David sought him out the next time he was in the area: 'I put my hand across the fruit and said, "Charlie, I just want to thank you for being so tremendously generous the other night in Guildford. I am David Shepherd … thank you for giving £11,000 towards wildlife conservation and for my little painting." His reply was immediate. "Oh, that's all right, mate. I sold the painting at a profit to somebody else the next morning."'

Whilst rejections to his enthusiastic offer to become a game warden in Kenya and his application to the Slade School of Fine Art undoubtedly knocked back David's confidence at the time, very little in his future life was to prove to do so and he coped with other family members taking the limelight with that self-same deprecation. In an interview with the *Express* newspaper in 1997, David commented on the fact that daughters Mandy and Melanie were becoming quite famous in their own right – Melanie for sharing and continuing his passion of wildlife conservation as CEO of the DSWF, and Mandy for her artwork. Of the latter, he said, 'Mandy has done a lot of work in Zambia where I am also quite well known. But one evening, at a big conservation party in Lusaka, I was introduced as Mandy's father. It definitely deflated my ego…'

Judy, David's sister, despite having become famous as an international showjumper in the 1960s and being extremely well known in the horse world (as she continues to be today) was nevertheless, well-used to being introduced to people as being 'David Shepherd's sister' – until one day 'I was pleasantly surprised to hear David introduced to someone as Judy Crago's brother … it quite made my day!'

### Always the exhibitionist!

At the very height of his success – and before he had his own extremely valid reasons for fundraising – David was frequently being asked for a painting to be donated to many worthwhile charities. Whilst it was all very flattering and certainly a boost to the artist's ego, it wasn't always possible to fulfil every request. Some did, nevertheless, appeal; especially those which – as with the occasion mentioned above – benefited local organisations. One in particular remained strong in the artist's mind, and he recalled it in the revised edition of *The Man Who Loves Giants* (1989):

> For many years now I have regularly given a small wildlife painting to raise funds for local charities at a black-tie dinner held in Guildford Civic Hall and organised by Guildford Rotary. The auction always takes place when everyone is nice and plastered – quite the best time to get money out of people – and Guildford is wonderfully generous. [On one occasion] I volunteered to actually paint an elephant painting in oils on the table at which I was sitting.
>
> I did most of the painting in advance to give it time to dry and then, come the evening… the auctioneer announced, 'David Shepherd is going to do something rather special.' We cleared away the tablecloth and I pulled out my oil paints from under the table where they had been hidden. Taking my dinner jacket off, I then climbed onto the table and spent five minutes 'finishing' the painting to the astonishment of all around me. Then, in a loud voice … I said, 'Has anyone got a power-saw?' … One gentleman sitting at his table on the balcony of the hall had been let into the secret: 'I've got one.' He then lowered the power-saw over the balcony on a rope, I pulled the toggle to start it and then, accompanied by clouds of sawdust and a ripping noise, I sawed through the table top of the still wet painting. The entire audience of some 250 people stared in astonishment. Even more amazed was the manager of the Civic Hall. He couldn't speak; he stood with his mouth open in complete bewilderment as he saw one of his tables being destroyed.

At Chester Zoo, Penny Rudd (chair of the North West Group of Flora and Fauna International) shared a few good social evenings with David over a glass or two of red wine – and one where the artist, as Penny describes it: ' … flamboyantly signed the bonnet of my car with car paint'. More impressive in Penny's mind, however, was his ability to 'brilliantly communicate with audiences about the need for action to save species'.

Through The Wildlife Art Society International (TWASI) David inspired many other wildlife artists to donate their artwork for conservation causes, some auctions for which were held at Christie's where David, as the auctioneer, ensured that they were hilarious – and profitable – events. Elsewhere, Karen McGowen's father was a trustee of the Wildlife Society in Malawi and remembers that David attended one of their fundraisers and that, apart from the original painting which David had donated, 'David's charisma along with flowing wine, kept the room vibrant and [that] he even got people to bid for a signed elephant dropping!'

* * *

## Just chatting

Mark Carwardine, zoologist, environmental activist, writer/author and wildlife photographer, quite often found himself on stage with David:

David and I gave many talks and speeches together over the years, about wildlife and conservation. We rarely planned anything in advance, preferring to bounce off one another and ad lib. Just chat and see where we ended up. He had a wicked sense of humour and we frequently found ourselves, on stage, collapsed in heaps of giggles. But he also had an awful lot to say – often saying it in a very long-winded way – and it could sometimes be quite difficult to get a word in edgeways. I remember, on one occasion, he just wouldn't shut up and we were rapidly running out of time. So I made a big play of grabbing the microphone cable and melodramatically feeling my way down to the cable to the plug. David, needless to say, kept going. Then I unplugged the microphone. He was in full flow and, for a few moments, still didn't realise what I had done. Then he stopped talking. And burst into that wonderful spontaneous, contagious laughter. The entire audience joined in.

** * **

## Time spent with ...

Evenings, daytime venues, a whole weekend, it was all the same to David who, throughout his public life, would give of his time (and artistic efforts) generously, especially when it came to fundraising. It wasn't exclusively to the benefit of his own charity though, and many others found themselves fortunate in being able to include a charismatic artist as part of their promotion for their particular event – with the proviso that at least a part of their revenue for the time would go to help the current projects being sponsored by the DSWF. There were many such joint ventures where the ticket profits would be split 50/50.

On other occasions not directly involved with the Foundation, David always gave his time for free – provided that the DSWF was likely to be rewarded in some small way, be it through publicity, the sale of raffle tickets or via a table or in a small tent at an outdoor venue through the sale of prints and merchandise. A brilliant salesman – of both himself and his 'product' – many were anxious to include his presence knowing that by doing so, audience numbers would be guaranteed.

Ego notwithstanding, David would hardly ever say 'no'. There were certainly few things that held his interest for which he wouldn't travel and agree to speak, or just to be there as a presence – a presence which all enjoyed. He enjoyed their company too, as one member of the DSWF who attended various such gatherings remembers: 'He just sparkled in whatever situation.'

## An Evening with ...

At the many events at which David was the main attraction, there were certain stipulations to be fulfilled. Unlike many of today's celebrities who might insist on the most bizarre of requirements before agreeing to perform on stage, his were requested more for practical reasons rather than arrogance and self-importance. Kay Roudaut who, for twenty years was mainly responsible for travelling with David and getting props, paintings and whatever else to the venues and who (with a transient team) checked that all was as it should be before David took to the stage, ensured that the organisers had provided, close to hand:

a) Brandy and ginger
b) A tall stool
c) Handheld microphone
d) Visual aids (paintings etc. as brought to the event).

Wherever David was expected to be fed or stay overnight, a further stipulation was that he should be offered no spicy food. As anyone in the family can verify, he was most definitely a plain food eating sort of man. Notes to organisers might well include the following: 'David likes simple English food … cheese, ham, beef, chocolate, ice cream and black tea. Dislikes curries or spicy foods and mayonnaise.' As to attire, unless it was a black-tie dinner, David's preferred wardrobe was of the 'safari' type.

At many events some of David's original artwork was on display, so what with the care needed to transport those alongside all the merchandise and equipment needed, it could quite often be a logistical nightmare requiring plenty of planning. The following itinerary is from a weekend at the Hurst Festival Event, West Sussex, in September 2012 and is typical of many similar occasions:

**Friday** 10.30 – Kay to arrive in David's car with 20 originals – list already supplied. Hang originals. Kay returns car to David's home, and picks up van in Guildford.

Volunteer stays overnight [at venue] with the originals to meet insurance requirements.

**Saturday** 09.00 – DSWF team arrives, unloads and sets up exhibition/sales.
11.00 – David and Avril arrive in their own car.
11.00 – 16.30 – Exhibition and sales throughout day.
18.30 onwards: 'An Evening Audience with David Shepherd' (as agreed format below)

- 19.30 – Introduction…
- 19.33 – Opening DVD (2 minutes)
- 19.34 – DS talks for 40 minutes
- 20.14 – DSWF DVD (8 minutes)
- 20.22 – DS resumes, talks for 10 minutes then takes questions
- 20.45 – Closing remarks …
- 20.50 – DS available for signing, more exhibition sales with drinks
- 22.00 – Evening ends

**Sunday** 11.00–16.30 –Exhibition and sales throughout the day
16.30 onwards – dismantle exhibition and take down originals.

The 'An Evening with …' format was by no means confined to British shores and many took place abroad, especially in America where, for instance, in March 1989 such an evening was held at the Joslyn Art Museum, Omaha, and was held as a joint benefit for the art museum, the Henry Doorly Zoo, the Western Heritage Museum and David's own Foundation. During the evening David autographed books and prints and introduced the auction of one of his paintings, a leather-bound book of prints and a limited-edition print.

*A Weekend with …*
Weekend roadshows and exhibitions were popular with both David and his audiences. They often involved a 'package' created by the organisers in conjunction with the DSWF and might include overnight stays in a hotel, an evening meal and after-dinner speech from David, plus an exhibition and sales of his artwork. Between 2000 and 2007, David participated in a number

of special weekend breaks at some of the ten hotels owned by the Forestdale chain and, according to Clive Jenns, their then Special Interest Breaks manager, they were 'always well-received with the guests and at the same time, raised some good money for the Foundation.'

Several weekends were spent fundraising on Guernsey – a small island, but one on which lived people with sufficient finance to be able to afford to give generously to a charity such as David's. His trips there initially began in 2007 and were a result of meeting Jayne Le Cras at a Lord Taverner's dinner on Sark. Sitting next to one another at the table, she and David soon discovered a mutual love of animals, and big cats in particular. Jayne had, amongst other things, previously worked as a keeper at Guernsey Zoo – and had been asked by the Born Free Foundation if she could consider looking after two rescued eight- or nine-week-old lion cubs from Romania until they were old enough to be taken to one of their two reserves in Africa. Jayne gladly took on the cubs and, as a consequence, her husband Steve asked if David would do a painting of them. David did so and, in personal gratitude but also, more importantly, to benefit wildlife, Jayne approached Melanie, then CEO of the DSWF, to see if they would be prepared to be a part of fundraising weekend on Guernsey. On the guarantee that at least £20,000 would be raised (the first event subsequently netted 'almost double that') thus began several weekends to the Channel Islands – one of which was aimed to coincide with the launch of 'Tiger Time' in 2011, a social-media campaign to raise awareness and funds to save the tiger in the wild.

* * *

## Children's art competitions

An itinerary for a weekend event with David on Guernsey in October 2011 – held at the Farmhouse Hotel, St Saviour – included judging the children's art competition. A part of the programme went as follows: 'Friday 28th … David chooses the category winners in the "Tiger Time" … competition run with all Guernsey schools. Three winners in each age category (7–10 years; 11–14 years; 15–18 years) will be awarded prizes and their work exhibited at the Farmhouse Hotel as part of the weekend event.'

This was just one example of many such competitions aimed at children – and of which David was always extremely supportive.

* * *

### School's out – and in!

No matter what else David did to raise awareness of the perilous situation of some aspects of wildlife, there was always a heartfelt need to educate the young. Never at all patronising or guilty of talking down to them, he would, at any opportunity that proved practicable with regards to his work commitments, always accept an invitation to enter a school classroom and chat to the assembly about conservation issues or various aspects of art. As Kay Roudaut remembers, 'David was brilliant with kids, he loved their cheekiness, their sense of humour.'

Writing in the spring of 2017, David expressed his delight at having recently been chatting with shortlisted entrants of the annual children's Global Canvas Art and Poetry Competition:

> The talent and passion of the children never fails to impress me and it gives me a sense of deep pride to think that these young people, inspired by DSWF, could be the next generation of wildlife guardians … it was an outstanding shortlist, and in my eyes everyone was a winner … That the winners also managed to raise so much money to protect the wildlife that we all love was the icing on the cake.

One of David's favourite questions to ask of a group of assembled schoolchildren was: 'What's the most dangerous animal on earth?' Invariably, enthusiastic youngsters would stick their hands up and, vying for his attention, excitedly shout out 'lions', 'tigers', 'sharks' and go on to list all manner of perceived danger. After a period of time, David would kindly tell them that they were wrong and that 'It is man … man is the most dangerous animal on earth …', thus beginning much thought-provoking discussion.

David's knowledge of wildlife conservation plus his artistic merits made him sought-after by many schools. In the early days of his fame, enterprising head and art teachers would ask him to visit and he would quite readily accept almost any invitation in the interests of education.

Parent Teachers Associations nowadays regularly approach the Foundation, be they a small village primary school, or those of a high profile such as Thomas's Battersea, where in recent times the Duke and Duchess of Cambridge's children, Prince George and Princess Charlotte, have been educated. At St Peter's School, East Grinstead, David's talk to the pupils inspired them so much that they decided to raise money for the DSWF by taking part in an inter-school cross-country race. At Aldro School, Godalming, he opened their art department many years ago, and visited again in 2013 to accept a cheque for money raised from all the pupils designing and selling Christmas cards. Head of Art, Loren Fenwick, remembers: 'The boys who met him loved him. He was so kind and playful with them, especially those who shared his love of trains.' Alice Phillips, headmistress at St Catherine's School, Bramley, said that David went to the school very early in her tenure in order to give a sixth-form lecture: 'I will always remember his humility and readiness to engage with the young people whilst also encouraging them to think big for their own world and their own futures.'

Specifically intended for schoolchildren, in 1995, David, in collaboration with Ginn (today a publishing imprint of Pearson, but still with a long-held, strong tradition for publishing quality educational resources) produced a fully illustrated paperback book entitled *Only One World* – in essence, a very brief résumé of all that he had written in previous books about his life to date but, nevertheless, with attractive illustrations and a very subtle yet definite emphasis towards wildlife conservation. Over a quarter of a century on, copies still remain in some school libraries and continue to be used as a teaching aid on occasion.

Sadly, not only are schools nowadays unable to invite random speakers without due clearance, they generally need to stick to a curriculum set by the various government authorities. Fortunately, for the benefit of wildlife conservation (and thereby David's legacy) the DSWF has since devised an educational file (initially sponsored by the retail group Marks & Spencer) to attract schools should they be so minded.

## *The things people say*

David was occasionally heard to remark that, on occasion, children asked far more intelligent questions and made many more constructive comments than did some members of adult audiences! In one such situation, fascinated by his talk, but nevertheless saddened by the accompanying film which happened to feature a lion attacking its prey, a female member of the audience was moved to ask whether there wasn't something that could be done to change the big cats' habits of generations of evolution and possibly convert them to vegetarianism or at least for the rangers to provide more aesthetically acceptable joints of dead meat. An amusing comment – and somewhat ironical bearing in mind the fact that the lady in question was wearing a leopard-skin coat. David, on realising that the woman was serious, didn't think too long before replying: 'No, madam ... it is difficult enough getting humans to change their habits ... and that includes wearing a second-hand coat ... Do you know that the one you are wearing would have caused the deaths of several animals?'

Another instance where conversation took an unexpected turn was when Avril and David happened to be in India and thought, like all good tourists, that they should visit the Taj Mahal:

Somehow the message got around that I was going to be there so a local Indian bureaucrat came with us and was almost in tears. 'David, our glorious Taj Mahal is falling down through pollution and the weight of tourist feet. I don't know what we are going to do about it.' My reply was brief: 'Build another one.' 'What do you mean?' he asked.

I explained that the Taj Mahal is man-made; the tiger is God-given. 'Stop the bloody poaching,' I said. 'You can build another Taj Mahal, but you can't build another tiger.'

## Desert Island Discs

Some of David's anecdotes were aired by him on *Desert Island Discs*. He is one of only a handful of people to have appeared more than once on this popular BBC Radio 4 programme – firstly when being interviewed by Roy Plomley in September 1971 and then again in January 1999 when Sue Lawley was the presenter.

**Record, book choices and luxury item(s) for the 1971 programme included:**

- Jean Sibelius: *Symphony No. 1 in E minor*
- The Syd Lawrence Orchestra: *Tuxedo Junction*
- Giacomo Puccini: *Love Duet* (with Maria Callas and Nicolai Gedda)
- George Formby: *Mother, What'll I Do Now?*
- Richard Strauss: *Tod und Verklärung* (Death and Transfiguration)
- Frederick Delius: *The Walk to the Paradise Garden*
- Stereo recordings of a steam locomotive
- Gustav Mahler: *Symphony No. 8 in E-flat major 'Symphony of a Thousand'*

**Book:** *Elementary Calculus Volume 1*

**Luxury:** The *Black Prince* steam locomotive, canvases and oil paint.

**Record, book choices and luxury item for the 1999 recording took the form of:**

- Sir Laurence Olivier: *Once More Unto The Breach* – speech from *Henry V* film
- Jean Sibelius: *Symphony No. 1 in E minor*
- Al Bowlly With the New Mayfair Orchestra: *Goodnight Sweetheart*
- Glenn Miller: *Tuxedo Junction*
- Clifton Parker: *Western Approaches* – from *The Guns of Navarone* film
- Sergei Bortkiewicz: *Piano Concerto No. 1 in B-flat major Op. 16*
- Edward Elgar: *The Light of Life – Meditation*
- Gustav Mahler: *Symphony No. 8 in E-flat major 'Symphony of a Thousand'*

**Book:** A *Collection of Beatrix Potter*

**Luxury:** Wind-up video player.

It would appear that his love of Sibelius' *Symphony No. 1 in E minor* and Mahler's *Symphony No. 8 in E-flat major* (the latter his overall record of choice on both occasions) remained with him throughout a long period of his life – as did the Glenn Miller-composed *Tuxedo Junction*. It is, however, interesting that although a record choice in both 1971 and 1999, for the first, David chose a Syd Lawrence Orchestra recording rather than, as he did in 1999, Miller's original rendition. As to the reason for his book choice of 1971 (*Elementary Calculus Volume 1*) that remains a total mystery. Whilst it is still possible to hear all of the 1999 *Desert Island Discs* with Sue Lawley online via BBC links, unfortunately the one recorded with Roy Plomley only runs for the first ten minutes of the programme and so the part where the interviewee is normally heard to choose their luxury item and one book – and give their reasons for doing so – is omitted.

***

## Radio and unexpected benefits!

In 1963, David made his third appearance on BBC Radio 2's John Dunn evening programme which had a regular listenership of around two million. Unsurprisingly, the host asked about David's *Wise Old Elephant* painting – or 'Elephant in Boots' as David had begun to scathingly refer to it due to the fact that Boots the chemists was where the print was being sold:

> It was a live programme and we were talking about my 'Elephant in Boots': laughter all round. I said to John, 'If I go on plugging Boots like this, it's time they did something for me': more laughter. Boots were obviously listening because, three days later, a gigantic box full of deodorants and hair sprays arrived for my wife, with 'the compliments of the company'. So my elephants have helped Avril too.

* * *

*Television*

David's first invite to appear on a television chat show came from David Frost in 1967. The programme was to cover the recent interest in mass-produced prints, and because of the success of David's *Wise Old Elephant*, Frost and his producers wanted a popular artist's opinion regarding the mass market and the somewhat 'snobby' attitude of the art establishment. David was paid £40 for his appearance (far more than he was asking for some of his paintings at the time) and it was after taking part in David Frost's show that he began to realise that it was time to progress upwards into limited editions in order to retain his credibility. With that in mind, *March Sunlight*, published that year, was to become David's last ever mass-produced print.

### The Man Who Loves Giants

Whilst *The Man Who Loves Giants* was used as the title for David's 1975 autobiography, it had, in fact, first been used for a documentary featuring David, his work and interests which was shown on BBC 2 at 2.20 p.m. on Christmas Day, 1971 – the voice-over being supplied by Hollywood actor and great friend of the Shepherd family, James (Jimmy) Stewart. It says a lot for David's popularity that the BBC felt a programme such as this could complete with more typical Christmas viewing such as the likes of Morecambe and Wise, who attracted huge audiences.

Beginning in Africa and touching on his incredible efforts towards wildlife conservation, the programme went on to document how David was asked by the RAF to reproduce, on canvas, the refuelling of an aircraft in flight and showed his dedication and diligence in restoring locomotives, founding the East Somerset Railway and, of course, his painting prowess.

Pamela Jackson, production assistant on *The World About Us* series which featured *The Man Who Loves Giants*, recollects David's huge enthusiasm for everything and the privilege of being able to get so close to the elephants – and also the fact that one of the wildlife rangers looking after them took rather a fancy to the desert boots they were all wearing; so much so that 'David asked me if it was possible for me to leave some with Nelson when we finished filming – so we came home minus one pair of boots but left behind a very happy ranger!'

## Nature Watch

David and his passion for elephants featured again some twenty years later (1990) in the *Nature Watch* series compered by Julian Pettifer, made by Central Television and shown on Channel 4. Entitled *All for the Elephant*, this particular episode focused on David's attempt to raise £1 million for elephant conservation – half of which sum was secured by the sale of prints of one of his paintings from that year, *The Ivory is Theirs*.

## In Search of Wildlife

In 1987, David was co-presenter on *In Search of Wildlife*, a series of six half-hour programmes for Thames Television, which were later also shown on US screens and helped increase awareness of

David's various conservation projects amongst American viewers. The programmes were well received on both sides of the Atlantic, the reason for which David attributed to the fact that they were different in format to many other wildlife films previously seen on television:

> First of all, I was painting the landscape and the animals concerned in each film, and painting being highly visual, is perhaps ideal for television. Moreover, I was the person who was learning. I have said many times that I am in no way an ecologist and in each of the films I was with an expert who was telling me all about the particular species we were featuring.
>
> The films were also different in so far as virtually all the dialogue was completely unprepared with no script and all was done on location. I think that the six films benefited from this spontaneity, but it created fearful problems for the producer. Whenever I saw anything new or exciting, I got carried away with the exhilaration of it all and I was then impossible to film!

## Last Train to Mulobezi

In 1976, BBC Television showed a documentary featuring David and his involvement with the rescue and preservation of two steam locomotives both built in Glasgow, one in 1896 the other in 1922, and a vintage (1927) passenger sleeping carriage from the Zambezi Sawmills Railway.

The *Last Train to Mulobezi* chronicled the story of the railway, the two engines and the carriage and how David eventually acquired them – and how it was hoped that all could be brought straight back to England. However, as events were subsequently to prove, logistics, both political and financial, made things difficult and only No. 993, – '7A Class 4-8-0' and carriage – was to eventually arrive in the UK at Manchester docks (see Chapter 9). It all went towards creating a fascinating programme.

### *Film night for the locals*

A few years after *Last Train to Mulobezi* was completed, David had cause to be back in Mulobezi – and so took a copy of the film with him and suggested that it might be screened for all the locals who had taken part. It was to be an evening that remained forever in David's mind:

> When we heard how many people from the surrounding villages were coming … (some walking twenty miles through the bush!) we realised that we must show the film in the open air. Power for the projector was supplied by a portable generator and the audience of several hundred Africans sat on the ground in front of a white sheet hung from a scaffolding frame. From the first moment that the film was on the screen, the noise was so great that we decided to turn the sound right off and run the film silent. As soon as the show was over, the audience clamoured for a second showing. This time I suggested that I should tell them a little bit about the film … I stood in the arena lit by the headlights of a Land Rover. They listened in rapt silence as I told the story. We then put the film on for a second time with the sound and you could have heard a pin drop.
>
> It amused me to notice the audience's reaction … When a particular friend of theirs, for instance the driver of the Class 10 who was well known to all of them for his eccentric behaviour, appeared, they erupted with laughter and cat calls. That's audience participation!

## Away Day

In August 1989, BBC 1 screened *Away Day*, in which David met up with Shakespearean actor Peter McEnery and they spent a day together on the Severn Valley Railway whilst sharing their mutual love of all things steam. The two obviously hit it off together and discussed, amongst other things, how much better it is when steam locomotives are given a name rather than simply being referred to by the number they are 'registered'. The half-hour programme is still available to watch via YouTube and makes for charming viewing whether or not one is a 'train freak' – as railway enthusiasts are described in the programme's synopsis and opening credits.

## This Is Your Life

As, by his own admission, David loved being the centre of attention, appearing on Thames Television's *This Is Your Life* in February 1990 was a self-indulgent delight to him and he gloried in being, quite literally, in the spotlight and having kind words said about him by family and friends. It was quite a line-up of guests too, as David recalled when writing about his experience some five years later:

I came on the stage at Teddington Studios and was confronted by some hundred of our friends, all of whom had been let in on the secret ... Right from the start I was so emotional I could hardly speak. Avril obviously came in first ... Then, one by one, friends who I had not seen for years, or who had played a significant part in my life ... Peter Mumford came on. He was the man who had taken pity on me when I was on my beam ends in Kenya, and given me a job in his hotel in Malindi. The late and much-missed Bill Travers came on with his wife, Virginia McKenna. Then, Robin Goodwin: the programme would not have been the same without him.

Perhaps the most moving thing of all was the fact that the researchers had flown over to Hollywood and interviewed James Stewart in Beverly Hills... [and] to Zambia to interview the President, Dr Kenneth Kaunda; and Prince Bernhard of the Netherlands, another close and very dear friend, then said some flattering things about me. He was followed by His Royal Highness Prince Michael of Kent ... By this time I was almost speechless with emotion.

I had noticed that there was one empty seat at the end of the row; next to three of our four daughters. Could this ... be for our youngest daughter, Wendy, who might be flying in from America? I did at least guess that much but there was more ... It happened that just before the programme was going to be televised, Avril and I were spending a day in London [and, during that day] Thames television [had] gathered all our grandchildren together in my studio [at Winkworth] and invited them to paint elephants.

As a climax to the programme, all the little ones came onto the set holding their artistic efforts, to the enthusiastic cheers of the audience.

## Animal Magic – *and more*

In addition to television programmes about himself, his paintings, conservation and his eclectic interests, over the years David appeared in many other programmes, including *The Painter and the Engines* (1967), as a celebrity guest on *The Golden Shot* (1969), the hugely popular *Animal Magic* hosted by Johnny Morris on children's television (1975), as a celebrity guest on the antiques programme *Going for a Song* (1976), in the tenth series of *Parkinson* interviewed by Michael Parkinson alongside photojournalist Don McCullin and opera and concert singer Ian Wallace (1981), and *Wildlife Talkabout* (1982).

## *Fundraising*

Although much of the above has been in aid of fundraising for his beloved wildlife, there's the well-known saying that 'charity begins at home' and with that in mind, David and Avril have never been afraid to throw open the doors of their home if it was likely to bring in much-needed money for the DSWF and the various projects it supports.

Such occasions might be something as simple as cream teas to include a look around the artist's studio and gallery or something far more substantial (and infinitely more expensive) such as the event organised at Winkworth Farm with William and Ffion Hague as guests of honour. As David remembered, 'Everybody paid £500 a head to eat very good canapés and [drink] champagne. Hague was a super guy and Ffion gave me a hug and said: "You're a star" – so that made me a Tory even if I wasn't one before.' That event was such a success that David and Avril then hosted a similar event at Brooklands some years later – at which the guest-of-honour was Iain Duncan-Smith and his wife Betsy. Although the tickets for this event were £100 more than at Winkworth, one arguably got more for one's money, as this time it was a sit-down dinner!

*Milestone birthdays*

David's 'milestone' birthdays were often used as a means of raising funds. His seventieth, for example, was celebrated actually on his birthday (25 April) in 2001, and was billed as being the 'Conservation Party of The Year'. Taking the form of a dinner at the Natural History Museum, 650 guests attended and, as well as a fine meal, were given splendid entertainment in the form of a *They Think It's All Over* quiz based on the popular television comedy panel game of the same name. Like the programme, it was compered by Nick Hancock with regular panellists Rory McGrath, David Gower and Jonathan Ross making up the team for that unique occasion. (Gary Lineker was another panellist on the television show and he and David Gower also did much to fundraise for the DSWF over many years – and also contributed to the Foundation's magazine *Wildlife Matters* in which their input helped many youngsters to become interested in wildlife and conservation.

David's seventy-fifth birthday 'bash' took place at The Dorchester hotel (also the venue for the DSWF Wildlife Ball held in November each year) and was hosted by actor Robert Lindsay and comedian Sandi Toksvig. It was on this occasion that David and Sandi were playing around with a 'Toylander' miniature replica of a Land Rover given for auction by the company and David famously lost control whilst driving it on the stage and very nearly quite literally crashed into the audience.

Eightieth birthday celebrations were held at the Natural History Museum again, in May 2011, in the presence of HRH Prince Michael of Kent (see Chapter 6). On this occasion, as well as a dinner and fundraising auction, the 600-strong audience enjoyed a sit-down chat show hosted by chat-show host extraordinaire, Michael Parkinson. David and Mark Carwardine were the two interviewees. In 2016, there were plans afoot to celebrate David's eighty-fifth year with a surprise party hosted by Julian Birley at the North Norfolk Railway where David's beloved steam locomotive *Black Prince* is kept. Sadly, due to David's health at the time that particular party never materialised.

## *Advertising*

In the 1950s, David produced some paintings which were to be used as advertising for British Railways, the best known of which is *Service by Night* which was intended to promote overnight/ sleeper services. The painting shows a steam engine leaving King's Cross and passing signal gantries set against a cloudy, smoky night sky, and was printed as a poster by Waterlow and Sons Ltd, in 1955:

> I was excited beyond measure when British Rail Eastern Region bought the painting, including the copyright, for £60; they wanted to make a poster of it to put up on stations all over the country. However, for this it had to be correct, and it was full of mistakes. I didn't know anything about signalling or which train would come out of which platform – I had one train coming out of the milk yard, so that had to go.
>
> When the painting had been passed in every detail, it went to print. All the copies had been produced when another major mistake, right in the foreground was noticed. I had managed to get the points wrong which meant that the train coming out of the picture would have promptly derailed. A poor man at the printers had to alter every single copy by hand …

In March 2017, David visited the National Railway Museum at York – and saw his original painting *Service by Night* for the first time in over sixty years. It is now on public display there but had hitherto been kept in storage.

There is some confusion over another promotional 'Travel by Train' painting from the same period. Commissioned by LNER as one of their 'England's Stately Homes' series, it depicts Newby Hall in Yorkshire. Still available to buy as a poster from the likes of the National Railway Museum, some sellers state 'Artwork by Shepherd' but interestingly, the artist's signature is just that – 'SHEPHERD' in capital letters – and not David's easily recognisable moniker. It is, in fact, by Charles Shepherd, who was famous for such poster paintings, not only for British Rail but also for the White Star Line, Royal Mail Line Mediterranean Cruises and Union-Castle Line.

*Wrist watches and spectacles*

In the 1960s and 1970s, the Rolex watch company began a series of advertising connected to outstanding achievements and famous people. Some of the advertisements are stylish, some of them are thought-provoking, and some humorous. All, however, represented a certain lifestyle to which some viewers and readers of the adverts would like to aspire. At possibly the most influential point of his artistic career, David was invited to be a part of this particular campaign, for which he and Avril both received Rolex watches in gratitude.

In 1998, the Specsavers company asked David to take part in one of their advertising campaigns, both on television, in magazines and on posters – the tagline for which was, 'My eyes are important to me ...' The television advert showed film of David's studio with him painting and mixing colours on a palette, and also completed examples of his steam engine and elephant paintings. It can still be seen online via YouTube. Both the television and print advertisements were hugely influential with the public and a year later, on the strength of the success of their original campaign with David, Specsavers launched a similar six-week advertising campaign featuring physicist Stephen Hawking.

* * *

## Off the wall!

Somewhat bizarrely, David's *Wise Old Elephant* painting hung on the wall of Del Boy and Rodney's kitchen during several episodes of the BBC Television sitcom, *Only Fools and Horses*.

Since then, many of David's paintings have sbeen used to 'dress a room' in several television programmes (including the likes of *Midsomer Murders*) – so much so that it's not unusual to be sitting with any family member watching television and to hear them suddenly comment: 'Oh ... look ... there's one of David's/ Dad's/Granddad's paintings!'

In late 2019, the Belvoir Street Theatre in Sydney, New South Wales, staged a production of *Packer & Sons* – an account by Tommy Murphy of the Packer family's media empire – a scene in which showed a cigar-smoking Kerry Packer talking to his young son, Jamie, whilst looking at an otherwise black, blank wall on which was hung a portrait of David's painting *Elephant Charge* (very similar to *The Ivory is Theirs*). The intention was presumably a metaphor indicating how the Packer dynasty had to approach the cut-throat media world, but it could so easily have simply been that Kerry Packer liked David's work and, in the 1990s, had commissioned an original directly from the artist.

* * *

*Audience recognition by subliminal means*
Some of David's paintings came to the eyes of many without them even being aware of it. In some instances, this might even have taken the form of a seasonal greetings card from family and friends as, during the early part of his career, David painted around thirty paintings intended for such use. Commissioned by W. N. Sharpe Ltd ('Manufacturers of Sharpe's "Classic" Boxed and Loose Autograph Christmas and New Year Cards') the company only paid the artist around £30 for each original, including the frame and the copyright but, as David philosophically remarked, 'I suppose that was a lot of money in those days.' As they were specifically painted for Christmas cards, it perhaps wasn't surprising that W. N. Sharpe insisted that all the artwork had to have snow featured and he was usually asked to also include a dog (or two). *St Paul's and Ludgate Hill 1900* (also known by other titles) proved to be one of the most enduring of these paintings and it was reproduced on several occasions. Being a period setting, it required a tremendous amount of research and all the detail was accurate, right down to the signage and advertising on the horse-drawn buses. Temple Bar,

which once stood at the western entry to the City of London, near the junction of Fleet Street and The Strand, was moved, stone by stone to Theobald's Park, Hertfordshire in 1878 – and there was to become the focus of another of David's Christmas card paintings entitled *Temple Bar, Theobald's Park at Christmastime*. It is worth noting because it features a pack of hounds, huntsman and the mounted field, a most unusual choice of subject matter as far as both David's interests and views on hunting and shooting were concerned.

During the period when David's parents ran the Frimley Hall Hotel, and when David was still under the tutelage of artist Robin Goodwin but still living at home, he painted a 'drunken fish' mural on one of the hotel walls. Some 9 m (30 ft) long, it consisted of fish in various stages of inebriation, pushing prams, blowing bubbles and engaged in all manner of bizarre occupations. At some point in the intervening years, someone must have painstakingly peeled off the painting and wallpaper (it was of the strong canvas-type) rolled it up and carefully stored it away as, during a refurbishment by new owners Trust House Forte in the 1980s, the mural was rediscovered. Recognising David's signature in the bottom right of the mural, they got in touch with him in order that painting and artist might be reunited. But, before that, all the time it was on display in the hotel how many people must have seen the painting without realising who the artist? Likewise, on a wall at The Potter's Heron hotel and restaurant, Ampfield, near Romsey, Hampshire, guests were quite likely to have admired a country landscape mural painted by David during his early years. As it measured some 2.74 m by 1.37 m (9 ft by 4½ ft) they could hardly have missed it! Sadly, The Potter's Heron in its original form was burnt to the ground in 1966, was rebuilt in 1969 and then, in 2018, suffered another fire which was thankfully not quite so disastrous, but by then David's mural was no more.

David's artwork also appeared as illustrations to books such as *Full Circle: The Story of Air Fighting*, written in 1964 by Air Vice Marshal J. E. (Johnnie) Johnson, and in 2000, in *Think Like a Bird: An Army Pilot's Story* by Alex Kimbell and, as mentioned in the previous chapter, on the cover of certain publications of Cornelius Ryan's *A Bridge Too Far*.

Audiences encountered David's work by other means too. For those who remember the days when, at the cinema, there was always a short Pathé film preceding the major screening, one of the 'shorts' that did the rounds of many towns and cities featured David and his paintings.

In it, the narrator told the cinema audience that David's painting of a steam locomotive 'was alive in atmosphere, in character and rhythm. Alive because the artist has the power of understanding his subject; living with it until he has the effect he desires ...'

A catalogue for an exhibition of *Paintings by David Shepherd*, held at Biddles, Guildford, in April 1954, includes the fact that 'David Shepherd was photographed for television and filmed by leading newsreel companies on the occasion of the London-New Zealand air race in 1953. His painting of the Dutch winner, purchased by Royal Dutch Airlines, now hangs at Schiphol airport, Amsterdam. Shots of him painting this picture appeared on cinema screens and in newspapers in Holland and New Zealand.'

## 12

# THE LAST WORD

'I'd like to be remembered as someone who did their bit for wildlife … and my ego is so enormous, I want to be there at my memorial service to hear what they say about me.' David had long maintained that he would have wanted to 'attend' his own funeral so that he could hear all the wonderful things that would, no doubt, be said about him. In that he was right; both at the funeral/celebration of his life on 27 September 2017, and at the memorial service held at Southwark Cathedral the following March. In addition, there were compliments and messages galore added to the *Book of Condolence* from people whose lives he had touched through his artwork and conservation efforts.

In a 1974 magazine article, when asked about his dislikes he responded that he would rather talk about things he did like: 'Life, for example. I will have to live to be 150 to get all the things done that I want to. I want a twenty-five-hour day. Life is so full and exciting.' His thoughts recorded in an article for the *Somerset & Avon Life* some twelve years later were in similar vein. When asked (at age fifty-five) whether he had any remaining ambitions, he replied, 'To live to be at least 150 years old and to be able to cram in everything I want to do. One ambition I will never achieve – but there is no harm in dreaming – is that one day I will drive *Black Prince* into Waterloo station.'

Generally a healthy man throughout life (he never stopped still long enough to allow illness to settle!) just after the Millennium, David developed prostate cancer. Appearing on BBC 2's daytime show *Esther* not long afterwards, in answer to a somewhat direct question from the programme's eponymous host: 'Come on David. Tell me ... You've been very ill, haven't you?' David responded, 'I haven't been ill at all.' 'Yes, you have,' countered Rantzen. 'You've had prostate cancer.' Typically flippant, David then replied 'Oh that ... That was huge fun.' Fun it was not. David received intensive radiotherapy every day for six weeks but, at the end of it all felt so good about being the centre of attention that he was delighted by the radiation team wanting to take photos: 'They took a photo of me on the machine wearing my knickers and Avril wrote all their names on my front with a felt-tip pen.' He told the tale that afternoon on *Esther* and it prompted laughter and a round of spontaneous applause.

Grateful for the cancer having been caught in time – and then only because of having undergone a medical for life insurance – David's life continued at its usual manic pace until, in the late 2000s when arriving at Maesgwyn, their cottage in the Brecon Beacons (see Chapter 3) he got out of the car to open the five-bar gate into the yard and suffered a minor heart attack. Avril drove him straight to the local hospital where he remained for several days for treatment and check-ups until, a while later, in a London hospital, he had stents fitted. Again, as with the cancer treatment, after a short convalescence David was soon back in his studio painting – and hosting his ever-popular chat shows (see Chapter 11) in many parts of the British Isles. The latter was tiring and the usual format (as described elsewhere) was altered so as to make such occasions less strenuous. Although his prodigious output of art never ceased (and he was painting until virtually his last days), the rate at which he worked lessened and, it has to be said, his work – quite understandably given his age and the Parkinson's disease which affected the last decade of his life – lost some of its earlier detail and outstanding atmospheric quality.

The family made sure of his daily exercise. Whilst a cycling machine regime was attempted for a while, it was a somewhat futile and boring exercise as far as David was concerned and it wasn't long before he rebelled against it. Thinking of his love of the countryside, it was then suggested that he walked every day with Maddy (a little rescued Jack Russell terrier of indeterminate age) up over the fields, beyond the stable complex and to a point where a gate defined the boundary between Brooklands and the neighbouring farm. Well-armed with a shepherd's crook for support, he undertook the daily mission with determination, but not necessarily with good grace and, on their return, after a coffee he would invariably retire to his studio in order to carry on with his latest project.

David's last solo exhibition was at the Rountree Tryon Galleries (then still in Bury Street, London, but now based at Petworth, West Sussex) in December 2014. Entitled *A Wild Lifetime*, in the catalogue introduction, gallery director Oliver Swann wrote:

> At the present time, there can be no other name more universally associated with the cause of Wildlife Conservation than that of David Shepherd. For most of his energetic life, he has crusaded tirelessly for a greater awareness and harmony between the growing demands of man at the expense of those creatures with whom he shares the planet. In addition to countless seminars, speeches and fundraising events in all corners of the globe, the vehicle for celebrating this cause has, of course, been his painting …

The exhibition included an extremely wide selection of his work and examples of his versatility spanning a speriod from 1963 to 2014 and was, as Oliver was further to opine: '… a unique witness/tribute to a very special and inspirational crusader.' It proved to be a brilliant swansong.

During the last week of July 2017, complaining of a pain in his leg (deep vein thrombosis was suspected) and generally feeling unwell, David was admitted to the East Surrey hospital at Redhill where he sadly died on 19 September. The Parkinson's had weakened a giant of a man who loved giants, be they elephants or steam engines, but he was, during his time in hospital, on some days able to engage with visiting family and friends in his typical fun-loving way. On days when he was tired, a smile might, however, be all he could manage. Mandy remembers when she and her nephew Luke (David's grandson and one of Wendy's two sons) were with David in hospital. Holding his right hand, she happened to comment to him how amazing it was to think of how many elephants this particular hand had painted – to which Luke responded that it was even more amazing to consider how many elephants that hand had saved, a reply to which David most definitely smiled.

* * *

## Media obituaries

On 22 September 2017, Matthew Bannister, host of *Last Word*, BBC Radio 4's weekly obituary programme, paid tribute to David – as did many newspapers, local, national and international.

From the *Surrey Advertiser* to *The New York Times*, and the likes of the *Guardian*, *Telegraph*, *Times*, *Daily Express* and the *Independent*, all contained details of David's extraordinary full and varied life. In addition, his life and death were covered by many magazines whose readers were likely to have known of the artist and conservationist through his many and varied eclectic interests and hobbies, plus on the websites of the likes of Stowe School and organisations of charitable groups of which he was, or had been, a patron or president. Whilst usually wonderfully self-publicising, there were, it seems, several organisations with which David was involved that he rarely if ever mentioned. An email of condolence from Fiona Dick at the Royal Surrey County Hospital is a typical example: '[he] was one of our longest-serving patrons. We [are] sad to know he is no longer quietly supporting us in the background.'

* * *

### St Swithun's and Southwark Cathedral

David's funeral – a celebration of his life – was held at St Swithun's Church, East Grinstead on 28 September 2017 and was followed by a private cremation attended only by Avril, David's sister Judy Crago and David's daughters. At the funeral service, in amongst the patriotic hymns and readings Judy talked of her childhood with David and their brother Peter; daughters' Mandy and Melanie of *Our Man Who Loved Giants*, while further family memories and reflections were offered by daughter Wendy and grandchildren Emily, Robin, Peanut, Thomas, Elliot, Justin, Rosie, Luke and Annabel. *A Letter from Avril* was read by Melinda. Family friend, writer, broadcaster and wildlife conservationist, Mark Carwardine, read his own poem *Larger Than Life*, written especially for David. At the end of the order of service, the words of George Bernard Shaw had been printed – and they were particularly apt when it came to considering David's life and what he had achieved: 'Life is no brief candle to me. It is a splendid torch, which I have got hold of for the moment and I want to make it burn as brightly as possible before handing it on to future generations.'

### In memoriam

The memorial service took place on 2 March 2018 at Southwark Cathedral. Several possible venues had been considered and discarded, either for reasons of practicality or accessibility. Guildford Cathedral was the family's initial choice due to David's local connection when they lived at Winkworth, and also the fact that he had been chosen to lay one of the foundation bricks when the cathedral was first built. Sadly, on enquiry it appeared that there would be insufficient seating for the size of congregation expected. London was the next option and the idea of St Paul's investigated. In the end, however, Southwark was considered most suitable. The chosen date was, though, to coincide with the spell of really bad weather which became known as 'The Beast from the East' – as a result of which, several guests who would have wanted to be there were physically prevented from travelling. Those who were able to attend heard Mandy and her daughter Rosie sing *Pie Jesu* from Andrew Lloyd Webber's *Requiem* and verbal tributes from David's sister Judy, Melinda, granddaughter 'Peanut', son-in-law Graeme, art gallery director Oliver Swann, and Julian Birley, family friend and former chairman of the North Norfolk Railway.

As an aside, in an effort to achieve David's lifelong ambition of getting *Black Prince* as near as possible to Waterloo station (see elsewhere in this chapter) Julian and members of the North Norfolk Railway had seriously considered transporting David's beloved steam locomotive all the way from Sheringham into London for the service. The firm who had supplied David with railway low-loader transportation in the past were keen to take her as a gesture of the affection they felt for David – and Julian had even got as far as travelling a possible route taking photos and working out the logistics of whether *Black Prince* atop a low-loader would be able to get to where she was needed. Unfortunately, despite such exhaustive attention to detail, practicalities dictated that the loco's presence at Southwark would not be possible. Apart from anything else, on being approached by the transport company regarding the idea, the London authorities whose permission was needed had thrown up their hands in horror as, irrespective of the disruption to the traffic, they were more than a little concerned about the effects that the combined weight of the low-loader lorry and *Black Prince* herself might have on under-street amenities such as the capital's sewerage system. Being over seventy tons, she would also have required the presence of a police escort. Had it have been feasible and had David been looking down on the cavalcade, he would have loved it as, whenever he'd been present when his steam locomotives had been moved from place to place by road, the longer the traffic jam, the happier and more excitable he became!

## *An influence on many*

Whilst David's skill as an artist, as outspoken ambassador for wildlife conservation, railway preservation and a fundraising figurehead for charity had long been appreciated by those who had come into direct contact with him, it was with his death that it became obviously apparent just how much his life and work had touched and influenced many more throughout the world. These comments, taken from notes of condolence to the family and the Foundation, are typical of the general feeling:

Possibly the vast majority of people who David impacted, never met him. By this I refer to the rangers, communities and people around the world. Whether communities are now able to harvest their crops due to sustainably reducing elephant raiding, having children and adults encouraged to splash paint on canvas, or accommodation built to provide frontline wildlife and community rangers somewhere dry and secure to stay, he has left us in a better, more enjoyable and positive world.

My mum bought me [a print] one of David's paintings when I was a little girl. It was dolphins swimming [*Ocean Rhapsody*, painted in 1996]. Whenever I had a nightmare I'd wake up and imagine I was swimming in with the dolphins and it would make me happy again. I met David and he signed my painting, and when he found out my birthday was Christmas Day he sent me a hand written card for years afterwards. That ... picture is one of the reasons I'm a conservationist today...

David. Thank you for your passion and enthusiasm. Thank you for inspiring new generations of wildlife lovers and conservationists. Thank you for taking a stand and never compromising.

I have followed David's work since I was a child (I am now 59) and along with the likes of David Attenborough and Peter Scott he influenced my own choice of career in the nature conservation and countryside management field.

Our pupils will remember all the lovely art projects ... and the lucky pupils who met him will never forget the time he spent with us ... telling us stories of his adventures ...

He was a man who took life by the throat and knocked seven bells out of it ...

While we mourn his loss, we also celebrate the man, his art, and all that he and the foundation have accomplished. He has left an indelible mark on the world with his humanity, creativity and action to create a world that embraces all life forms.

Of those that knew David personally, Julian Birley was moved to contribute the following:

I am privileged to have been able to call David a dear friend leaving me with so many much-treasured memories. Through his foresight, dedication or simple madness he rescued steam engines that would otherwise have succumbed to the cutter's torch allowing my generation and those after me to learn, understand and above all enjoy one of the greatest gifts this country gave to the world: Railways.

Mark Carwardine described David as being: '... a whirlwind of energy and enthusiasm – his passion for wildlife and conservation inspired everyone in his path.'

Nigel Colne, a trustee of the DSWF remembered that:

Over 20 years of working closely with David made me appreciate what a tenacious and outspoken advocate he was. He was shocked and saddened by the steep decline in the numbers of so many iconic species at the hands of man; at the insatiable appetite for tusks, horn, and animal parts particularly because of the demand from China and South East Asia. He abhorred the brutality of modern poaching and the evil influences behind this trade. He dedicated his life to fighting these issues and there is no doubt that he and his

Foundation have played a really valuable part in informing public and political consciousness around the world.

Like many others, Pamela Jackson has many memories of her time with David, firstly as a BBC production assistant on *The Man Who Loves Giants* and subsequently as a family friend:

> My overriding memories of David are of his passion for everything he did, and his generosity, fun, enthusiasm and friendliness. I miss him but am so pleased that I had the privilege of working with him and knowing him for so many years.

Then this, from Jonathan, the son of actor Bill Pertwee (Bill and David coincidentally happened to find themselves at several fundraising and book-signing events together):

> As a young lad growing up in East Horsley during the 1970s, I remember how I felt about animals and endangered wildlife and around 1975 committed myself to the HELP THE WHALE campaign and from then on did all I could to protect animals. I was lucky that my parents had a similar passion and my mum would often arrange coffee mornings to raise money for other animal causes. My father, at the time away filming *Dad's Army*, bought me the coin collection, or the first few to start me off ... he sat me down and explained the importance of all these endangered species. A decade later he would come across our champion of such concerns, David Shepherd ... who seemed to embody the perfect approach; passion, commitment and heart... Whatever goes on in our lives, it often seems of little relevance when we compare it to the love of endangered species and their survival.

David Gower, retired cricketer and an Honorary Vice President of DSWF said that he would: '... miss all the teasing that we inflicted on each other whenever our paths happily crossed, that sort of teasing that comes only from mutual respect ...' and, in an interview for the *Mail on Sunday* in May 2013, admitted that his prized possession, above all others, was 'A David Shepherd oil painting called *Rhino in The Kaokoveld*. I bought it about 20 years ago for £20,000. It marries my two loves – David's work and wildlife, which stems from my childhood in East Africa.'

* * *

## Impulsive and impetuous

David always painted in oils on canvas – and in a style much admired by many. When asked in 1999 by Sue Lawley during his second appearance on BBC Radio's *Desert Island Discs* why he'd chosen that particular medium, he replied that he'd always done so: 'It's more exciting and suits my personality ... I couldn't do watercolours as I'm as impulsive and impetuous in my painting as I am in life and I'd probably go through the paper ... sometimes I don't know when a picture is finished and although one should never overwork a painting, oils let you do more ... as Robin [Goodwin] used to tell me, "Never let a painting go unless you are happy with it."'

* * *

*From cricketer to artist – 'my hero, my inspiration...'*
Wikipedia mentions that 'Robert Charles "Jack" Russell, MBE ... is an English retired international cricketer, now known for his abilities as an artist ...' According to Jack, writing a guest blog for the DSWF with the title of *David Shepherd, My Hero, My Inspiration*, he owes all his success to David, whose work first inspired him:

'... when I saw a David Shepherd original oil painting for the first time [it] blew me away! It was at one David's exhibitions near Bristol promoting wildlife conservation in the 1980s. Right, I thought, there must be a way of doing this, I'm going to have a go. At the time people were telling me that to learn to paint you first have to learn to draw so during a long rain delay at a county match

I left the ground and went to the shops and bought a sketchpad and some pencils ... I was too shy at first to let people see what I was doing [but] ... [a]t the end of that season [1987] I took a number of sketches into a Bristol gallery to have them framed just to put them on our walls at home. However, the gallery owner ... told me that if I came back with enough sketches he would hold an exhibition ... He was true to his word and ... [t]o my amazement, all 40 sketches sold out within 2 days! I was in a state of shock but my career as a professional artist had begun...

All this is down to David. Or rather David's unquenchable enthusiasm for life and his paintings. If he could paint such amazing pictures having learnt from scratch, then so could I. That's what gave me the confidence to go for it. I know he had Robin Goodwin to guide him in the early years but basically he started from nothing and that was a big motivation for me ... His sheer determination to succeed was a guiding light. I can remember in my early years when I was throwing 9 out of 10 canvases in the bin because they weren't good enough, it was David's determination not to give up that kept me going ... Taking a closer look at his work he taught me the lesson of creating the illusion of three dimensions on a flat surface. Whether it's a tusk coming out of the canvas, or the buffer beam on a steam locomotive, or the branches of a tree, his skill of having something leap out at you is one of his greatest assets. Not all artists can achieve that. It's something I strive for every day!

## A neglected knighthood

As well as touching the hearts and lives of many and earning their admiration and respect, David received a great number of official accolades and awards – all of which are listed in full elsewhere (see Honours and Awards). They include those from abroad and at home. In the UK, he was given both the OBE and CBE but there are many who think he should have been honoured further and the subject of a neglected knighthood was mentioned by several in the emails and letters following his death. There can be absolutely no doubt at all that David would have greatly relished having his shoulder dubbed by a sword held in the hand of one of the Royal Family and it was a matter of personal regret to him that such an occasion never happened. The oversight was also a cause for good-natured family banter, especially when, in the 2009 New Year's Honour's List, Graeme, David's son-in-law (husband of Melanie and father of Emily and Peanut) was created a knight as a result of his outstanding military career – including being director of UK Special Forces and Commander of the British Field Army.

## A last memory

As a son-in-law with far less credentials than Graeme, perhaps one of my fondest and most abiding memories of David was of when, in the spring of 2017, I volunteered to help him clear the greenhouse at Brooklands Farm and remove unwanted plastic trays in which plants had previously been delivered. He was – despite by then showing signs of being a little old and frail – typically still dedicated to getting things done and, for some reason known only to himself, had set aside that particular day in order to complete the task. Wandering out to the greenhouse together, David asked me what we could do with them:

> 'Well, as I see it, we have two options: we could send them to landfill where they'll lay dormant without rotting for centuries or we could burn them.'
>
> 'Will they burn?' asked David.
>
> 'Oh yes, but with all the chemicals and oils involved in their manufacture, they'll produce lots of black smoke …'
>
> Burning was eventually decreed to be the lesser of the two evils so we set to and wheelbarrowed the trays up to the field behind the stables where there was a large wire-mesh brazier made expressly for the purpose of burning paper, scrap wood and the like. A base fire was soon started and the plant trays gradually added. Extraordinarily beautiful multicoloured flames shot into the air – and the promised dense smoke soon materialised – and David's face lit up like a small child on Fireworks Night.

'I never thought they'd do that … we'd better not tell Avril …'

'She might know when she realises that flights to Gatwick [Brooklands was under one of the Gatwick flight-lines] have had to be diverted due to an unexpected intense fog-cloud … I can just see the *Daily Mail* newspaper headlines now: "GATWICK BROUGHT TO A STANDSTILL BY WORLD-RENOWNED WILDLIFE ARTIST AND CONSERVATIONIST …"'

Giggling in his inimitable way, David seemed greatly amused at the prospect and, once the fire had died down to a safe level, we headed back to the house for lunch. With a grin and a twinkle in his eyes, he turned and said, 'I know it might not have been environmentally friendly … but I really did enjoy that!'

As did I – and all the time spent in his company over the quarter or a century or so that I was privileged to know this extraordinary man. It might be a cliché to say that 'we shall never see his like again' but, in this particular instance, I fear it will more than likely prove to be true. His name will, however, live on through his art and the David Shepherd Wildlife Foundation.

# *ODE TO DAVID SHEPHERD*

Mark Carwardine is a zoologist, an environmental activist, an award-winning writer, a television and radio presenter, a widely published wildlife photographer, a best-selling author, a wildlife tour operator and leader, a lecturer and a magazine columnist – he was also a very great friend to David for over forty years and penned this poem, which he read at David's seventieth birthday celebrations held at the Natural History Museum. It is a good biographical résumé!

Seventy years old
Or so we are told
Three score years and ten.
Which means he was born
Before the war
But after Sir Christopher Wren.

He must be proud of the fact
That when he was in on the act
When the first flint tools were made.
And that even today
He remembers the way
In which dinosaur eggs were laid.

As a young lad
He wasn't too bad
He dreamed of the Ngorongoro Crater.
To work in the Serengeti
Meet a wild yeti
But all that was to come much later.

He applied – the fool!
To art school
And fell into a trap.
Cos when they saw
Him trying to draw
They told him he was … not quite as good as they hoped.

Then – out of the blue
A call came through
But he thought he was going insane.
Are you deaf?
It's the RAF!
And we'd like you to paint our plane.

They sent him far
To Africaaa (sorry!)
And he painted planes galore.
But his heart really lay
More in Mother Nature's way
So he painted wild beasts much more.

He directs his oils
To far-away soils
With a *delicate* splash of paint
He takes great care
With a bloody great bear
Damian Hirst he definitely ain't.

With a touch of sienna
A laughing hyena

Comes to life on the page in a flash.
A quick dab of blue
And the tail of a gnu
Suddenly has style and panache.

His painting knows no bounds
From sun-dried termite mounds
To Her Majesty the Queen Mum.
From pampered pets
To Harrier jump-jets
And the wrinkles on a pachyderm's bum.

He looks quite debonair
With his sticky-up hair
And genuine safari suit.
With trousers to match
He's quite a catch
Well, the baboons think he looks rather cute.

Of course, safari suits were born
Just to be worn
While striding over African plains.
But David wears his
When doing the biz
In Reading and Luton and Staines.

He went to the Palace
And meant no malice
But nearly made the Queen faint,
Cos he was covered in lots
Of *nearly*-dry spots
Of elephant-coloured paint.

Then there are trains
Which make different stains
Because David just loves to get dirty.
But not the kind

With leaves on the line
That crawl in late at nine-thirty.

Like a great whale
The sheer scale
Of his passion for trains makes you wince.
He set up a railway
And the very next day
Bought the *Green Knight* and *Black Prince*.

*And* wildlife can depend
On no better friend
Than the man who loves giants.
His Foundation will aid
With funds it has made
And using the appliance of science.

Would you believe it, perchance?
David went to a dance
And strutted his stuff on the floor.
Avril was there
Determined not to stare
From behind the fire exit door.

He tried to impress
With his art, no less
And took her to wine and dine.
He showed her his etchings
His paintings, his sketchings
And sang 'Oh my darling turpentine'.

With Avril in his head
*David* decided to wed
But persuading *her* took him a while.
As you might have supposed
He went and proposed
In, well, true David style.

Not on a beach of white sand
No piña colada in hand
Not drenched in soft golden sun.
But – I have to confide
It was round the backside
Of Battersea Power Sta-tion.

She said 'No'
He said 'Oh!
But I don't want you to be just a friend.'
Well, he may be a blighter
But David's a fighter
And he talked her round in the end.

The next thing
Is offspring
And of those they've had *only* four.
But they were all girls
With blonde fluffy curls
So I don't think they'll have any more.

The thing about them
All their names begin with 'M'
OK – except one – so don't frown.
Melinda, Mandy, Mel,
Just Wendy they couldn't spell
But then – 'W' is 'M' upside-down.

The latest word's
New members of the herd
Because now he's a grandfather, *too*.
Nine he's had
All call him 'granddad'
But he's still *Sir!* To me – and you.

So, he's a difficult man
With whom to plan

So busy you must fight for a date.
But please don't worry!
He says in a hurry
I'm free on the 25th – between seven and eight. [April 25th being
    David's birth date.]

You may think he looks placid
But a cheetah on acid
Lives life at a more sedate pace.
He shows no sign of slowing
Just keeps on going
Faster than the entire human race.

Conservation, trains
Painting, aeroplanes
The star of screen and stage.
David Shepherd, OBE
A great person to be
But most ... I'm impressed by his age.

Mark Carwardine
April 2001

# HONOURS AND AWARDS

Bearing in mind his achievements, it is perhaps, something of a surprise that David was never offered a knighthood. He was, nevertheless, officially honoured in many other ways, both in the UK and abroad.

1954: Member of the Society of Aero Artists.

1962: *Wise Old Elephant* published and became best-selling print.

1967: *March Sunlight* judged 'the top selling print' of the year.

1971: Honorary Degree in Fine Arts by the Pratt Institute of New York.

1973: The Order of the Golden Ark; personally awarded by HRH Prince Bernhard of the Netherlands for his services to conservation, in particular, raising money for the WWF's 'Project Tiger'.

1979: Member of Honour of the World Wide Fund for Nature.

1979: Officer of the Order of the British Empire (OBE) for services to wildlife conservation.

1986: Fellow of the Royal Society of Arts.

1988: Zambian Order of Distinguished Service; awarded by President Kenneth Kaunda.

1989: Fellow of the Royal Geographical Society.

1989: Honorary Doctorate of Science of Hatfield Polytechnic (now the University of Hertfordshire).

1996: Officer (Brother) of the Order of St John.

1996: Voted 'Best Selling Published Artist of the Year'.

2002: Recommended for award for 'outstanding contribution to both the [art] industry and the world as a whole' by The Fine Art Trade Guild after being approached by the Fine Art Committee.

2004: Granted the Freedom of the City of London.

2008: Commander of the Order of the British Empire (CBE) for services to charity and wildlife.

2012: Conservation Award from Wetnose Animal Aid.

2012: True Englishman Award from the St George's Day Club.

2016: Lifetime Achievement Award at the *Daily Mirror*/RSPCA's Animal Hero Awards for a lifetime's commitment to wildlife.

# DAVID SHEPHERD 'COLLECTABLES'

During his lifetime the locations of David's solo exhibitions were, quite literally, worldwide and included those held in London, New York, Johannesburg, Lusaka, Nairobi, Nevada and San Francisco. In addition, examples of his paintings can be seen in the permanent collections of the Chesterfield Museum; National Railway Museum at York; Airborne Assault Museum, Duxford; Tank Museum, Bovington; Fleet Air Arm Museum, Ilchester; RAF Museum, London; the Merseyside Maritime Museum, Liverpool and the Guildhall Art Gallery, London.

*The 'David Shepherd Originals Circle'*
A year after David's death in 2017, a major worldwide search was launched in order to try and locate the owners and whereabouts of any of David's original artworks. Organised by the DSWF, the network was created so that anyone who wanted could share stories and anecdotes connected to their paintings, limited edition prints and sketches that had been done by David over his long career. As the organisers say: 'Our aim is to celebrate David's work together and build an important catalogue of his work around the world – something that has never happened before.'

To find out more, take a look at www.davidshepherd.org/art/david-shepherd-originals-circle

Your artwork is likely to be an original if:

- It is signed by David Shepherd.
- The brush or pencil marks are clearly visible.
- It is open and not behind glass – oil or acrylic paintings, in particular, are rarely enclosed.

Your artwork is NOT an original if:

- It has a number written in a bottom corner – this is likely to be a limited-edition print.
- It is mounted – generally only prints are displayed in a mount.
- It has a title or name of the artwork/artist printed at the top or bottom.

*Prints*

Most of David's prints are photo lithographs. In 1992 (and for the following decade) there began a limited 'Gold Edition' series of David Shepherd prints – each typically with a run of between 200 and 495 – which were high-quality silkscreen prints published on watercolour paper. These are absolutely identical in quality, irrespective of whether or not the numbers in the margin are the first or last of the edition, unlike days of old when etchings and lithographs were printed using an ink-covered plate and the quality of the reproduction would depend on how much ink remained on the plate as the printing process progressed. It might be of academic interest to know that David kept the first copy of most prints; with either system, however, it is virtually impossible to detect any difference between the first and last off the press. As far as collectors are concerned, silkscreen prints are often considered to be somewhere between signed limited edition prints and an original painting in terms of kudos and value.

*Gold Edition titles*
1992: *Cheetah*
1993: *Africa*

1994: *Amboseli*
1995: *The Last Refuge* (of Giant Pandas)
1996: *Mountain Lion*
1997: *Leopards*
1998: *The Bandipur Tiger*
1999: *Storm over Africa*
2000: *Indian Summer* (tigers running into water)
2000: *Portrait of a Tiger* (to celebrate the Millennium)
2001: *The White Tiger of Rewa*
2002: *In the Cool of Evening* (a lion, lioness and two cubs)

## Market demands

In general, limited editions signed by David became an excellent investment and, at the height of his popularity, demand often far outreached supply, thus creating a strong secondary market, which, as Jean Winch, David's business manager since 2002 explained, saw some titles escalate enormously in price. A signed limited edition might quite easily sell out on the day of publication and a waiting list of potential purchasers would often be quite lengthy – and contain a number of well-known names.

For those wishing, or only able to, spend a few hundred pounds as opposed to several thousand for an original painting, a signed limited edition generally proved a sensible purchase, and one which was unlikely to lose money.

## The David Shepherd Archive Collection

In 2011, to celebrate David's eightieth birthday and in association with Gateway Publishing Limited, the 'Archive Collection' was launched. In large format, the book is a collection of some 120 of David's paintings – some well known, others less so – stitched and hand-bound in English vellum and leather. Strictly limited to 1,000 copies, each book is numbered and signed by David and a proportion of the money from each sale is allocated directly to the DSWF.

## Wedgwood plates and others

In 'Man on the Move', the title of a feature article all about David which appeared in the November 1974 issue of *Signature*, the magazine of Diners Club Ltd, Frederick Radford, told his readers that David 'hopes shortly to design exclusively for Diners Club members a limited edition of porcelain plaques in bas-relief of all the Big Five animals (the elephant, the lion, the leopard, the buffalo and the rhinoceros) to be made at the famous Danish porcelain factory of Bing & Grøndahl'.

Whether he did or not, David's artwork has appeared as a series on several collectors' editions of decorative plates. His first such was seemingly for Wedgwood when, in conjunction with the World Wildlife Fund (WWF) they produced a series of plates, the central part of which featured some of the animals from his original African artwork on 'Queen's Ware' earthenware with a clear glaze applied. According to Wedgwood: '[The] decorations… [are] taken from artist's original work then applied to plate using lithograph. The plate [is] then… edge-lined in green.'

As a follow-up, a 'deluxe fine bone-china' limited edition of 500, each containing six plates in a set, was produced in order to further raise funds for the WWF. Other limited editions were not, however, quite so 'limited' as the series of eight depicting hippopotamus, zebra, cheetah, elephants, lion, giraffe, rhinoceros and tiger, were produced and sold worldwide as a 'limited edition' of 25,000.

According to Jamie Breese, writing his online 'Treasure Hunters' column for the *Mirror* newspapers in 2012: 'They … were made by Wedgwood for the David Shepherd Wildlife Collection commissioned by Spink Modern Collections. Each plate has a 22-carat gold rim and a facsimile signature by the artist.' (Those in the earlier earthenware editions had only David's initials forming part of the artwork and lithograph.)

Limited edition bronzes of David's painting subjects are also collected by enthusiasts. One such is *The Gentle Giant* (of an elephant) by sculptor Richard Sefton. Such bronzes are numbered and signed by both the sculptor and the artist.

# DAVID SHEPHERD WILDLIFE FOUNDATION

David Shepherd Wildlife Foundation (DSWF) was established by my late grandfather, David Shepherd, in 1984 and was born from his passion to give back to the wildlife to which he felt he owed a huge debt due to his enormous success as a world-renowned artist. To date, the Foundation has given away nearly £12 million in grants directly to conservation initiatives across Africa and Asia to fight wildlife crime and to protect some of the planet's most vulnerable and endangered species.

Our mission is to increase awareness in people around the world about the need to protect and conserve wildlife and their habitats. We wish to ensure the value of ecosystems and the wilderness are recognised, ensuring sufficient energy, resource and innovation are applied to their survival.

- We **FIGHT** wildlife crime through ranger empowerment, law enforcement programmes and international policy.
- We **PROTECT** endangered species in their natural habitat and key environmental landscapes.
- We **ENGAGE** with local communities and international audiences to educate and raise awareness to end wildlife crime.

DSWF focuses on eight core endangered species: elephants, rhinos, tigers, painted dogs, snow leopards, pangolins, lions and chimpanzees. We also fund support for wildlife rangers.

As we face the world's sixth mass extinction with over 1,000,000 species now at risk from vanishing forever, and some within mere decades, the fate of the natural world rests in our hands. The devastating impact that humans inflict on wildlife and the environment is within our grasp to reverse.

DSWF invests in economically and socially vulnerable communities most affected by human-wildlife conflict and wildlife crime. We take a holistic approach to conservation, recognising the essential role that communities and education both play in ensuring conservation successes. We also recognise the need to tackle environmental and wildlife crime from grassroots to the world stage across all forums and platforms in order to generate change.

My grandfather was unafraid and unashamed to address controversial and often unpopular conservation narratives in his outspoken and brave approach to ensuring wildlife and the natural world were given an equal voice to our own.

We are incredibly grateful for the generous support and friendship of all of our friends and supporters around the world who choose to stand with us and fund our work and keep our critical projects alive and operational.

As the future health of our planet, its ecosystems and wildlife become more important than ever before, continuing my grandfather's legacy to turn the tide on extinction has never been more critical.

Georgina Lamb, Chief Executive
**David Shepherd Wildlife Foundation**

To find out more please contact us at 01483 272323 or go to: *www.davidshepherd.org*

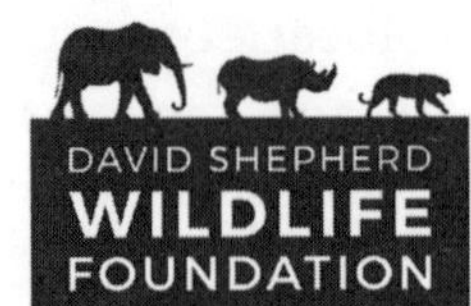


Reg Charity number 1106893